"OF ALL THE CONTESTANTS ON *TOP CHEF,* RICHARD BLAIS WAS EASILY THE MOST FASCINATING TO WATCH.** His food pays solid respect to the past while looking fearlessly to the future. *Try This at Home* takes Richard's years of thinking, experimenting, trying and failing, and trying and succeeding, and brings it all home in thrilling and decidedly useful ways. This is the fast, accessible route to looking like a genius at your next dinner."

—ANTHONY BOURDAIN

"I'VE KNOWN RICHARD FOR A LONG TIME NOW AND HIS COOKING HAS ALWAYS BEEN A HUGE INSPIRATION.** *Try This at Home* totally captures his creativity, his talent, and his awesome sense of humor."

—SEAN BROCK

"THE MOST INNOVATIVE CHEF ON *TOP CHEF,*** Richard Blais brings us creative, thought-provoking recipes for the home cook. Let him make you look like a rock star."

—GRANT ACHATZ

"I'VE BEEN ROOTING FOR RICHARD BLAIS SINCE HIS FIRST SEASON ON *TOP CHEF*** and always wondered, How'd he do that? Now I finally have the answers . . . and I will definitely try these recipes at home!"

—ZOOEY DESCHANEL

"RICHARD HAS CREATED A BOOK THAT I WISH I HAD WRITTEN—**a book that will inspire not only professionals to look at food technique and flavor in a different way, but that any casual cook can work out of each and every day. For a guy who's not even Jewish to teach me about better brisket was a welcome miracle, and the potato chip omelet shouldn't be dismissed as gimmickry. We make it every week now in our house! Richard's genuine passion as a chef, innovator, and artist comes shining through, but his influence as a father and husband makes this book truly special. *Try This at Home* is a must for anyone who enjoys cooking."

—ANDREW ZIMMERN

"THIS IS A COOKBOOK FROM A SERIOUS CHEF WHO KNOWS HOW TO MAKE FUN OF HIMSELF AND LIGHTEN UP THE WHOLE PROCESS.** Cooking need not be an overly complicated, overwrought process with eighteen ingredients and fourteen pans. Though you can try using a good iSi siphon and a smoking gun (not that kind of smoking gun). And occasionally some nitrous oxide. Oh, and good ingredients, of course. Plus a spirit of fun. You have the cookbook. Now, as your mother would say, 'Go play!'"

—TOM COLICCHIO
FROM THE FOREWORD

TRY
AT
H

THIS OME

SUBTITLE: Recipes from My Head to Your Plate
AUTHOR: Richard Blais
FOREWORD: Tom Colicchio
PUBLISHER: Clarkson Potter | New York

Copyright © 2013 by Trail Blais, Inc.
Photographs copyright © 2013 by John Lee

All rights reserved.
Published in the United States by Clarkson Potter/
Publishers, an imprint of the Crown Publishing Group,
a division of Random House, Inc., New York.
www.crownpublishing.com
www.clarksonpotter.com

CLARKSON POTTER is a trademark and POTTER with colophon
is a registered trademark of Random House, Inc.

Library of Congress Cataloging-in-Publication Data
has been applied for.

ISBN 978-0-307-98527-9
eISBN 978-0-307-98528-6

Printed in China

Design by Laura Palese
Cover photographs by John Lee

10 9 8 7 6 5 4 3 2 1

First Edition

There are many people who have helped me in my career, but only one who has changed my life for the better at every turn. Before her, frankly, my character was a bit questionable. I've become better in many ways and good at many things, as a husband, a dad, a businessman, a winner, and now, an author. All of those are because of her support, friendship, and guidance. THANK YOU, JAZMIN BLAIS, FOR MY LIFE AS I KNOW IT. YOU MAKE IT TRULY SPECIAL.

MUSTARD CAVIAR, PAGE 212

CONTENTS

FOREWORD BY
TOM
COLICCHIO

"DON'T PLAY WITH YOUR FOOD! EAT IT!"

How often did we hear *that* refrain from our moms while growing up?

But why not play with our food … and then eat it?

I think this is the question that greets Richard Blais when he wakes each morning and that then rides on his shoulder throughout the day, muttering in his ear. It's the notion that keeps him in his notebooks and in the kitchen.

It was clear to me from my first encounters with Richard and his food that he was a very talented guy with a very different way of looking at food. Like most successful chefs, he definitely marches to his own beat and has his own style. There is a reason Richard considers himself the Willy Wonka of cooking: He has the ability to find something fun and unusual and amusing to riff off of in a bowl of macaroni. Hence, his successful marriage of artistic creativity and scientific curiosity that lets him take "playing with your food" to new heights, as he wields his microplane and reimagines dishes in new, delightfully inventive, flavorful ways.

But, like Wonka, Richard's ability to find the whimsy in food goes hand in hand with a seriousness of purpose. In his sojourns on *Top Chef,* he maintained a staunch professionalism and kept his engagement in the competition solely about the food. I saw him push himself, and, as a result, I saw him grow in his craft. Kids learn through play—why can't chefs, too?

Luckily for the rest of us, Richard didn't heed his mom, nor does he plan to cease playing with his food any time soon. And now, in *Try This at Home,* he has managed to cleanly and clearly break down his process so that you can have a good time trying out some of his methods in your own kitchen. This is a cookbook from a serious chef who knows how to make fun of himself and lighten up the whole process. Cooking need not be an overly complicated, overwrought process with eighteen ingredients and fourteen pans. Though you can try using a good iSi siphon and a smoking gun (not *that* kind of smoking gun). And occasionally some nitrous oxide. Oh, and good ingredients, of course. Plus a spirit of fun.

YOU HAVE THE COOKBOOK. NOW, AS YOUR MOTHER WOULD SAY, "GO PLAY!"

THE MOST THRILLING
ASPECT OF COOKING

is making people happy. I often start imagining a dish before I even step into the kitchen. It's taking a classic preparation—like the linguine and clams I grew up eating at Long Island Italian restaurants—and tweaking it, or remixing it, so it still resembles the original but is a more interesting and flavorful version. I embrace food that is different and unique. That's who I am as a professional chef and as a home cook. I like to put a dish through the wringer by reimagining it, adjusting textures, temperature, and taste along the way. No matter how refined a dish I may create, no matter what manner of luxurious or unusual ingredient I might work with, at the end of the day, I know that what I do is about pleasing people and satisfying my guests in a special and profound way.

What I love about cooking is re-creating traditional dishes to make them delicious and an *experience.* I prod my diners for an emotional reaction—a chance to revisit childhood, or a special time and place, or to find whimsy in overwrought dishes that we sometimes eat. When I competed on *Top Chef*, I made linguine and clams in front of a national audience. But my dish was a plate of linguine fashioned out of thinly shaved sweet potato and paired with conch and oregano. As the judges praised my dish, I said, "I pretty much hate everything I cook."

I meant that my dishes are never truly "finished," because as I'm ready to plate one, I start thinking about how I can improve it. I keep a sketchbook with me at all times for recording moments of inspiration or planning events or holiday meals. I sketch composed dishes or elements of a dish, trying to get the first few iterations of it down before I even touch a pan. I love to tinker with my food and come up with ways to make it more delicious.

I didn't spend my summers braising meat at my grandmother's farmhouse in Provence. Instead, I was eating SpaghettiO's, and the only chef I knew then was Chef Boyardee. My first cooking job was at a McDonald's on Long Island. It was where I *wanted* to work when I was a teenager: I went there when my Little League team won a game, when my mom didn't have time to make dinner, and when my dad picked me up for my weekend with him (I was adopted by my stepfather in second grade). I started at the counter, but I didn't like wearing the name tag and visor, and in my first hour on the job, I had to serve a girl from school I had a crush on. The embarrassment sent me into the kitchen, which turned out to be a far more anonymous—and interesting—place, plus it was where all the cool kids worked. They were older than me and most played football at school, and they took pride in trying to be the fastest at making a batch of twenty-four hamburgers. Growing up in a lower-middle-class family had made me humble. I didn't have a strong sense of belonging in the world, but I found that in the kitchen.

My station included one warming box for fish fillets and another for chicken nuggets, plus a small deep fryer, a small table for toasting buns, and a few hanging hydraulic guns filled with sauces. We were heating, reheating, and assembling. But it was a great first step in my career: I learned the grace to move quickly in a cramped space, and the ability to both follow orders and give them. (I also learned what to do during an armed robbery, but that's another story.) I may have won *Top Chef All-Stars*, but starting my career at McDonald's also shaped me as a chef.

After a short stint at college ended, I walked a mile between my afternoon gig flipping upscale burgers to my evening job broiling steaks and steaming lobsters. I had dreadlocks, wore way-too-baggy pants, listened to the latest rap remix on my Walkman, and drank Olde English by the forty. I was cooking most days of the week, but it was really just

I EMBRACE FOOD THAT IS DIFFERENT AND UNIQUE. THAT'S WHO I AM AS A PROFESSIONAL CHEF AND AS A HOME COOK.

a job. Then I got a job at a Rockville Centre restaurant called Tuscany, which had received a good review in the *New York Times*. It was the type of place that serves shrimp cocktail in a martini glass, Caesar salad in a bowl made of Asiago cheese, and an ostrich fillet with twenty-nine garnishes. This kind of food was trendy in New York during the mid-to-late 1990s, and Tuscany was the closest to a "city" restaurant that I could find in my branch of suburbia. It was a great training ground: There was a steady and talented kitchen team. The books that the owner kept in his office—*White Heat* by Marco Pierre White, and cookbooks by Lidia Bastianich, David Burke, and Charlie Trotter, among others—opened up a new world to me.

At Tuscany, I lost the dreadlocks and found my passion and ambition. I then enrolled in the Culinary Institute of America. I learned so much in cooking school; I was a poster boy for great classical kitchen training, a model student. So much so that I was asked to stay on for a prestigious fellowship in the fish kitchen after graduating. From there, I embarked on a rotation of working with some of the best chefs in the world, doing stints in the kitchens of Thomas Keller, Ferran Adrià, and Daniel Boulud.

Eventually I was offered an opportunity to run my own restaurant, called Fishbone, in Atlanta, and I jumped at it. But when I moved to the South in 2000, the food there seemed decidedly un–New York. To me, polenta was better than grits, pimento cheese was just a weird substance sold in plastic tubs, and boiled peanuts were the food of gas stations. The South is known for its incredible time-honored traditions. Yet when I got to Atlanta, it was in the middle of a restaurant revolution: inventive chefs were applying modern twists to many regional dishes. I felt I had the flexibility and space to be übercreative for the first time. I was both fearless (I was dubbed the "Bad Boy of Brunoise" by a local critic) and naive. I could make lasagna out of artichokes and serve it with halibut, and the diners appreciated it.

The city was growing at the same time I was getting more comfortable and confident in my own style. I gained an appreciation for the ingredients and techniques of the South. I can now make a brisket that puts many true Southerners to shame, and at my restaurant Flip Burger Boutique, we feature both a "country-fried" burger topped with pimento cheese and a burger topped with a red wine reduction and blue cheese foam. The South and I have harmonized well: I consider myself lucky to be in a city where there's plenty of interest in a cooking revolution. What's true and important is that I am a chef who makes unique food, and as I happen to be based in the South, I draw from my surroundings.

And then, after a few years in Atlanta, TV happened. When I got the call inviting me to appear on *Top Chef* in 2007, I was hesitant; I thought I was a good candidate for a guest judge, not a contestant. It turned out to be a life-changing experience. The resulting fame is neat, but I'm still most comfortable in a kitchen—that's where I feel at home and can be most creative and have fun.

Some people think I'm a "molecular chef" because they've seen me whip out a tank of liquid nitrogen on TV. I do use science and technology as tools to further my cooking, and I enjoy it. I'll embrace a unique ingredient or technique in the pursuit of flavor first. I'm obsessed with what the Japanese refer to as umami, which literally means "delicious taste" and is more of a sensation than a flavor; it's the flavor of savory or what makes your mouth water. It occurs naturally in foods such as tomatoes, seaweed, and shiitake mushrooms. I try to incorporate umami in many of the foods I cook.

But I'm also a classically trained chef—and a husband and father. So I know what it means to balance my desire to push the concept of what I can make noodles out of with my desire to put dinner on the table. At home, I don't have unlimited resources, professional equipment, pricey and rare ingredients, an army of prep cooks, and all day to prepare. At home, I cook just like everyone else. I like a roasted chicken or a simple grilled steak for dinner, pancakes and eggs for breakfast, and a pimento cheese sandwich for lunch (I have truly become a convert). I'm going to show you how to cook those everyday dishes that I love, plus fun variations of them when you have the time or inclination.

Many of these recipes will be familiar, and the ones that aren't likely have familiar roots. For example, you can make my cheeseburger, and then if you want to take it a step further, you can make a Swiss cheese foam to go on top of it. You can make your kids the eggs I make for my daughter Riley at breakfast, or you can try cooking them sous vide (how I like them). You can make a classic Reuben sandwich, or you can try it with tongue, which I love. These are all dishes within any good home cook's reach, so I'm going to urge you to try new things. Throughout the book, I call out opportunities for a more challenging or exciting way to make a dish by using a new technique, an unusual ingredient, or a special piece of equipment. These variations—we'll call them 2.0s—will help you be more creative in your kitchen.

Some of the dishes here are great versions of traditional dishes and some are what I think of as "culinary remixes." Enjoy the ride!

MY FAVORITE PIECES OF EQUIPMENT

DUTCH OVEN/BRAISING POT: A good cast-iron Dutch oven with a lid is my go-to pot for many of my favorite things to cook, and a number of recipes in this book call for one.

ELECTRIC KNIFE: This is an extremely underrated tool. The kind of precision it offers is great for cutting through large blocks of meat, like big old-fashioned roasts, and layered foods like finger sandwiches for hors d'oeuvres. Use for Tuna Prime Rib (page 225) and Roast Beef Tenderloin (page 237).

IMMERSION CIRCULATOR/SOUS VIDE MACHINE: This uses a method of slowly cooking food that is sealed in plastic in water at precisely controlled, steady temperatures. I recommend the Sous Vide Supreme and the immersion-circulators from PolyScience or Julabo. Use for Sous Vide Eggs (page 69), Mashed Sous Vide English Peas (page 131), Sous Vide Chicken (page 184), Lobster Sous Vide (page 219), and Sous Vide Steak (page 238).

ISI SIPHON: A siphon is essentially an old-fashioned whipped cream canister. I use the iSi brand because I like its sleek efficiency and the fact that it comes in both a professional size and a more user-friendly one for home cooks. If you're just whipping cream, you can use what you've been using for that purpose. But if you want to try whipping up foams and unique sauces, the iSi siphon is a great thing to have around. (A small 1-pint siphon that is perfect for a home cook is available from online retailers—just be sure you get the canister type, not the kind for making carbonated sodas.)

LIQUID NITROGEN: Want to make ice cream in five minutes, with no cranking, no rock salt, and no waiting to eat it? Of course you do. Liquid nitrogen is the answer. You don't need a chemistry degree, but you do need a little ingenuity to get your hands on a canister. (And some good-quality cryogenic gloves—no joke.) Liquid nitrogen must be stored and transported in a special container called a deur, or it will evaporate very quickly. You can search your local Yellow Pages or look online for a supplier. You can borrow or rent a five-liter deur to transport the liquid nitrogen; five liters, at about $2 a liter, is enough to make a couple of quarts of ice cream.

Liquid nitrogen can be entirely safe to cook with, but you have to use caution. I tell my cooks to respect liquid nitrogen and to treat it like they do hot fryer oil. It is best to wear gloves, closed-toe shoes, and long pants (in case of drips) when dealing with liquid nitrogen. And you should do so in a vented area. Prolonged contact can burn you—just like hot oil would—and the vapors can cause a harmful condition in a closed space. Always make sure that the vapors have burned off any food before consuming it.

MANDOLINE: This is a great tool for slicing, especially very thin, exact, and consistent slices. Use caution when using a mandoline, as the blades are often razor sharp.

MICROPLANE: This invaluable tool is often very sharp, which means you have to be a bit more careful with it than with a regular grater, but it also means that you can use it to easily and finely grate or zest a wide range of ingredients.

MORTAR AND PESTLE: Whether I'm making pesto or just need to crush or grind pepper, I always have a mortar (the bowl) and pestle (the heavy little bat) on hand.

PRESSURE COOKER: A pressure cooker cooks food at a really high temperature by increasing the air pressure surrounding it, greatly reducing the cooking time. A lot of people have a pressure cooker collecting dust at home already. Check your grandma's cupboard! Use for Chicken Stock (page 44), Braised Bacon (page 45), Boiled Peanuts (page 89), and Bolognese (page 153).

SMOKING GUN: One of the most common questions I get is "Where did you get that little electric smoker you used on *Top Chef*?" And, yes, that's usually from college students. The mini electric smoker is one of my favorite devices because it's much easier to use it than to brine and cure salmon. All you do is fill it up with hickory chips and turn it on; the smoke infuses the salmon so that the scent is there, but the fish retains its moist texture. I use The Smoking Gun, a handheld battery-operated electric food smoker made by PolyScience.

SPOON: I pretty much always carry a spoon (a nice antique one) in my back pocket, and I advise you to do the same—at least when you're in your kitchen. I use it to taste everything I cook, as well as for basting meat or fish or making a quenelle (an oval- or egg-shaped scoop or portion of food, traditionally pureed fish, but also things like ice cream or mashed potatoes).

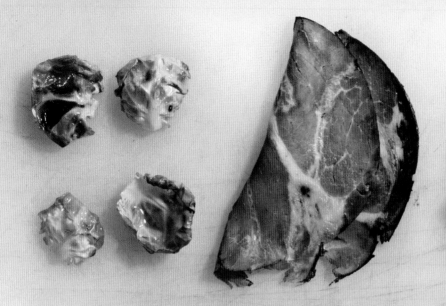

NOTES ON PLATING

THIS MAY SURPRISE YOU, BUT I REALLY CAN'T STAND PLATING—
the careful arrangement of food on plates that we do in restaurants. It bothers me because I feel it gets in the way of flavor. I bet if you rattled off your top three foods, you'd find they aren't at all about presentation. Bolognese, goulash, a good curry—sure, they're beautiful in the eye of the beholder, but let's be honest, they are also kind of messy.

It's not that I don't care how my food looks when I serve it, just that I think we need to get away from some of the pretensions of plating. I'm always searching for a way to make the food look *unpresented*. I tell my cooks to make it look like it fell from the sky, but to bear in mind that this means softly falling from the sky, as if on a parachute made of clouds. Does it look like the wind naturally set it there? Or does it look like someone preciously squirted and swooshed a masterpiece? I'd rather the former.

And in reality, I don't care if each plate looks like the one before it. Consistency is important when it comes to taste and flavor, but it's overrated when it comes to plating. As a matter of fact, I think it's almost romantic that each plate is a little different, like people or (I know this is a bit cheesy) snowflakes.

When you put delicious food on a plate, think about how it will be eaten. Is the sauce close enough to the protein? Will it be easy to taste all the elements together? Those are the most important aspects of plating your food.

THE ESSENTIAL SPICE SHELF

4-SPICE POWDER

BARBECUE SPICE

CARAWAY SEEDS

CHIPOTLE CHILE
POWDER

CLOVES

CORIANDER SEEDS
(GROUND)

CUMIN SEEDS
(GROUND)

ESPELETTE PEPPER

KOREAN BARBECUE
SPICE

MALDON SALT

OLD BAY SEASONING

OREGANO (DRIED)

PÂTÉ SPICE

RAS EL HANOUT

SMOKED PIMENTÓN

TANDOORI SPICE

WHITE PEPPERCORNS

SOUS VIDE COOKING 1

MEAT	TEMP
Beef short ribs	179°F
Boneless skinless chicken breast	144°F
Duck confit (leg)	167°F
Lamb loin (chop)	138°F
Lobsters	126.5°F
Pork belly	140°F
Pork chops (thick)	138°F
Rib-eye strip or steak	136°F
Root vegetables	194°F

Aioli (Smoked Aioli) 24 | Three Great Mustards: Beer Mustard, Pastrami Mustard, Violet Mustard 26 | Two Great Ketchups: Umami Ketchup, San Marzano Ketchup 29 | Sri-Rancha 30 | Ranch Caviar 32 | Balsamic Vinaigrette 33 | Mustard Vinaigrette 33 | Citrus Herb Vinaigrette 34 | Sauce Maria Rosa 34 | Tomato Sauce 35 | Pork BBQ Sauce 35 | Tartar Sauce 36 | Blue Cheese Dressing (Blue Cheese Foam) 38 | Buttermilk Herb Dressing 39 | Bear-naise with Brown Butter 40 | Bottled Pepper Vinegar 41 | "Everything Bagel" Vinaigrette 43 | Pressure-Cooker Chicken Stock 44 | Pressure-Cooker Braised Bacon 45 | Clarified Butter 45 | Snail Butter (Asian Snail Butter) 46 | Toasted Herb Bread Crumbs 47 | Candied Onions 48 | Candied Spiced Pecans 49 | Hab Spice 50 | Pastrami Spices 50 | Cranberry-Grenadine Jelly 51 | Gentlemen's Chutney 51 | Pickling: Pickling Brine, Pickled Celery, Pickled Radishes, Pickled Strawberries, Pickled Peaches 52

A
PANTRY
ARSENAL

Do you want to make your food taste so much better without having to enroll in cooking school? The best advice I can give you is to be assertive. One way to distinguish your food from someone else's—whether it's to impress your family, for friends at a dinner party, or to best a fellow contestant on a television cooking show (insert laugh)—is with bold-flavored herbs, spices, and condiments.

The hallmark of my food is aggressive seasoning. "More fresh herbs! More acidity!" is a call my sous-chefs constantly hear from me, because those are my key tools for making up the flavor in my dishes. I concentrate on harnessing strong-flavored ingredients—so bring on the fresh lemon juice, tear up the parsley leaves, splash on the Worcestershire sauce. The most important thing in my pantry at home is my spice rack, which is loaded with spices, mixes, and blends. (Buy bulk spices; they're cheaper and they stay fresher longer, whether it's something commonplace like oregano or something exotic like ras el hanout.) The most important thing in my fridge? My condiments, including different kinds of mayonnaise, ketchup, chutney, and vinaigrette.

There isn't a condiment I don't like (in other words, I don't question it when somebody puts ketchup on their scrambled eggs or mayo on their fries). And my favorite, bar none, is tartar sauce. Early in my career, when I was training with French chefs, I would have blanched at the thought of a sauce that didn't rely on expertly minced, precisely blended ingredients; but as I've matured, I've come to embrace the pleasure of chunky sauces laden with hand-ripped herbs, chopped hard-boiled egg, and bits of cornichon—my mouth waters writing about it. Ketchup is another favorite, especially a version I make with precious San Marzano tomatoes, which come from a village near Pompeii at the foot of Mount Vesuvius.

When my family and I sit down for dinner, there is always a collection of condiment jars set out on the table. Both of my daughters enjoy a good drizzle of red wine reduction or a chunky salsa verde on their veggies . . . or mac 'n' cheese.

So here are some must-have recipes that will help you appreciate and adopt my almost obsessive desire to season (herbs, spices) and complement (condiments) my food.

"MORE FRESH HERBS! MORE ACIDI

1 large egg

4 garlic cloves,
finely minced

Juice of 1 lemon
(about 3
tablespoons)

1 tablespoon Dijon
mustard

1 teaspoon cider
vinegar

2 teaspoons kosher
salt

½ teaspoon freshly
ground white
pepper

¾ cup extra-virgin
olive oil

Dash of hot sauce,
or to taste
(optional)

MAKES ABOUT 1 CUP

AIOLI

To me, mayonnaise is a true "mother sauce," which means you can use it as a
base for just about any other type of sauce, even salad dressing and dips.
And you don't need me to tell you that it's great as is in a sandwich.
I have a T-shirt that says "I ♥ mayo," and I especially like the French
garlic mayonnaise called *aioli*.

1. Fill a small saucepan with 3 inches of water and
bring to a boil over medium heat. With a slotted spoon,
lower the egg into the water and boil for 6 minutes. Remove
the egg and put it in a small bowl of cold water until cool
enough to handle. Peel the egg.

2. Put the egg, garlic, lemon juice, Dijon, vinegar,
salt, and white pepper into a blender and puree on low
speed. With the blender running, add the oil in a steady,
slow stream, blending until emulsified and thickened. Add
the hot sauce, if using, and blend on high speed for about
1 minute. Transfer to an airtight container and store in the
refrigerator for up to 3 days.

SERVE WITH: PORK-BELLY SANDWICH (PAGE 104),
CHARRED ARTICHOKES (PAGE 128), CHICKEN
SALAD (PAGE 185), CRAB CAKES (PAGE 211),
LOBSTER ROLLS (PAGE 216)

2.0 SMOKED AIOLI

Barbecue is very popular in Atlanta, and I've developed a taste for smoked meat since moving here. One day while eating barbecue, I wondered what would happen if I put a pot of homemade mayonnaise into a cold-smoker. So I tried it, and it infused my mayo with a great hickory-smoked flavor. When I don't make my own mayonnaise, I like the brand Kewpie. It's a Japanese product that has a chubby baby licking his lips on the label (which is part of what makes it officially legit in my book).

To make Smoked Aioli, simply add ¾ teaspoon hickory smoke powder (which you'll find sold with spices and other seasonings at supermarkets or online) to the egg mixture before adding the olive oil.

THREE GREAT MUSTARDS

BEER MUSTARD

For some reason, I used to be embarrassed that I liked honey mustard. In retrospect, it's probably because it's such a simple, sweet condiment that lots of children love. So, I thought, what is the anti-child's ingredient? Beer. I make a sweet honey mustard that any chicken finger would love and then ratchet it up by adding beer extract. It rounds out the sweetness and gives it a bit of a hoppy edge. (Beer extract is available at home-brew equipment suppliers and good spice shops; you can also find it online at SpiceBarn.com.)

1 cup Aioli (page 24) or good-quality store-bought mayonnaise

½ cup Dijon mustard

2 tablespoons agave syrup

1 teaspoon ground cinnamon

½ teaspoon beer extract

Pinch of cayenne pepper

In a small bowl, whisk the aioli, Dijon, agave, cinnamon, beer extract, and cayenne together until well combined. Store in an airtight container in the refrigerator for up to 1 month.

SERVE WITH: VIDALIA ONION RINGS (PAGE 86)

PASTRAMI MUSTARD

You eat a pastrami sandwich slathered with mustard, so why not add pastrami spices to the mustard and use it to flavor another dish, such as grilled salmon? Sometimes cooking is about connecting the dots: Ask yourself, for example, what else is good with mustard? A turkey sandwich is one answer, and wouldn't that taste even better with the pastrami spices? That's all it takes to make new and interesting dishes.

1½ tablespoons coriander seeds 1½ teaspoons yellow mustard seeds	1½ teaspoons black peppercorns	1 teaspoon paprika	1 cup Beer Mustard (opposite)

1. Put the coriander and mustard seeds in a small skillet and toast over medium heat, swirling the pan, until fragrant. Transfer the seeds to a mortar and pestle or spice grinder, add the peppercorns, and grind until fine. Transfer to a small bowl.

2. Add the paprika and mustard and stir until well combined. Store in an airtight container in the refrigerator for up to 1 month.

SERVE WITH: **CORNED BEEF ON RYE (PAGE 102)**

VIOLET MUSTARD

If honey mustard is for kids, violet mustard is for old ladies. I say this only because a restaurant critic once wrote that one of my flowery mustards smelled like the inside of a grandmother's purse. I loved my grandmother's purse . . . with its cool, snappy clasp.

2 tablespoons candied violets ¼ cup honey	¼ cup balsamic vinegar ¼ cup Dijon mustard	¼ cup whole-grain mustard ½ teaspoon kosher salt	1 teaspoon freshly ground black pepper

1. Mince the violets on a cutting board until very fine, or mash until pulverized using a mortar and pestle.

2. In a small bowl, stir together the honey, vinegar, and Dijon and whole-grain mustards until combined. Add the violets, salt, and pepper and mix thoroughly. Store in an airtight container in the refrigerator for up to 1 week.

SERVE WITH: **A CHEESE PLATE OR, FOR A FLORAL NOTE, CORNED BEEF ON RYE (PAGE 102)**

WO GREAT KETCHUPS

MAKES ABOUT 2 CUPS

UMAMI KETCHUP

This is like ketchup on steroids—it's bold and dark, and it has a temper. The use of the word "ketchup" here is liberal. You could call it oyster sauce, syrup, or glaze as well. You can overdose on this. Seriously, too much of the umami ingredients can make your heart rate increase, so a little goes a long way. Also, umami has a tendency to bloom in a dish, so even if the first taste seems like it needs more, wait a few minutes before dousing it with more. Patience, grasshopper.

1 cup tamarind concentrate

¾ cup San Marzano Ketchup (opposite)

2½ tablespoons fish sauce

2 tablespoons sugar

1 teaspoon Worcestershire sauce

2 garlic cloves, finely minced

2 red Thai chiles, finely minced

In a medium bowl, whisk the tamarind, ketchup, fish sauce, sugar, Worcestershire, garlic, and chiles together until well combined. Store in an airtight container in the refrigerator for up to 3 weeks.

SERVE WITH: FRENCH FRIES (PAGE 85), VIDALIA ONION RINGS (PAGE 86)

SAN MARZANO KETCHUP

San Marzano tomatoes are from a region near Naples, and their sweet-tart flavor and thin skins make them ideal for canning. This recipe is a mash-up of sorts, almost blasphemy: slow-cooked tomatoes spiked with prepared ketchup. The combination really encapsulates my philosophy in the kitchen: No ingredient is sacred. Good old ketchup is as valuable as a San Marzano tomato. (And each adds something to the other.)

2 tablespoons olive oil

1 yellow onion, chopped

1 garlic clove, chopped

2 tablespoons tomato paste

½ cup firmly packed light brown sugar

¼ cup cider vinegar

One 28-ounce can San Marzano tomatoes in juice, crushed with your hands

1 tablespoon soy sauce

1 teaspoon kosher salt

¾ teaspoon chipotle chile powder

½ teaspoon dry mustard

⅛ teaspoon ground cloves

⅛ teaspoon ground allspice

1. Heat the olive oil in a medium saucepan over medium heat. Add the onion and garlic and cook until soft and fragrant, 3 to 4 minutes. Add the tomato paste and cook, stirring occasionally, until it begins to deepen in color and caramelize, about 3 minutes. Add the brown sugar and continue cooking, stirring often, for another 5 minutes.

2. Add the vinegar, tomatoes, soy sauce, salt, chile powder, mustard, cloves, and allspice and stir well to combine. Cover the pan and cook, stirring occasionally, until the mixture reaches a thick, ketchup-like consistency, about 30 minutes.

3. Transfer the mixture to a blender and puree until smooth. Set a fine-mesh strainer over a bowl and pass the ketchup through it, pressing on the solids with a rubber spatula or a spoon to push through any large pieces. Let cool completely. Store in an airtight container in the refrigerator for up to 3 weeks.

NOTE: *If you add some prepared ketchup to the puree (¼ cup), the emulsifiers in the store-bought stuff will make your ketchup a bit closer to what most people find texturally acceptable for something called a "ketchup."*

SERVE WITH: ANYTHING YOU LIKE WITH REGULAR KETCHUP, SUCH AS FRENCH FRIES (PAGE 85)

2 cups store-bought ranch salad dressing | Juice of ½ lemon (about 1½ tablespoons) | ¼ cup Sriracha hot sauce

SRI-RANCHA

I love ranch dressing. It's such an anti-fine-dining condiment. I love the combination of ranch and Sriracha because it cools as it burns. The play of the heat off the herby creaminess of the dressing is amazing. For something really crazy, pour this into an ice cream maker and turn it into a frozen savory condiment; serve it with thick ridged potato chips.

Put the ranch dressing into a small bowl, add the lemon juice and Sriracha, and whisk until fully incorporated. Store in an airtight container in the refrigerator for up to 2 weeks.

SERVE WITH: FRENCH FRIES (PAGE 85), CRUDITÉS (PAGE 139)

2 cups store-bought ranch salad dressing

¼ cup (2 ounces) American paddle-fish caviar (or other cheap caviar)

MAKES ABOUT 2³/₄ CUPS

RANCH CAVIAR

Ranch caviar is what your redneck cousin might create if he won the lottery: He'd buy expensive caviar and fold in some creamy ranch.

Put the ranch dressing into a small bowl and gently fold in the caviar until fully incorporated. Store in an airtight container in the refrigerator for up to 2 weeks.

SERVE WITH: FRENCH FRIES (PAGE 85) OR AS A SAUCE FOR SEARED/FRIED/GRILLED SEAFOOD

¼ cup balsamic vinegar

2 teaspoons molasses

1¼ tablespoons minced garlic

1 teaspoon minced white onion

1 teaspoon Dijon mustard

½ teaspoon salt

½ teaspoon black pepper

¾ cup extra-virgin olive oil

Juice of ½ lemon

MAKES ABOUT 1 CUP

BALSAMIC VINAIGRETTE

Balsamic vinaigrette, it seems so . . . eighties, but with its natural sweetness and woody, aged flavor, it's of tremendous value. Here we are spiking up the savoriness with the mustard, garlic, and molasses, which gives it, well, nuance. Serve as a dressing with some hearty bitter greens, or brush it over a steak right off the grill.

In a bowl, whisk the balsamic, molasses, garlic, onion, mustard, salt, pepper, oil, and lemon juice until well combined. Store in an airtight container in the refrigerator for up to 2 days. Whisk to incorporate before serving.

2 teaspoons sherry vinegar

2 teaspoons red wine vinegar

2 teaspoons sugar

1 teaspoon Dijon mustard

1 teaspoon whole-grain mustard

⅓ cup extra-virgin olive oil

1 teaspoon chopped fresh thyme

1 teaspoon thinly sliced fresh chives

Kosher salt and freshly ground black pepper to taste

MAKES ABOUT ½ CUP

MUSTARD VINAIGRETTE

This herb vinaigrette is a basic and easy way to dress a salad. It's a classic recipe inspired by a brief stint in Miami. My wife, Jazmin, and I used to frequent a little bistro that served the most amazing mustard vinaigrette. This is my homage.

In a small bowl, whisk the sherry and red wine vinegars, sugar, and Dijon and whole-grain mustards together. Whisking constantly, slowly drizzle in the olive oil, whisking until emulsified and thickened. Whisk in the thyme and chives, season with salt and pepper, and stir. Store in an airtight container in the refrigerator for up to 1 month.

SERVE WITH: CORNED BEEF HASH AND EGGS IN A CAN (PAGE 75)

- Juice of ½ lemon
- 1 teaspoon Dijon mustard
- 1 teaspoon sugar

- ⅓ cup extra-virgin olive oil
- Kosher salt and freshly ground black pepper to taste

- 1 teaspoon minced fresh tarragon
- 1 teaspoon minced fresh flat-leaf parsley

- 1 teaspoon minced fresh basil

MAKES ABOUT ½ CUP

CITRUS HERB VINAIGRETTE

A great multipurpose vinaigrette to use for delicate greens or when you want a touch of fresh acidity.

In a small bowl, whisk the lemon juice, Dijon, and sugar together until combined. Whisking constantly, add the oil in a slow, whisking steady-stream, until emulsified and thickened. Season with salt and pepper and stir in the tarragon, parsley, and basil. Store in an airtight container in the refrigerator for up to 1 month.

SERVE WITH: SWEET CHERRY TOMATO SALAD (PAGE 122)

- ⅔ cup Aioli (page 24) or good-quality store-bought mayonnaise
- ⅓ cup San Marzano Ketchup (page 29) or store-bought ketchup

- 3 tablespoons chopped fresh cilantro
- 1 teaspoon grated lime zest
- 2 teaspoons fresh lime juice

- ½ teaspoon Cholula hot sauce
- 3 drops Worcestershire sauce

- ¼ teaspoon kosher salt
- ⅛ teaspoon freshly ground black pepper

MAKES ABOUT 1 CUP

SAUCE MARIA ROSA

By this point, you probably know I hold very little sacred when it comes to traditional recipes. This has as its base Thousand Island dressing, which some people call Sauce Marie Rose. My remix replaces the usual lemon juice with lime juice spiked with Cholula hot sauce and Worcestershire. I call it Maria Rosa. Why not?

In a small bowl, whisk the aioli, ketchup, cilantro, lime zest and juice, Cholula, Worcestershire, salt, and pepper together until well combined. Store in an airtight container in the refrigerator for up to 2 weeks.

SERVE WITH: CORNED BEEF ON RYE (PAGE 102)

- 3 tablespoons olive oil
- 1 large yellow onion, minced
- 8 garlic cloves, minced
- Two 28-ounce cans San Marzano tomatoes in juice
- One 4-inch piece Parmesan cheese rind
- ¼ cup finely diced charcuterie scraps, such as prosciutto or hard salami rinds (optional)
- 4 teaspoons dried oregano
- Kosher salt and freshly ground black pepper to taste
- 18 to 20 fresh basil leaves
- 5 to 6 leaves from an organic or nonsprayed tomato plant (optional)

MAKES ABOUT 6 CUPS

TOMATO SAUCE

I wish I was Italian. I pretend by keeping this classic sauce in the fridge at all times. It's especially handy for busy weeknights.

1. Heat the oil in a large saucepan over medium heat. Add the onion and garlic and cook until softened, about 5 minutes. Add the tomatoes, mash coarsely with a potato masher, and bring to a simmer. Reduce the heat to low and simmer for 1 hour.

2. If the tomatoes are still chunky, mash them again with the potato masher. Add the cheese rind, diced meats, if using, and oregano and cook until very thick, about 30 minutes more. Season the sauce with salt and pepper and stir in the basil and tomato leaves, if using. Remove from the heat and let cool to room temperature.

3. Transfer the sauce, including the Parmesan rind, to an airtight container and store in the refrigerator for up to 1 week or in the freezer for up to 3 months. Discard the cheese rind before serving.

SERVE WITH: SPAGHETTI AND MEATBALLS (PAGE 148), MOROCCAN TUNA BOLOGNESE (PAGE 154), BRAISED SQUID "CANNELLONI" (PAGE 165), VEGETABLE LASAGNA (PAGE 155), FRESH RAVIOLI (PAGE 170), PRAWNS 'N' POLENTA (PAGE 215)

- 8 cups pork stock
- ¼ cup cider vinegar
- 2 tablespoons light brown sugar
- Kosher salt and freshly ground black pepper to taste

MAKES ABOUT 2 CUPS

PORK BBQ SAUCE

This challenges the idea of barbecue sauce but carries its essential flavors, acidity, and sweetness with the stock's meatiness. Add some chipotle and/or pineapple juice, even coffee, to ramp it up. Or use the reduced stock as a sauce for roasted vegetables or to glaze any meat.

1. In a sauce pot over medium heat, bring the stock to a boil, reduce the heat, and simmer. Cook until reduced by 75 percent or until the sauce coats the back of a spoon.

2. Mix in the vinegar and sugar. Cook until the sugar is dissolved, about 2 minutes. Season with salt and pepper, then remove from the heat.

1 cup Aioli (page 24) or good-quality store-bought mayonnaise

1 hard-boiled egg, chopped

¼ cup (about 7) cornichons, minced

¼ cup capers, rinsed and minced

1 small stalk celery, minced

½ small jalapeño, seeded and finely minced

2 tablespoons fresh flat-leaf parsley leaves, roughly torn

2 sprigs fresh tarragon, leaves removed and chopped

Grated zest and juice (about 1½ tablespoons) of ½ lemon

Kosher salt and freshly ground black pepper to taste

MAKES ABOUT 1¼ CUPS

TARTAR SAUCE

I first discovered tartar sauce in the backseat of my parents' 1973 Pinto, eating takeout from an Arthur Treacher's Fish & Chips when I was seven years old. It was the first time I realized you could add things to mayo to make it even better. Whaaat!? That is genius. For tartar sauce, it's pickles, lemons, herbs, and other stuff, but open your fridge and see what you could toss into mayo to make a more creative sauce. Tartar sauce changed my life. I hope my version changes yours.

In a medium bowl, whisk the aioli and chopped egg until combined. Add the cornichons, capers, celery, jalapeño, parsley, tarragon, and lemon zest and juice and stir well until combined. Season with salt and pepper and mix well. Store in an airtight container in the refrigerator for up to 1 week.

SERVE WITH: FILLET OF FISH SANDWICH (PAGE 93)

- 3 tablespoons sherry vinegar
- 1 shallot, very finely minced
- 2 cups Aioli (page 24) or good-quality store-bought mayonnaise

- ¼ cup low-fat buttermilk
- ¼ cup fresh flat-leaf parsley leaves, finely chopped

- 3 sprigs thyme, leaves removed and finely chopped
- 2 scallions, green parts only, thinly sliced
- 1 teaspoon kosher salt

- 1 teaspoon freshly ground black pepper
- ⅓ cup crumbled blue cheese

MAKES ABOUT 2½ CUPS

BLUE CHEESE DRESSING

I don't think there's a more masculine flavor than blue cheese. Like an old pair of socks, or a barnyard, it cuts through almost anything. It's a natural foil to anything overly sweet or sour or meaty. Freezing this recipe in an ice cream machine makes for an adventurous condiment for a nicely charred steak.

1. Pour the vinegar over the shallot in a small bowl and let stand for 10 minutes.

2. In a medium bowl, whisk the aioli and buttermilk together until smooth. Add the shallot mixture, parsley, thyme, scallion greens, salt, and pepper and whisk until smooth. Using a rubber spatula, fold in the blue cheese until combined. Store in an airtight container in the refrigerator for up to 1 week.

SERVE WITH: GRILLED RIB EYE (PAGE 238), SWEETBREAD NUGGETS (PAGE 90), BURGERS (PAGE 101)

2.0 BLUE CHEESE FOAM

Foams have become more widely known thanks to cutting-edge chefs. I like them, though not because they are considered sophisticated—I just find them so interesting on the plate. Blue cheese, for instance, is a rather dense ingredient, so turning it into something light as air, which you can do easily within an iSi siphon (see page 14), is unexpected.

To make blue cheese foam, put 2 cups heavy cream and 4 ounces crumbled blue cheese in a medium saucepan and warm gently over medium-low heat, stirring frequently, until the cheese is completely melted and the liquid is smooth. Pour the cream into a pitcher or bowl and refrigerate, covered, until cold. Transfer the cold mixture to an iSi siphon and charge with 2 charges. Let the canister sit for 5 minutes, then shake it vigorously before dispensing.

- 1 cup low-fat buttermilk
- ½ cup sour cream
- 2 tablespoons red wine vinegar
- 2 tablespoons fresh lemon juice
- 1 tablespoon honey
- 1 garlic clove, finely minced
- 1 tablespoon minced fresh basil
- 1 tablespoon minced fresh tarragon
- 1 tablespoon minced fresh flat-leaf parsley
- ½ teaspoon celery seeds
- 1 teaspoon kosher salt
- ¼ teaspoon freshly ground black pepper

MAKES ABOUT 2 CUPS

BUTTERMILK HERB DRESSING

I like ranch dressing, which is basically what this recipe is, so much that I mix it with Sriracha (see page 30) and even caviar (see page 32), and I've been known to freeze it into a savory ice cream or dehydrate it and pulverize it into a powder. What's funny is that I don't really care to use it to dress a salad!

In a medium bowl, whisk the buttermilk, sour cream, vinegar, lemon juice, honey, garlic, basil, tarragon, parsley, celery seeds, salt, and pepper together until well combined. Store in an airtight container in the refrigerator for up to 1 week.

SERVE WITH: FRENCH FRIES (PAGE 85)

10 tablespoons (1¼ sticks) unsalted butter

3 large egg yolks

1 tablespoon champagne vinegar

2 teaspoons fresh lemon juice

2 teaspoons chopped fresh tarragon

Dash of Tabasco or other hot sauce, or to taste

Kosher salt to taste

MAKES ABOUT 1½ CUPS

BEAR-NAISE WITH BROWN BUTTER

Most French culinary instructors would never mess with a classic hollandaise. Good thing I'm not one of them. I brown the butter first, which adds color and richness to the proceedings. The result is not as pristine as traditional hollandaise, but it's got a deeper, more intense flavor. The name? I use it on my daughter's eggs, and her nickname is Riley Bear. (Alternatively, serve it with bear steak.)

1. Melt the butter in a small skillet over medium-low heat. Cook, swirling the pan frequently, until the milk solids turn golden brown and the butter has a nutty aroma, about 5 minutes. Remove from the heat and let cool.

2. Fill a small saucepan with 1 to 2 inches of water and bring to a slow simmer over medium-low heat. In a medium heatproof bowl, whisk the yolks and vinegar together until combined. Set the bowl over the simmering water, making sure the bottom of the bowl is not touching the water, and whisk constantly until the yolks are very fluffy and hold the trail of the whisk, 2 to 3 minutes. If the water in the pan begins to boil, remove the bowl, so as not to overcook the yolks, and reduce the heat to low, then return the bowl to the pan and continue whisking.

3. Remove the bowl from the heat and, whisking constantly, very gradually drizzle in the browned butter, whisking until thick and creamy. Whisk in the lemon juice, tarragon, and hot sauce and season with salt. Cover the bowl and set it over the saucepan of warm water (off the heat) until ready to serve. Whisk well before using.

SERVE WITH: RILEY'S SCRAMBLED EGGS (PAGE 68)

| 1 cup brown rice vinegar | 1 cup sugar | 6 Thai chilies, halved lengthwise |

BOTTLED PEPPER VINEGAR

Put the vinegar and sugar in a small saucepan over medium heat and cook, stirring, until the mixture begins to boil and the sugar is completely dissolved. Remove from the heat and add the chilies. Let cool completely before storing in an airtight container in the refrigerator for up to 2 weeks.

SERVE WITH: TANDOORI FRIED CHICKEN (PAGE 183)

1 teaspoon red wine vinegar

1 teaspoon sherry vinegar

1 teaspoon Dijon mustard

½ teaspoon poppy seeds

½ teaspoon sesame seeds

½ teaspoon dried onion flakes

½ teaspoon chopped fresh oregano or ¼ teaspoon dried

¼ teaspoon garlic flakes

⅓ cup extra-virgin olive oil

Kosher salt and freshly ground black pepper to taste

MAKES ABOUT ½ CUP

"EVERYTHING BAGEL" VINAIGRETTE

Sometimes the leftovers from a meal inspire me to create the next one. The idea for this vinaigrette came to me after I looked into the bottom of a paper bag that had once contained a dozen bagels. The crumbs and spices that remained were quickly mixed into a vinaigrette and drizzled on smoked salmon for breakfast. It was delicious! So, take a long look before you throw something away . . . it may be the start of your next great idea.

In a medium bowl, whisk the red wine and sherry vinegars, Dijon, poppy and sesame seeds, onion flakes, oregano, and garlic until well combined. Whisking constantly, slowly drizzle in the olive oil until emulsified and thickened. Season with salt and pepper and whisk again. Store in an airtight container in the refrigerator for up to 2 weeks.

SERVE WITH: BARELY SMOKED SALMON (PAGE 64)

Carcass of
1 roasted chicken

1 yellow onion,
chopped

2 stalks celery,
chopped

2 medium carrots,
chopped

2 sprigs fresh
thyme

1 bay leaf

2 tablespoons
kosher salt

½ teaspoon white
peppercorns

3 quarts water

MAKES ABOUT 3 QUARTS

PRESSURE-COOKER CHICKEN STOCK

Who has a freezer full of chicken carcasses and a giant stockpot that an eight-year-old can fit in? No one. Instead, make chicken stock using just one chicken carcass in your pressure cooker, which saves time, money, and energy. The technique intensifies flavor and minimizes evaporation, increasing the yield. It's so economical.

1. Put the chicken carcass, onion, celery, carrots, thyme, bay leaf, salt, and peppercorns in a pressure cooker and pour the water over the ingredients. Attach the lid and set the pot over medium-high heat. When the pot begins to hiss, reduce the heat to medium-low and cook for 25 minutes. If the pot is not hissing, raise the temperature slightly until it does.

2. Remove the pot from the heat and let stand until the pressure subsides completely before removing the lid. Pour the contents of the pot into a colander set over a large bowl and let stand until the liquid has drained completely; discard the solids.

3. Pour the stock through a fine-mesh strainer into a plastic container and let cool to room temperature. Cover the container with the lid and store in the refrigerator for up to 1 week, or freeze in separate containers for up to 3 months.

1½-pound piece slab bacon or pancetta | 1 yellow onion, roughly chopped | 2 sprigs fresh thyme | 1½ cups water

MAKES 1½ POUNDS

PRESSURE-COOKER BRAISED BACON

I love the backwardness of this recipe: You take cured pieces of pork and then rehydrate them to make them velvety and soft. It's like painting a masterpiece and then painting over the canvas again, to make it more of a masterpiece.

1. Put the bacon, onion, thyme, and water in a pressure cooker and attach the lid. Set the pot over medium-high heat. When it begins to hiss, reduce the heat to medium-low and cook for 20 minutes. If the pot is not hissing, raise the temperature slightly until it does.

2. Remove the pressure cooker from the heat and let stand until the pressure subsides before removing the lid.

3. Transfer the bacon to a plate and let cool to room temperature (discard the cooking liquid). Wrap tightly in plastic wrap and refrigerate for up to 1 week. Cut to the desired thickness to serve.

SERVE WITH: BURGERS (PAGE 101), ICEBERG CARPACCIO (PAGE 120)

2 sticks unsalted butter |

MAKES ABOUT ¾ CUP

CLARIFIED BUTTER

1. Melt the butter slowly in a small saucepan over low heat. Continue cooking until the butter stars to bubble and foam rises to the top, 2 to 3 minutes. Remove from the heat and let stand for 5 minutes.

2. With a spoon, skim off the white foam sitting on the top of the butter and discard. Slowly pour the clear butter into a small container, leaving behind any solids in the bottom of the pan. Store clarified butter in the refrigerator in an airtight container for up to 1 month.

NOTE: *You can also pass the butter through a cheesecloth-lined fine-mesh strainer for perfectly clear clarified butter.*

| 1 tablespoon olive oil | 6 garlic cloves, finely minced | 1 teaspoon kosher salt | ½ cup fresh flat-leaf parsley leaves, finely chopped |
| 1 tablespoon finely minced white onion | ½ pound (2 sticks) unsalted butter, softened | 2 teaspoons finely grated lemon zest | |

MAKES 1 CUP

SNAIL BUTTER

You may notice there are no snails in this recipe! The point is to evoke their savoriness, their umami. This is just a lovely, garlicky, herbed butter that will make almost anything delicious.

1. Heat the oil in a small skillet over medium heat. Add the onion and cook until softened, 4 to 5 minutes. Add the garlic and cook, stirring, until softened, 3 to 4 minutes. Transfer to a small bowl and let cool completely.

2. In the bowl of a standing mixer fitted with the paddle attachment, whip the butter on medium speed until lightened in color and creamy. Add the garlic mixture, salt, and lemon zest and mix well. Add the parsley and mix on low speed until just combined. Store in an airtight container in the refrigerator for up to 10 days.

SERVE WITH: PORK-BELLY-STUFFED BAKED POTATOES (PAGE 134), CLAMS STEAMED IN GINGER BEER (PAGE 206), CLAMS STUFFED WITH PANCETTA (PAGE 208)

2.0 ASIAN SNAIL BUTTER

Snails are loaded with umami, and their earthy flavor adds great depth and dimension to a rich, creamy butter. Since we are making snail butter without snails, you can replace their umami flavor with some traditional Asian ingredients. This is a more intense, hot (there's a minced chile in it), and herbaceous version. I love cilantro like Bobby Flay loves cilantro . . . that's a lot. Some people hate cilantro. (Please do not serve this to Fabio Viviani.)

Replace the parsley with 2 charred scallions (blackened on a grill pan), finely chopped, and ¼ cup chopped mixed fresh cilantro, basil, and (a touch of) mint—or any combination thereof. Mix the herbs into the seasoned butter, then add a splash of fish sauce and 1 minced red chile and mix until well combined.

3 cups finely torn stale sourdough or white bread

2 tablespoons extra-virgin olive oil, or as needed

Kosher salt and freshly ground black pepper to taste

¼ cup chopped fresh herbs (dill, parsley, thyme, rosemary, sage, or a combination of whatever you have on hand; you can use dried herbs instead, but use half as much)

5 garlic cloves, minced

TOASTED HERB BREAD CRUMBS

These toasted bread crumbs are an easy way to make a great textural difference in any dish. They add an addictive buttery crunch to whatever you sprinkle them on: pasta, cooked vegetables, or even raw seafood. They are an essential pantry staple in my house. And if you ever find yourself in a thirty-minute cooking competition and you're running out of time, use this for a quick burst of flavor and texture.

1. Preheat the oven to 300°F. Scatter the torn bread on a baking sheet and toss with enough olive oil to lightly moisten but not saturate it, about 1 tablespoon. Season well with salt and pepper, scatter the herbs over the bread, toss well, and spread out. Bake until the bread is dried and beginning to turn golden, about 10 minutes. Remove from the oven.

2. Meanwhile, heat 1 tablespoon oil in a small skillet over medium heat. Add the garlic and cook until softened, about 5 minutes. Add the garlic and oil to the bread crumbs, toss to combine, and spread out. Return the crumbs to the oven and bake until golden brown, 6 to 8 minutes. Cool the bread crumbs completely on the baking sheet (they can then be crushed finer with your hands, if you'd like).

3. Store the crumbs in an airtight container at room temperature for up to 2 weeks.

SERVE WITH: POTATO "LINGUINE" (PAGE 157), SPAGHETTI CARBONARA (PAGE 150), MACARONI AND HEADCHEESE (PAGE 166)

2 tablespoons
unsalted butter

3 yellow onions,
halved through
the root ends and
thinly sliced

2 garlic cloves,
chopped

3 sprigs fresh
thyme, leaves
removed

1 tablespoon sugar

1 tablespoon kosher
salt

1 teaspoon freshly
ground black
pepper

¼ cup sherry
vinegar

MAKES ABOUT 2 CUPS

CANDIED ONIONS

Because I don't have a real sweet tooth, I prefer the word "candied" in front of words like onion or garlic, where the sugar serves to draw out the intensity of the allium flavor. This is a nice item to have on hand during holiday or high entertaining seasons. You can also use it to garnish any sandwich or pasta dish.

1. Melt the butter in a large saucepan over medium-low heat. Add the onions, garlic, and thyme leaves and stir. Cover and cook, stirring frequently, until the onions are deep golden brown, 45 to 60 minutes.

2. Add the sugar, salt, and pepper, stir, replace the lid, and cook for 10 minutes.

3. Add the vinegar and scrape up any browned bits in the pan, mixing it into the onions. Cook until the liquid has evaporated, about 10 minutes. Transfer to a container and let cool completely, then cover and refrigerate for up to 2 weeks.

SERVE WITH: BURGERS (PAGE 101)

¼ cup sugar

¼ cup water

1 cup whole pecans

¼ cup confectioners' sugar

1 teaspoon togarashi (Japanese chile pepper blend) or 1 teaspoon smoked paprika with a pinch of cayenne pepper

MAKES 1 CUP

CANDIED SPICED PECANS

This is one of my favorite snacks, and I'm particular about it. For me, candied nuts need to be coated almost as if in glass, so that they crackle, and here the sweetness is balanced with the spice and heat.

1. Preheat the oven to 325°F. Line a baking sheet with parchment paper.

2. Put the sugar and water in a small saucepan and stir over medium heat until the sugar is completely dissolved. Remove from the heat and stir in the pecans until coated. Let stand until the syrup is cool.

3. Stir the confectioners' sugar and togarashi together in a medium bowl. Drain the pecans in a fine-mesh strainer set over a bowl and shake off the excess syrup (the leftover syrup can be saved and used again to make more nuts). Add the nuts to the confectioners' sugar and use a large rubber spatula to toss them until evenly coated in sugar. Use your hands to shake off the excess sugar, and spread the nuts in an even single layer on the baking sheet. Bake until the sugar melts and the nuts are golden and glistening, about 15 minutes.

4. Cool the pecans completely on the pan. Store in an airtight container at room temperature for up to 1 week.

SERVE WITH: ROCKET SALAD (PAGE 125), PECAN TREACLE TART (PAGE 265)

| 3 tablespoons black peppercorns | ¼ cup kosher salt | 1 tablespoon onion powder | 1 tablespoon granulated garlic |
| 2 tablespoons coriander seeds | 2 tablespoons dried dill | | |

MAKES ABOUT ³/₄ CUP

HAB SPICE

Montreal's professional hockey team is nicknamed the Habs (an abbreviation of *les habitants,* the informal name given to the original settlers of New France in the seventeenth century). You may know this spice mix as Montreal Steak Seasoning, which is how it's marketed in the spice aisle in grocery stores. It's really all about the coriander and dill—they leave an impression of sweetness. This mix can brighten seafood as well as meat.

1. In a small skillet, heat the peppercorns and coriander seeds over low heat, swirling the pan, until toasted and fragrant, about 5 minutes. Transfer to a plate and let cool completely.

2. Coarsely crush the toasted spices in a mortar and pestle or spice grinder, or put on a flat surface and crush with the bottom of a heavy pan. Transfer to a small bowl, add the salt, dill, onion powder, and garlic, and stir together until well combined. Store in an airtight container at room temperature for up to 6 months.

SERVE WITH: **TUNA PRIME RIB (PAGE 225)**

| 2 tablespoons whole coriander seeds | 1 tablespoon yellow mustard seeds | 1 tablespoon black peppercorns | 1½ teaspoons paprika |

MAKES ABOUT ¹/₄ CUP

PASTRAMI SPICES

Heat the coriander, mustard seeds, and peppercorns in a small skillet over medium-low heat, swirling the pan, until toasted and fragrant, 2 to 3 minutes. Cool completely before coarsely grinding in a mortar and pestle or pulsing in a spice grinder. Stir in the paprika. Store in an airtight container at room temperature for up to 6 months.

USED IN: **CORNED BEEF HASH AND EGGS IN A CAN (PAGE 75)**

| 2 cups pure cranberry juice | ¼ cup grenadine | 4 gelatin sheets |

MAKES ABOUT 2 CUPS

CRANBERRY-GRENADINE JELLY

A "mixologist" might say that grenadine, a sugary pomegranate-based syrup, is disgusting. But to me, its nuclear red color and cloying sweetness has a place in sauce making, or, in this case, jelly making. It's kind of an adult version of the canned cranberry sauce that people serve on Thanksgiving. It is particularly good with rich savory food, like lamb chops.

1. Pour the cranberry juice and grenadine into a small saucepan and bring to a boil over medium-high heat. Reduce the heat to maintain a simmer and cook until the liquid has reduced to 1 cup, about 15 minutes.

2. Meanwhile, in a small bowl, immerse the gelatin sheets in cold water and soak until pliable, about 10 minutes.

3. When the cranberry mixture is reduced, squeeze the excess water from the gelatin, add the gelatin to the hot cranberry mixture, and stir until dissolved. Transfer to a small bowl and let stand until completely cool. Store the jelly in an airtight container in the refrigerator for up to 6 weeks.

SERVE WITH: **QUAIL POTPIE (PAGE 192)**

| 4 tomatoes, peeled, cored, and coarsely chopped

1 peach, peeled, pitted, and chopped | 1 red apple, peeled, cored, and chopped

1 yellow onion, finely diced | 1 stalk celery, finely diced

½ cup white vinegar | 1½ teaspoons kosher salt

¼ cup pickling spice |

MAKES ABOUT 2 CUPS

GENTLEMEN'S CHUTNEY

1. Put the tomatoes, peach, apple, onion, celery, vinegar, and salt in a large heavy saucepan over medium-high heat.

2. Wrap the pickling spice up into a bundle in a square of cheesecloth, tie with kitchen twine, and add to the pot.

3. Bring the mixture to boil. Reduce the heat to low and simmer, stirring frequently, until very thick and the liquid has evaporated, 2 to 2¼ hours.

4. Remove the spice bundle and discard. Transfer the chutney to a storage container and cool completely at room temperature. Chutney can be stored in an airtight container in the refrigerator for up to 1 month.

USED IN: **PIMENTO JACK CHEESE SANDWICHES (PAGE 98), MACARONI AND HEADCHEESE (PAGE 166)**

PICKLING

Pickling is the perfect catchall for the economical cook.
Stems, peels, roots, seeds, scraps, and trim can all be
turned into go-to condiments and garnishes simply by salting
them and then letting them swim in a spiced sugar-and-
vinegar mixture. And you can store your pickled foods in
the refrigerator for weeks. Don't worry if you haven't done
it before; I didn't try it until after I'd been to cooking
school, but there's not much to it. Just have fun!

PICKLING BRINE

1 cup sugar
1 cup water

½ teaspoon coriander seeds
½ teaspoon allspice berries

2 whole cloves
1 bay leaf

2 cups cider vinegar or white vinegar

1. Put the sugar, water, coriander seeds, allspice berries, cloves, and bay leaf in a small saucepan and stir over medium heat until the sugar is completely dissolved. Remove from the heat and let stand until cool, then add the vinegar.

2. Transfer to a nonreactive container with a lid and refrigerate until cold before using; the brine can be refrigerated for up to 6 weeks.

PICKLED CELERY

Most people think of celery as a throwaway ingredient, good only for crudités or as a background singer in the great French sauce triumvirate (along with carrots and onions) known as mirepoix, but not me. I love its flavor and crunch, especially when it's been pickled.

3 stalks celery

1 tablespoon kosher salt

About 3 cups Pickling Brine (page 53)

1. Thinly slice the celery stalks and transfer them to a small bowl. Sprinkle the salt over the celery, toss well, and let stand at room temperature for 15 minutes.

2. Transfer the celery to a colander and rinse very well under cold running water. Shake the colander vigorously to remove excess water. Put the celery into a nonreactive container and pour in enough pickling liquid to just cover. Cover and refrigerate for at least 1 hour before using. Pickled celery will keep in the brine for 2 to 3 days in the refrigerator.

SERVE WITH: SWEETBREAD NUGGETS (PAGE 90), SWEET CHERRY TOMATO SALAD (PAGE 122), CHICKEN SALAD (PAGE 185)

PICKLED RADISHES

Radishes are special. I think of celery as pop music, and radishes as alternative, because radishes bite you back when you eat them. Pickling them relaxes their harshness in every way.

8 radishes

1 tablespoon kosher salt

About 3 cups Pickling Brine (page 53)

1. Thinly slice the radishes and transfer them to a small bowl. You can also halve or quarter them lengthwise, depending on their use. Sprinkle the salt over the radishes, toss well, and let stand at room temperature for 15 minutes.

2. Transfer the radishes to a colander and rinse very well under cold running water, shaking vigorously to remove excess water. Put the radishes in a nonreactive container and pour in enough pickling brine to just cover. Cover and refrigerate for at least 1 hour before using. Pickled radishes will keep in the brine for 2 to 3 days in the refrigerator.

SERVE WITH: PORK-BELLY SANDWICH (PAGE 104)

PICKLED STRAWBERRIES

Pickling fruit is fun. It is a very adult preparation, because it takes some imagination to consider pickling anything other than a vegetable. It also takes a certain palate to appreciate the intense sweet-tart ratio. Besides preserving the fruit, the sugar and acid brine can enliven not-so-ripe fruit.

1 cup fresh
  strawberries,
  hulled

About 3 cups
  Pickling Brine
  (page 53), chilled

1. Slice the strawberries ¼-inch thick and transfer them to a small bowl. Pour in enough of the cold pickling liquid to just cover. Cover and refrigerate for 1 hour.

2. Drain the berries and use immediately.

SERVE WITH: RICOTTAGE CHEESE CREPES (PAGE 74)

PICKLED PEACHES

Pickled peaches get a hit of acidic bite that enhances their natural sweetness. Some diners think it's unusual that I pickle peaches, but the truth is, it's a fairly common practice: pickled peaches are a staple of classic Indian chutneys as well as Southern barbecues, where they garnish fried chicken.

2 ripe peaches,
  pitted and sliced
  into eighths

2 tablespoons
  kosher salt

½ to 1 cup
  champagne vinegar,
  or as needed

1. Put the peach slices in a small bowl, sprinkle the salt over them, and toss well. Cover tightly with plastic wrap and refrigerate for 4 hours.

2. Transfer to a colander and rinse very well under cold running water, shaking vigorously to remove excess water. Put the peaches in a nonreactive container. Pour in enough vinegar to cover. Cover and refrigerate for at least 2 hours before using. Pickled peaches will keep in the refrigerator for up to 3 days.

SERVE WITH: ANY SUMMER SANDWICH OR A CHEESE PLATE

Greek Yogurt with Tandoori Honey and Freeze-Dried Fruit (Yogurt Foam) 60 ▌Oatmeal Risotto 63 ▌Barely Smoked Salmon with Pumpernickel-Avocado-Egg Salsa and "Everything Bagel" Vinaigrette 64 ▌Potato Chip Omelet 67 ▌Riley's Scrambled Eggs with Asparagus and Hollandaise (Sous Vide Eggs) 68 ▌Pancakes with Warm Maple Syrup and Coffee Butter (Whipped Maple Syrup) 70 ▌Cinnamon-Brioche "French Toast" Skewers 73 ▌Ricottage Cheese Crepes (Homemade Ricotta Cheese) 74 ▌Corned Beef Hash and Eggs in a Can with Mustard Vinaigrette 75 ▌Country-Fried Steak with Sausage-Milk Gravy and Arugula Salad 77

WAKING
UP

In the restaurant world, brunch is the meal that most chefs want to avoid. Because the standard bacon-and-eggs fare is generally not considered "serious" cooking, most chefs send in their B-teams. And you can't blame them: There's less emphasis on how things are prepared and how they look on a plate. Diners' desires are pretty simple: good coffee and fluffy, buttery pancakes or meltingly cheesy omelets.

But that's what makes breakfast a great meal to remix. It's an opportunity to slip modern food to a half-awake crowd that isn't expecting creativity and experimentation and therefore doesn't come to the table with any hesitations or premeal jitters about what crazy things we might serve them. I've found that as long as it's delicious, people are pretty open to creative dishes in the morning, like pancakes with whipped caramel and coffee butter that I served while running a small Atlanta restaurant called Element.

That's one of the reasons that I love serving breakfast in my restaurants, but it's also because, in a sense, I've been reinventing breakfast my whole life. When I was growing up, no one was around when I got ready for school; my mom was at work and I was responsible for taking care of myself, including my own breakfast. Let me just say that I came up with some weird stuff. I also experimented with food when we dined out. I remember going to an IHOP with my mother and grandmother when I was about nine years old. I ordered pineapple juice and coffee for myself, and I tried the boysenberry syrup (What's a boysenberry? I wondered). I covered my bacon with the syrup, and I still am obsessed with the combination of sweet and salty.

Among my adult experiments with breakfast dishes, one morning more than any other stands out for me: I was preparing breakfast for my toddler. I'd blanched fresh asparagus in a pot of salted water. A farm-fresh egg was gently simmering in a glass jar to make the egg into a perfectly spherical disk and keep its texture moist and custardy. And with my whisk, I was emulsifying a little olive oil and butter into some egg yolks and vinegar for a hollandaise.

At 7:30 a.m., my guest was ready to eat. I could tell, because she was pointing to her lips and smacking her belly—a move common among French royalty in the seventeenth century. And as a princess of that time may have done, she tasted her food and then proceeded to throw every single asparagus tip onto the floor. The egg was met with curiosity at first, surely because she was amazed at the texture and shape, so amazed at how easily the egg squished in her hand, almost like Play-Doh. The egg was now squished into her chubby creases, hair, and fingernails. I was rejected: a professional chef who couldn't get a one-year-old to eat breakfast.

The next day I tried again. This time I tossed asparagus in olive oil, roasted them until they shriveled, and shook some vinegar over them. I cooked the egg in the microwave and chopped it up. There was no sauce, and scant seasoning. And there it was: a successful plate-cleaning breakfast, and a professional epiphany.

Babies don't care about exact shades of green. They don't care about the history of French cuisine or molecular gastronomy. They only care about flavor . . . as should I. I encourage you to do the same—but don't be scared of having some fun with the breakfast basics that we all love. And a thank-you to Miss Riley Maddox Blais for the cooking lesson.

"FRENCHED" TOAST
AROMATIC SPICES + WHIPPED MAPLE

WHIPPED OIKOS YOGURT
+ FREEZE DRIED FRUIT

PORK BELLY + EGGS

PANCAKE

COFF

MAPLE

COUNTRY FRIED STEAK
BUTTERMILK GRAVY
WILD ARUGULA

CORNED BEEF

SOFT BOILED EGG
LAMB — NAM
GRITS

NAM
COFFEE — YOGURT — SMOKE

- 1 cup plain Greek yogurt
- 1 teaspoon ground tandoori spice mix
- ¼ cup honey

- 1 cup all-natural granola
- 1 cup diced fresh fruit, such as pineapple, bananas, or berries, or a combination

- 1 cup freeze-dried fruit, such as pineapple, bananas, or berries, or a combination
- 8 small fresh cilantro sprigs (optional)

- 8 fresh basil leaves, torn (optional)
- 8 fresh mint leaves, torn (optional)

SERVES 4

GREEK YOGURT WITH TANDOORI HONEY + FREEZE-DRIED FRUIT

When we eat breakfast out, my wife always orders yogurt and invariably she's presented with something that looks a little beige, a little white, and a lot boring. Those sad meals were the inspiration for this dish; I became fascinated with how I could remix breakfast yogurt to make it interesting. Per usual, I headed to the spice rack, where I found the tandoori spice blend.

1. Divide the yogurt among four small serving bowls.

2. Put the tandoori spices in a small dry skillet and toast over low heat until very fragrant, 2 to 3 minutes. Remove from the heat and add the honey. Stir well to combine.

3. To serve, drizzle some warm spiced honey over the yogurt in each bowl. Divide the granola and fresh and freeze-dried fruit among the bowls, top each serving with one-quarter of the cilantro, basil, and mint, if using, and serve immediately.

2.0 YOGURT FOAM

Want to make the yogurt even lighter and frothier, to turn it into something ethereally creamy and elegant? Make yogurt foam.

In a medium bowl, whisk the yogurt until it is loosened and creamy and resembles a thick soup. If the yogurt is still very thick after whisking, loosen it with a splash of whole milk. Transfer the yogurt to an iSi siphon (see page 14) and insert a charge. Shake 5 or 6 times, then discharge the yogurt into four serving bowls and garnish with the tandoori honey and fruit.

1 cup steel-cut
  oats

3 cups water,
  Pressure-Cooker
  Chicken Stock
  (page 44), or
  store-bought
  low-sodium broth

¼ cup golden
  raisins

2 tablespoons
  sherry vinegar

1 tablespoon packed
  light brown sugar,
  plus extra for
  serving (optional)

Pinch of kosher
  salt

1 overripe banana,
  mashed

A Parmesan cheese
  wedge for shaving
  (optional)

SERVES 4

OATMEAL RISOTTO

My wife loves oatmeal for breakfast, and one day, when I looked inside a
can of the good steel-cut oats she keeps in our pantry, I realized that
the oats resemble rice—and my risotto-style oatmeal was born. Oatmeal is a
dried food, and, like anything that's dried, it needs to hydrate thoroughly
for optimal flavor, so letting the oatmeal stand overnight is worth it. The
mashed superripe banana blends beautifully with the homey, earthy oats. I
like aggressive shavings of Parmesan cheese, too.

1. Combine the oats and water in a medium bowl, cover, and let stand overnight at room temperature.

2. Put the raisins in a small bowl and pour the vinegar over them. Let stand while you cook the oatmeal.

3. Pour the oats and water into a medium saucepan and bring to a boil over medium-high heat. Add the brown sugar and salt, reduce the heat to a simmer, and cook, stirring occasionally, for about 20 minutes. The oatmeal is done if it's "squeaky" to the bite, not squishy.

4. Fold in the mashed banana and continue cooking, stirring occasionally, until heated through, about 2 minutes.

5. To serve, divide the oatmeal among four bowls. Drain and sprinkle 1 tablespoon of the vinegar-soaked raisins over each bowl. With a vegetable peeler, shave 3 or 4 strips of Parmesan, if using, over each serving.

Cooking spray

½ cup hickory chips
Four 4-ounce center-cut skin-on wild salmon fillets

2 cups cubed or roughly torn (½-inch pieces) pumpernickel bagel, pumpernickel bread, lightly toasted, or toasted pumpernickel croutons

½ small red onion, finely chopped

1 tablespoon capers, drained

1 ripe avocado, halved and pitted

8 cherry tomatoes, peeled

1 large hard-boiled egg, white and yolk separated

2 tablespoons chopped fresh flat-leaf parsley

1 teaspoon chopped fresh tarragon

Kosher salt and freshly ground black pepper to taste

"Everything Bagel" Vinaigrette (page 43) for serving

SERVES 4

BARELY SMOKED SALMON WITH PUMPERNICKEL-AVOCADO-EGG SALSA + "EVERYTHING BAGEL" VINAIGRETTE

It's not a stretch to say that Long Island natives are familiar with deli culture—we practically invented it. I love a bagel with smoked salmon for breakfast, but I like the smoked salmon to have just a hint of smoke, so that its velvety texture and delicate flavor aren't obscured. The best way to do this is to control the smoking process by doing it yourself; I use a stovetop smoker for this recipe, which allows you to regulate the smoky flavor to your liking (see Note for an alternative). But if you don't want to bother, prepared smoked salmon is fine.

1. Spray the rack of a stovetop smoker with cooking spray and set the salmon on it. Pour the hickory chips into the chamber of the smoker, close the lid three-quarters of the way, and heat over medium heat. After about 5 minutes, when the chips begin to smolder, open the lid and place the salmon on the rack over the chips. Close the lid and remove from the heat. Let stand for 5 to 6 minutes.

2. Meanwhile, in a large bowl, combine the bagel, onion, and capers. With a small melon baller, cut balls from the avocado and add to the bowl along with the tomatoes. Finely chop the hard-boiled egg white and add it, along with the parsley and tarragon. Season with salt and pepper and gently toss with a rubber spatula. Drizzle enough vinaigrette over the pumpernickel mixture to moisten. Toss very gently.

3. To serve, transfer the salmon to four plates. Divide the pumpernickel salsa among the plates. Drizzle the remaining vinaigrette over the salmon and crumble the egg yolk over the salmon. Serve immediately.

NOTE: *If you don't have a stovetop smoker, you can easily replicate one with two stacked 9-x-11-inch aluminum foil pans or an old rectangular cake pan. Put the hickory chips in the pan and use a double layer of aluminum foil to cover it for smoking. If you don't have a small rack that rests on top of the chips, simply roll pieces of aluminum foil into tight sturdy rods and lay them close together in the pan; spray them with cooking spray before you heat the hickory chips. Place the salmon on the rack or foil rods and smoke as directed.*

12 large eggs

3 tablespoons heavy cream

½ teaspoon freshly ground white pepper

1 tablespoon finely chopped fresh flat-leaf parsley

1 tablespoon minced fresh chives

6 cups plain kettle-cooked potato chips

2 tablespoons unsalted butter or vegetable oil

SERVES 4

POTATO CHIP OMELET

This is an American-style Italian frittata or Spanish tortilla, an open-faced omelet that's a great last-minute brunch dish. The potato chips are layered throughout yet still retain their firm texture. (You don't even need to add salt to the eggs, because the potato chips provide the seasoning.) You can enjoy this warm or at room temperature, with sour cream on the side. Or if you're a ketchup-on-your-eggs person, use the San Marzano Ketchup (page 29). (After I came up with this dish, I saw similar versions done by José Andrés and Ferran Adrià. A good idea is a good idea no matter how many people come up with it.)

1. Preheat the oven to 375°F. In a large bowl, whisk the eggs, cream, white pepper, parsley, and chives together until combined. Fold in the potato chips until they are completely covered in the egg mixture, but try not to crush the chips too much. Let stand for 10 minutes, until the chips soften slightly.

2. Heat the butter in an ovenproof 12-inch nonstick skillet over medium-high heat, swirling the pan to coat the bottom completely, until very hot. Carefully pour in the egg mixture and spread it evenly in the pan, then immediately reduce the heat to low. Cook until the eggs are set and the bottom is light golden, about 15 minutes. If the bottom is golden but the eggs are still runny on the top, transfer the skillet to the preheated oven and bake until the eggs are completely set, 3 to 4 minutes.

3. To serve, invert a large flat plate over the pan and flip the pan and the plate to invert the omelet onto the plate. Let stand for at least 5 minutes before cutting into wedges and serving.

1 pound thin asparagus, trimmed

1 teaspoon olive oil

Kosher salt and freshly ground black pepper to taste

4 large eggs

1 tablespoon whole milk

Bear-naise with Brown Butter (page 40) for serving

4 slices white or whole wheat sandwich bread, toasted and cut diagonally in half for serving

SERVES 4

RILEY'S SCRAMBLED EGGS WITH ASPARAGUS + HOLLANDAISE

The most humbling and educational cooking experience of my life was when my young daughter Riley rejected the breakfast I had painstakingly, lovingly, and preciously concocted for her one early morning. My perfectly cooked eggs were mush in her hands and my beautiful asparagus tips were thrown over my head. Here's how she likes it.

1. Preheat the oven to 450°F. Toss the asparagus with the oil on a baking sheet until coated and season with salt and pepper. Roast, shaking the pan halfway through, until the asparagus is beginning to brown but is still crisp-tender, about 10 minutes. Remove from the oven, cover, and keep warm.

2. In a microwavable bowl, whisk the eggs and milk until combined. Season with salt and pepper, stir to combine, and cook on high power, stopping the microwave and stirring every 10 seconds, until the eggs are set but not dry, 1½ to 2 minutes.

3. To serve, put the roasted asparagus on four warmed plates and divide the eggs among the plates. Drizzle some Bear-naise over each plate and serve immediately with the toast.

2.0 `SOUS VIDE EGGS`

This is an adult way to make eggs. These are eggs for
people, like me, who are interested in consistent, and
custardy and moist, texture; who don't like their eggs
dry; and who appreciate the virtues of sous vide, a
convenient and exact cooking technique. The French term
sous vide literally means "under vacuum," and it refers
to a technique that is associated with more experimental
chefs but in fact is used by chefs in all kinds of
restaurants. It's not complicated: it involves slowly
cooking food that is sealed in plastic in water at
precisely controlled, steady temperatures. I'm not the
first person to figure out that eggs are great cooked sous
vide—this method ensures a soft texture every time. Try
this when you have a Sunday morning to experiment. Once
you get the hang of it, it'll be the thing you do even on
the busiest workdays.

Preheat the sous vide machine to 168°F. Whisk the eggs, milk, and salt and
pepper to taste, until combined. Transfer the eggs to a sous vide bag and seal, but
do not vacuum-seal. Immerse in the water bath and cook for 10 minutes. Using
tongs, remove the bag from the water. Wrap it in a towel and squeeze gently with
your hands to mix and scramble the eggs. Return the bag to the water bath and
continue cooking until set, about 5 minutes more. Open the bag and remove the
eggs. Serve garnished with minced fresh chives and additional truffle salt and
pepper sprinkled over the top, if desired.

2 cups high-quality store-bought pancake mix (such as Robby's pancake mix)

¼ cup all-purpose flour

2 cups whole milk

2 large eggs

4 tablespoons unsalted butter, melted

½ cup brewed coffee

6 tablespoons unsalted butter, softened

Pure maple syrup, warmed, for serving

Sliced fresh strawberries or blueberries, sprinkled with sugar, for serving

SERVES 6 (MAKES ABOUT 18 PANCAKES)

PANCAKES WITH WARM MAPLE SYRUP + COFFEE BUTTER

If I entered a competitive-eating contest, it'd be one for pancakes. I like mine crispy edged, yet soft and tender inside. After years of tinkering, I've found that the best way to get this texture is to start with a fresh pancake batter, but you don't even have to make it yourself. (I love the buttermilk-based Robby's pancake mix available at RobbysPancakeMix.com or Amazon.) If you can, let the batter sit overnight in the refrigerator to hydrate and swell—that extra time makes for the fluffiest pancakes, I promise you. I love the play of the sweet maple syrup with the creamy, slightly bitter nature of the coffee butter in this recipe.

1. In a medium bowl, whisk the pancake mix, flour, milk, eggs, and melted butter together until smooth. Cover the bowl tightly with plastic wrap and refrigerate for at least 2 hours, and as long as overnight.

2. Put the coffee in a small saucepan, bring to a simmer over medium heat, and cook until reduced by about half. Remove from the heat and cool completely.

3. Put 4 tablespoons of the softened butter in a small bowl and whisk in the cooled reduced coffee until completely incorporated. Set aside until ready to serve.

4. Melt 1 tablespoon of the butter on a pancake griddle or heavy skillet over medium-low heat. Add the batter by ¼-cup amounts to make 4- to 5-inch pancakes and cook until bubbles appear on the surface and the bottoms are browned and crisp, 3 to 4 minutes. Flip the pancakes and continue cooking until browned on the bottom, 2 to 3 minutes more. Transfer to a plate in a low oven to keep warm until ready to serve. Continue with the remaining batter, adding the remaining butter as needed.

5. To serve, put 3 warm pancakes on each plate. Top each serving with 1 tablespoon of the coffee butter and some warm syrup, garnish with the fruit, and serve immediately.

2.0 WHIPPED MAPLE SYRUP

Maple syrup is sweet and delicious, but I give it more textural interest by using Versawhip, a soy protein. It's one of the cooler so-called "molecular" ingredients that chefs play with; it's probably no coincidence it's also one of the most forgiving and easy to use. It aerates maple syrup until it's the consistency of whipped cream, without using any cream. Versawhip is available from the manufacturer Will Powder (WillPowder.net); the online gourmet retailer L'Epicerie (Lepicerie.com); and Amazon.

To make whipped maple syrup, put 1 cup of pure maple syrup and 2 teaspoons Versawhip in the bowl of a standing mixer fitted with the whisk attachment. Mix on low speed until dissolved, then increase the speed to medium-high and whip until the syrup holds soft peaks. The whipped syrup can be held at room temperature for up to 1 hour.

MAKES ABOUT 3 CUPS

- 4 large eggs
- 1 cup whole milk
- 1 vanilla bean, split, seeds scraped out, and seeds pod reserved
- 1 teaspoon kosher salt

- 1 teaspoon ras el hanout (Moroccan spice blend; optional)
- Four 2-inch-thick slices brioche
- 12 cinnamon sticks

- 2 tablespoons unsalted butter, plus (optional) more for serving
- 2 dried hibiscus flowers, crushed (optional)

- ½ teaspoon dried lavender flowers (optional)
- Pure maple syrup, warmed, for serving

SERVES 4

CINNAMON BRIOCHE "FRENCH TOAST" SKEWERS

I made this French toast for a very sophisticated audience when I did a cooking segment on the PBS Sprout kids' program *The Sunny Side Up Show*, where I appeared with the resident star, a squawking chicken puppet named Chica. The recipe is standard egg-dipped French toast, but I cut slices of day-old brioche into long rectangles and use cinnamon sticks to skewer them, so the overall effect is of French-toast-on-a-stick.

1. Preheat the oven to 300°F. Place a cooling rack over a baking sheet and set aside.

2. In a shallow dish, whisk the eggs, milk, vanilla seeds, salt, and ras el hanout together.

3. Cut the crusts from the brioche slices and cut each slice crosswise into 3 strips. Insert a cinnamon stick into one end of each strip. Dip each piece of bread in the egg mixture, letting it soak for at least 5 seconds on each side, and transfer to the cooling rack to drain.

4. Heat a pancake griddle or electric skillet over medium-low heat. Add the butter, the vanilla pod, and hibiscus and lavender flowers, if using, and cook until the butter is melted and bubbling. Add half of the soaked bread pieces and cook, turning once, until golden, 2 to 3 minutes per side. Transfer them to the rack-lined baking sheet and keep warm in the oven while you cook the remaining bread.

5. To serve, stack 3 skewers on each of four plates. Spread a little more butter on them, if desired, drizzle warm syrup over them, and serve.

1 cup all-purpose
   flour

½ cup plus
   1 tablespoon
   whole milk

2 large eggs

3 tablespoons
   unsalted butter,
   melted and cooled,
   plus more for
   cooking

1 tablespoon sugar

½ teaspoon finely
   grated lemon zest

1½ cups fresh
   ricotta

2 tablespoons
   truffle or
   wildflower honey

Freshly ground
   black pepper to
   taste

1 teaspoon fennel
   seeds

½ cup agave syrup

SERVES 4

RICOTTAGE CHEESE CREPES

Ricotta cheese is like cottage cheese that went to college. It's refined. My mom was into cottage cheese diets in the 1970s, when I was growing up. I never liked it, but I found fresh ricotta to be a revelation—it may look like a curdy mess, but its flavor is clean and elegant. Agave nectar, the increasingly popular sugar substitute, combined with the fresh, licorice-like flavor of fennel is a great counterbalance to ricotta's creamy richness. Serve with Pickled Strawberries (page 55) to add a burst of bright color and sweet-tart tang to the dish.

1. Put the flour, milk, eggs, melted butter, sugar, and lemon zest in a blender and blend until smooth. Transfer to a bowl and refrigerate, covered, for at least 1 hour, and as long as overnight.

2. When ready to make the crepes, remove the batter from the refrigerator and let come to room temperature.

3. Meanwhile, place the ricotta in a fine-mesh strainer set over a bowl and let drain for 15 minutes. Transfer to a small bowl and stir in the honey and pepper; set aside.

4. Toast the fennel seeds in a small dry skillet over low heat, swirling the pan, until fragrant, 2 to 3 minutes. Stir in the agave syrup and remove from the heat. Reheat gently before serving if necessary.

5. To cook the crepes, brush a 10-inch crepe pan or nonstick skillet with melted butter and heat over medium-low heat. Pour in 2 to 3 tablespoons of batter and quickly swirl the pan to cover the bottom of the pan with batter. Cook until set and beginning to brown, about 1 minute. Flip with a large offset spatula and cook the other side until beginning to brown, about 1 minute. Transfer the crepe to a large plate and cover with a towel to keep warm while you continue making crepes, stacking the finished crepes on the plate.

6. To serve, spread about 2 tablespoons of the ricotta mixture over the surface of a crepe and fold into quarters. Repeat with the remaining ricotta and crepes. Serve 2 to 3 stuffed crepes per person, drizzled with warm fennel agave.

2.0 HOMEMADE RICOTTA CHEESE

This dish is even better if you make the ricotta yourself. And it's easy.

Heat 3 cups whole milk and 1 cup heavy cream in a saucepan over medium heat, stirring frequently to prevent scorching, until it reaches 200°F. Remove from the heat and, stirring the mixture clockwise, pour ⅓ cup distilled white vinegar and ½ teaspoon kosher salt; it will begin to coagulate immediately and white curds will float in the liquid (whey). Cover and let stand for 12 minutes.

Line a colander or fine-mesh strainer with cheesecloth and set the colander in a larger bowl. Gently ladle the curds into the colander, and let drain for 30 minutes. Transfer the ricotta to an airtight container and store in the refrigerator for up to 5 days.

MAKES ABOUT 1½ CUPS

- 1 tablespoon olive oil
- 1 large russet (baking) potato (about 12 ounces), peeled and cut into ¼-inch dice
- 1 small yellow onion, chopped
- 2 garlic cloves, chopped

- 1½ cups minced Brisket with Coriander, Black Pepper, and Brown Sugar (page 250)
- 1 teaspoon Pastrami Spices (page 50)
- 1 teaspoon caraway seeds, toasted
- 1 teaspoon red wine vinegar

- ½ teaspoon paprika
- Dash of Tabasco or other hot sauce, or to taste
- Kosher salt and freshly ground black pepper to taste
- 4 large eggs (in the shell)

- 2 tablespoons chopped fresh flat-leaf parsley (optional)
- 1 tablespoon chopped fresh dill (optional)
- ½ cup Mustard Vinaigrette (page 33) for serving
- Toasted sourdough or baguette slices for serving

SERVES 4

CORNED BEEF HASH + EGGS IN A CAN WITH MUSTARD VINAIGRETTE *(page 57)*

I take blue-collar pride in having grown up eating canned foods, and I am not embarrassed about that—although it took me a longer time than most to realize that fresh food is inherently better than canned. Like a lot of chefs, I try to eat local and organic, and I source high-quality ingredients whenever I can. So I show my fondness for canned food in the most playful way: by presenting homemade food in cans. I take leftover brisket, chop it, mix it with potatoes, and serve it in one-inch-high cans, with a soft-boiled egg on top.

1. Heat the oil in a large skillet over medium-high heat. Add the potatoes and cook, stirring frequently, until they begin to brown, 6 to 8 minutes. Reduce the heat to medium, add the onion and garlic, and cook, stirring, until softened, 5 to 6 minutes. Add the minced brisket, pastrami spices, caraway, vinegar, paprika, hot sauce, and salt and pepper and cook, stirring, until the meat is heated through and the potatoes are soft. Cover the pan and keep warm over very low heat.

2. Meanwhile, bring a medium pot of water to a boil. Ease the eggs into it. Reduce the heat to a simmer and cook for exactly 6 minutes. Remove the eggs with a slotted spoon and briefly run cold water over them to stop the cooking, then peel the eggs immediately.

3. When ready to serve, using a slotted spoon, dip each egg into a fresh pot of barely simmering water for 15 seconds to rewarm. Drain well.

4. To serve, stir the chopped parsley and dill, if using, into the beef hash. Divide the hash among four 6- to 8-ounce clean shallow (about 1-inch-high) cans and set on serving plates. Crack the eggs and place an egg on top of each serving of hash. Drizzle 2 tablespoons of the mustard vinaigrette over each serving and season the eggs with salt and pepper. Serve immediately with toast on the side.

Two 12-ounce flat-iron steaks or one 1½-pound flank steak

2 large eggs, beaten

2 teaspoons Dijon mustard

½ teaspoon Tabasco or other hot sauce, or to taste

1 cup all-purpose flour

2 teaspoons turmeric

½ teaspoon freshly ground white pepper, plus more to taste

Kosher salt and freshly ground black pepper to taste

Peanut or vegetable oil for frying

12 ounces bulk pork breakfast sausage

2 garlic cloves, minced

2 teaspoons grated fresh ginger

1 teaspoon chopped fresh sage or ½ teaspoon dried

½ teaspoon chopped fresh rosemary or ¼ teaspoon dried

1½ cups heavy cream

3 cups wild or baby arugula

½ lemon

SERVES 4

COUNTRY-FRIED STEAK WITH SAUSAGE-MILK GRAVY + ARUGULA SALAD

To a transplanted Yankee living in the South, batter-frying a piece of steak sounded atrocious at first. But sometimes something that sounds so wrong can turn out to be very, very right—this is delicious. I boost the traditional flavors with lots of fresh herbs and spices, and serve it with a very untraditional arugula salad dressed with an intense squeeze of lemon. Herbs + Acid = Big Flavor.

1. Preheat the oven to 250°F. Set a cooling rack over a baking sheet and set aside.

2. Cut each steak on a sharp bias in half or divide the flank into 4 equal pieces, cut on a sharp bias. In a shallow dish, whisk the eggs, Dijon, and hot sauce together. In another shallow dish, stir the flour, turmeric, and white pepper together; season generously with salt and black pepper and stir well.

3. Fill a large skillet with ½ cup of oil and heat over medium-high heat until rippling. While the oil is heating, dip each steak in the seasoned flour, shaking off the excess, then dip the steaks into the egg wash, allowing excess to drain, and back into the seasoned flour, shaking off the excess; dip the steaks again in the egg wash and coat again in flour, shaking off the excess. When the oil is hot, place the breaded steaks in the pan and cook, turning once, until golden brown, about 4 minutes on each side. Transfer the steaks to the rack-lined baking sheet and keep warm in the oven while you make the gravy in the skillet.

4. In a medium bowl, mix the sausage, garlic, ginger, sage, and rosemary together until well combined. Drain all but 1 tablespoon of the oil from the skillet and return to medium heat. Add the sausage and cook, breaking it up with a spoon, until well browned, 5 to 6 minutes. With a slotted spoon, transfer the sausage to a plate. Drain the excess fat from the skillet and return the pan to the heat. Add the cream and bring to a boil. Reduce the heat to medium-low and simmer the cream until reduced by half, about 5 minutes. Return the sausage to the pan and season the gravy with salt and generous amounts of black and white pepper. Let the gravy bubble for 2 to 3 minutes.

5. To serve, in a medium bowl, toss the arugula with a squeeze of lemon juice to coat, and season with salt and black pepper. Distribute the warm steaks among 4 plates, top with the sausage gravy, and add some of the arugula to each plate. Serve immediately.

Tomato-Salsa Jelly and Corn Chips 82 | French Fries with Fresh Herbs, Sea Salt, and Sri-Rancha 85 | Vidalia Onion Rings with Beer Mustard 86 | Pressure-Cooker Boiled Peanuts 89 | Sweetbread Nuggets 90 | Fillet of Fish Sandwich with Malt Vinegar Jelly and Tartar Sauce 93 | Pâté Melt 94 | English Muffin Pizzas 95 | Pimento Jack Cheese Sandwiches 98 | Burgers with Candied Onions, Braised Bacon, and Cheddar (Cheese Wizard) 101 | Corned Beef on Rye with Sauce Maria Rosa and Brussels Kraut (Corned Tongue) 102 | Pork-Belly Sandwich 104

NEW CLASSICS + OLD-SCHOOL FAVORITES

I learned to cook at my *grand-mère's* French farmhouse. She and I spent days at the stove braising meat as the cat napped in the sun. Together we made crusty baguettes and velvety-rich veal stew with the local red wine.

Actually, none of that is true. I didn't have the kind of experience growing up that you hear from a lot of chefs. As I mentioned in the introduction, my start was in the kitchen of a McDonald's, during my teen years. I now co-own and operate a chain of casual, fun restaurants that specialize in gourmet burgers, specialty condiments, and toppings, called Flip Burger Boutique. I also have a place called HD1, which serves up a similar twist on hot dogs and sausages. Given where I started and my restaurants today, you might expect me to say that working at McDonald's gave me a road map to my future, but that isn't what happened. For many years, I worked in some of the best restaurants in the country and even had my own fine-dining restaurant, but all the while, some of my favorite dishes to cook were reimagined versions of the comfort foods that we all love: burgers, French fries, onion rings, even chicken nuggets. Reinvented versions of these familiar foods, what I serve at Flip Burger Boutique and HD1, can be approachable starting places for anyone interested in tasting something new while not straying too far from their comfort zone.

While my food is influenced and inspired by how I learned to cook in many other, and better, restaurant kitchens, McDonald's left an indelible mark on me. That Filet-O-Fish sandwich allowed my love affair with tartar sauce (see page 36) to continue into my early adulthood, which in turn led to the creation of many of the condiments you see in the first chapter of this book. The McDLT (McDonald's Lettuce and Tomato), a long-discontinued burger, came in a two-part box that separated the hot ingredients from the cold ones so diners could assemble the sandwich right before eating it—that's deconstructed cuisine! The sundaes topped with hot fudge and crunchy peanuts gave me an appreciation for contrasting temperatures and the play of salty and sweet in a dish. Cooking French fries was a lesson in how the temperature of frying oil affects flavor. The Shamrock Shake, popular for its green hue and limited seasonal availability, remains a lesson in both aesthetics and marketing.

While many of the snacks and sandwiches in this chapter might seem familiar at first, as with many of my recipes, I push the envelope on what each dish is, coming up with new ways to make it more exciting and delicious. These are my favorite sandwiches and snacks of today.

FRIED CLAMS
DILL
BLACK GARLIC AIOLI

"XO"
VINAIGRETTE

THE JUICY LUCY
BURGER — AMERICAN CH?

CHEESE WIZARD
IS.

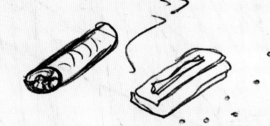

COBSTER ROLL
LOBSTER KNUCKLE SP?
LOB — STEER — BE?

CHICHARRONS
CHIPS
BEEF TENDONS
SEAWEED SALT

GENTLEMENS RELISH

ROAST CHICKEN
KUMQUAT
GREEN OLIVE

FOR THE TOMATO-SALSA JELLY

6 tomatoes, finely chopped

1 red onion, finely chopped

1 red bell pepper, seeded, cored, and finely chopped

1 jalapeño, seeded and finely chopped

1 bunch fresh cilantro, leaves removed and chopped (stems reserved for garnish)

1 tablespoon kosher salt

½ teaspoon freshly ground black pepper

Gelatin sheets as needed

FOR THE CORN CHIPS

1 cup Maseca instant corn masa flour

1¼ cups water

½ teaspoon kosher salt, plus more for sprinkling

Vegetable oil for deep-frying

¼ cup finely chopped reserved cilantro stems

SERVES 4 TO 6

TOMATO-SALSA JELLY + CORN CHIPS

This dish was an amuse-bouche at Element, my upscale restaurant in Atlanta. We served one corn chip adorned with a shimmery, wiggly jelly, along with a shot glass of a liquid-nitrogen frozen margarita (of course). The salsa jelly is a riff on tomato water, but it's even more flavorful.

1. TO MAKE THE SALSA JELLY: Put the tomatoes, onion, red pepper, jalapeno, cilantro, salt, and pepper in a medium bowl and mix well.

2. Line a deep bowl with a double layer of cheesecloth. Pour the salsa into the center of the cheesecloth and gather the cloth around it tightly to create a bundle. Tie the bundle together tightly with a long length of kitchen twine, then tie the string around the handle of a wooden spoon, making sure the bundle is close to the handle, and suspend the bundle over another deep bowl to catch the liquid. Refrigerate overnight.

3. Remove the salsa from the refrigerator and gently squeeze the bundle to drain any remaining liquid into the bowl. Leaving the bundle suspended over the bowl, let the liquid stand until it comes to room temperature.

4. Remove and discard the bundle and measure the liquid. Put 2½ gelatin sheets for every 1 cup liquid in a large bowl and cover with cool water; let stand for 5 minutes.

5. Squeeze the excess water from the softened gelatin sheets, put them in a small saucepan set over low heat, and stir constantly until the gelatin is completely melted.

Whisking constantly, pour the gelatin into the salsa liquid, whisking until thoroughly combined. Pour the liquid into a 9-×-13-inch baking dish and refrigerate until set, at least 2 hours.

6. When the jelly is set, cut it into ½-inch squares and transfer to a bowl.

7. TO MAKE THE CHIPS: In a medium bowl, combine the masa, water, and salt until thoroughly mixed. Knead the dough until soft and pliable, 2 to 3 minutes. The dough can rest, covered, until ready to fry. Tortillas can be shaped ahead; keep covered if not cutting and frying right away.

8. Divide the dough into Ping-Pong-ball-sized portions and roll into balls. Work with one piece at a time, keeping the remaining dough covered with plastic wrap. Flatten each dough ball between two sheets of plastic wrap, then roll with a rolling pin into a tortilla about 1/16 inch thick, or press in a tortilla press.

9. Heat a large dry skillet over medium heat. Working in batches, cook the tortillas just until set but not brown, about 2 minutes per side. Prick each tortilla several times with the tines of a fork to prevent it from puffing while frying.

10. Fill a medium heavy pot with at least 3 inches of vegetable oil. Attach a deep-fry thermometer to the side of the pot and heat the oil over medium-high heat to 360°F.

11. Meanwhile, cut the tortillas into quarters. Fry in batches, turning frequently with a skimmer or tongs, until light golden brown, 2 to 3 minutes. Transfer to a paper-towel-lined bowl and toss with salt while still warm.

12. Serve the warm chips topped with 2 or 3 salsa jelly cubes each, garnished with the chopped cilantro stems.

3 large russet
(baking)
potatoes, peeled

About 3 cups peanut
oil

About 1½ cups
melted lard or
vegetable oil

Sea salt to taste

1 tablespoon
chopped fresh
flat-leaf parsley

1 tablespoon
chopped fresh dill

1 teaspoon finely
chopped fresh
rosemary

2 teaspoons finely
grated lemon zest

A Parmesan cheese
wedge for shaving

Sri-Rancha (page
30) for dipping

SERVES 4 TO 6

FRENCH FRIES WITH FRESH HERBS, SEA SALT + SRI-RANCHA

Nothing is more delicious than a classic French fry—a simple combination of potato, oil, and salt—but French fries are hard to do right. My go-to frying technique is straightforward, but the secret to my fries is in the seasoning: When the fries are hot out of the oil, I toss them with bright, fresh herbs, sea salt, and a little shaved Parmesan cheese.

1. Halve the potatoes lengthwise. Lay them flat side down on the cutting board and cut lengthwise into ¼-inch-thick slices, then stack the slices a few at a time and cut into ¼-inch-thick batons. Transfer to a large bowl and cover with water. Let soak for at least 4 hours, or up to 6 hours, at room temperature to remove excess starch.

2. Fill a large heavy pot with the peanut oil and lard; the oil should be at least 3 inches deep. Attach a deep-fry thermometer to the side of the pot and heat the oil over medium-high heat to 230°F.

3. Meanwhile, drain the potatoes and pat them very dry with paper towels. Line a baking sheet pan with parchment paper and set aside. Working in batches, fry the potatoes until soft and limp but not brown, about 5 minutes. Spread them out in a single layer on the lined baking sheet and freeze until frozen hard, about 1 hour. Set the pot of oil aside.

4. When the fries are frozen, reheat the oil to 350°F. Working in batches, and adjusting the heat to maintain the oil temperature, fry the potatoes until golden brown, 3 to 4 minutes. Transfer to a large paper-towel-lined bowl and toss with salt while still warm. Once all the potatoes are fried, toss them with the parsley, dill, rosemary, lemon zest, and more salt until evenly seasoned.

5. Transfer the fries to a serving platter and, using a vegetable peeler, shave thin strips of Parmesan over the top. Serve warm with the Sri-Rancha for dipping.

2 large Vidalia
  onions
2 cups low-fat
  buttermilk
3 cups all-purpose
  flour

1 cup rice flour
4 cups soda water
One 16-ounce bottle
  beer

1 teaspoon honey
Kosher salt

Vegetable oil for
  deep-frying
Beer Mustard (page
  26) for dipping

SERVES 4

VIDALIA ONION RINGS WITH BEER MUSTARD

Onion rings are awesome, but you have to eat them immediately, or they get soggy (why you shouldn't order them for takeout). I start with sweet Vidalia onions and marinate them in buttermilk, then coat them in a tempura-style batter and fry them until they're golden and crunchy. The beer mustard has a sweet-tart, aromatic essence that's a perfect foil for the mild fried onions. And the best part is I can order these when I'm leaving one of my restaurants, and they're still hot and crunchy when I get home.

1. Slice each onion crosswise into even, ¼-inch slices. Separate the slices into individual rings; remove the 4 center rings from each slice and reserve them for another use. Put the separated onion rings into a large shallow bowl or baking dish and cover them with the buttermilk.

2. In a large bowl, whisk together 1 cup all-purpose flour, the rice flour, soda water, beer, and honey until smooth. Put the remaining all-purpose flour into a large shallow pan and season it generously with salt.

3. Fill a large heavy pot with at least 3 inches of vegetable oil. Attach a deep-fry thermometer to the side of the pot and heat the oil over medium-high heat to 350°F.

4. Working in batches, lift the onion rings from the buttermilk and shake off the excess, transfer them to the flour mixture and toss until coated, then dip one by one into the batter, shaking off the excess, and add to the hot oil. Fry, turning the onions often with tongs, until golden brown, 3 to 4 minutes; adjust the heat as necessary to maintain the oil temperature. Drain on paper towels and sprinkle the rings with salt while still warm.

5. Serve warm with the beer mustard for dipping.

| 1 pound (about 6 cups) peanuts in the shell | ¼ cup Cajun spice mix | Four 12-ounce bottles light beer |

PRESSURE-COOKER BOILED PEANUTS

When I first moved to the South, I noticed crocks of boiled peanuts in grocery stores and gas stations. The contents of those crocks didn't look particularly appealing, but when I finally tried boiled peanuts I found they were soft, starchy, and almost creamy inside—like a potato but with a more intense, nutty flavor. I now use boiled peanuts to garnish a number of dishes, such as my Chicken Cutlets (page 188). They're also delicious on their own as a snack, especially if you boil them in beer for added zest—a big step up in flavor from the gas station version.

The pressure cooker cuts the time that it takes to soften a tough nut in half. If you don't have a pressure cooker, just simmer away in a pot on the stove.

1. Put the peanuts, spice mix, and beer in a pressure cooker and attach the lid. Set the pot over medium heat. When it begins to hiss, reduce the heat to medium-low and cook for 1 hour. If the pot is not hissing, raise the temperature slightly until it does. Shake the pot every 10 minutes or so to prevent the spices from sticking to the bottom.

2. Remove the pot from the heat and let stand until the pressure subsides before removing the lid, then drain the peanuts; save the cooking liquid. Let the peanuts cool, then store in a resealable plastic bag in the refrigerator for up to 3 weeks. Transfer the spiced beer to an airtight container and store in the refrigerator for up to 1 week to use to cook more peanuts, poach fish, or make beer batter.

- 1 pound veal sweetbreads
- 2 cups low-fat buttermilk
- One 750-ml bottle dry white wine
- 3 stalks celery, chopped
- 1 yellow onion, chopped
- 1 carrot, chopped
- 1 jalapeño, chopped

- Vegetable oil for deep-frying
- 3 large eggs, beaten
- 1½ cups all-purpose flour
- 1 teaspoon kosher salt, plus more to taste
- 1 teaspoon freshly ground white pepper

- ½ teaspoon freshly ground black pepper
- ½ teaspoon ground turmeric
- ½ teaspoon packed light brown sugar
- Mustard
- Pinch of celery salt
- ¾ cup hot sauce, such as Frank's

- 2 tablespoons cold, unsalted butter, cut into 8 pieces
- Pickled Celery (page 54) for serving
- 2 chives, finely chopped for serving (optional)
- 1 cup Blue Cheese Dressing (page 38) for serving

SERVES 4

SWEETBREAD NUGGETS

I'm a nose-to-tail guy, which means I like to cook all parts of an animal, including the unpopular ones (tongue, cheeks, ears). This stuff can be a hard sell on a restaurant menu, but I like to give my guests the chance to try something unfamiliar. So I prepare sweetbreads (the thymus glands of young calves or other animals) Buffalo-chicken-wing-style, because who doesn't like that? Also, sweetbreads are texturally similar to chicken, so it's an easy substitute.

1. Rinse the sweetbreads under cold water, then transfer them to a small bowl, cover with the buttermilk, and refrigerate for 1 hour.

2. Combine the white wine with 2 cups water in a large saucepan. Add the celery, onion, carrot, and jalapeño to the pot and bring to a boil. Rinse the sweetbreads and add them to the saucepan. Once the liquid returns to a boil, reduce the heat to low and simmer gently for 10 minutes. Remove the pan from the heat and let the sweetbreads cool in the liquid for 30 minutes. Drain the sweetbreads and refrigerate, covered, until completely cooled.

3. Shape the cooled sweetbreads into small nuggets and return to the refrigerator until ready to fry.

4. Fill a medium heavy pot with at least 3 inches of vegetable oil. Attach a deep-fry thermometer to the side of the pot and heat the oil over medium-high heat to 350°F.

5. Meanwhile, put the eggs in a medium bowl. Put the flour, kosher salt, white pepper, black pepper, turmeric, brown sugar, mustard, and celery salt into a medium shallow baking dish and combine with a fork. Transfer the

sweetbread to the bowl of eggs and, with a slotted spoon, toss to coat evenly. Using the fork, shake the excess egg from the sweetbread and transfer to the seasoned flour, tossing until coated. Shake off the excess and return them to the egg wash. Turn to coat, shake off the excess egg, and dredge the pieces in the flour again. Shake off the excess flour and put the pieces on a plate.

6. Working in 2 or 3 batches, fry the sweetbread pieces, turning frequently with a strainer or tongs, until golden brown, about 5 minutes. Return the oil temperature to 350°F between batches. Transfer the hot sweetbreads into a large paper-towel-lined bowl to drain.

7. Heat the hot sauce in a large skillet over medium heat. Stir frequently until it begins to simmer. While whisking continually, add the butter, a few pieces at a time, until completely melted and smooth before adding more. Add the sweetbread to the skillet and toss until evenly coated and hot.

8. Transfer the nuggets to a platter, scatter pickled celery and chives over top, and serve with blue cheese dressing for dipping.

FOR THE JELLY

1 cup malt vinegar

1 teaspoon
agar-agar

FOR THE FISH

Four 5-ounce
portions cod
fillets

Vegetable oil for
deep-frying

1 cup all-purpose
flour

Kosher salt to
taste

Beer batter (see
page 86)

Store-bought
brioche rolls,
split and toasted,
or soft sandwich
buns, toasted

Tartar Sauce (page
36) for serving

MAKES 4 SANDWICHES

FILLET OF FISH SANDWICH WITH MALT VINEGAR JELLY + TARTAR SAUCE

The key to a fried fish sandwich is a great batter, and mine is a classic. The alcohol burns off when it's cooked, but it leaves a rich flavor in its wake. The malt vinegar jelly was inspired by a trip to London, where I got to watch Arsenal, my beloved soccer team, while munching away on traditional fish 'n' chips. I wished, though, that they didn't turn soggy when the malt vinegar was poured on them. So I turned the vinegar into a jelly using agar-agar, a gelatin made from seaweed that will stay gelled at warm temperatures. So you get the same great bang of flavor without soggy batter. Any kind of bun will do, but please toast them for that extra layer of crunch.

1. TO MAKE THE JELLY: Bring the malt vinegar to a boil in a small saucepan over medium-high heat. Slowly add the agar-agar and whisk rapidly until dissolved. Reduce the heat to medium-low and simmer for 2 to 3 minutes. Pour the mixture into a shallow pan or pie plate and cool completely.

2. Put the jelly into a food processor and pulse briefly until it is the consistency of soft jelly. Transfer to a cookie sheet, let set, and cut into sheets that loosely resemble a slice of cheese! (Leftover jelly can be stored in an airtight container at room temperature for up to 3 weeks.)

3. TO MAKE THE FISH: Fill a medium heavy pot with at least 3 inches of vegetable oil. Attach a deep-fry thermometer to the side of the pot and heat the oil over medium-high heat to 320°F. Place a rack over a baking sheet and set aside.

4. Put the flour in a shallow pan or pie plate and season with salt. Lightly dust the cod fillets in flour, shaking off the excess. Prepare the beer batter. When the oil is hot, dip the floured fillets in the batter to coat, let the excess drip off, and add to the hot oil. Fry, turning several times with tongs, until golden brown, about 5 minutes. Transfer the fish to the rack-lined baking sheet and sprinkle with salt while still hot.

5. To serve, spread 2 tablespoons of the jelly on the top half of each roll and ¼ cup tartar sauce on each bottom. Put the warm fish fillets on the bottoms, assemble, and serve immediately.

FOR THE PÂTÉ

- 1 pound boneless pork shoulder, finely minced
- 4 ounces fatback, finely diced
- ¼ cup water
- ¼ teaspoon pink salt
- 2½ teaspoons kosher salt
- ½ teaspoon freshly ground black pepper
- ½ teaspoon dried thyme

FOR THE SANDWICH

- ½ cup crème fraîche or sour cream
- 2 tablespoons freshly grated Parmesan cheese
- 1 large egg yolk
- 1 to 2 drops white truffle oil
- ½ teaspoon sugar
- 2 tablespoons Dijon mustard
- 1 teaspoon prepared horseradish
- 8 slices rye bread
- 4 thick slices Gruyère cheese (about 2 ounces)
- 8 cornichons, thinly sliced lengthwise
- ½ cup arugula leaves
- ¼ cup lingonberry preserves or jam
- 2 tablespoons unsalted butter

MAKES 4 SANDWICHES

PÂTÉ MELT

People often think that pâté is difficult to make. Mine is a very quick version made with braised pork shoulder; I think of it as "pressed pork." A few years ago, my team and I wanted to come up with a sandwich for our late-night bar menu. Chef Mark Nanna collaborated with me on it, and he gets credit for coining the name "pâté melt." It's like a patty melt. For the condiment, I remembered a jar of lingonberry preserves I bought for my daughter Riley at IKEA. The sweet-tart flavor works well with the salty cured meat.

1. TO MAKE THE PÂTÉ: Put the pork, fatback, water, and pink salt in a medium saucepan, bring to a simmer over medium-low heat, and simmer, stirring occasionally, until the water has evaporated, 10 to 15 minutes. (There will still be some liquefied fat in the mixture.)

2. Transfer the mixture to a medium bowl, add the kosher salt, pepper, and thyme, and stir well to combine. Line a 1-quart rectangular terrine mold or an 8 × 4-inch loaf pan with plastic wrap and pour the pork mixture into it. Wrap the mold tightly in plastic wrap. Place a heavy object on top of the pâté and press down to compact it. Put the mold in the refrigerator and refrigerate for at least 2 hours, or preferably, overnight.

3. WHEN READY TO ASSEMBLE THE SANDWICHES: Remove the pâté from the refrigerator and let stand for 30 minutes.

4. Invert the pâté onto a cutting board. Halve it crosswise, then slice each piece horizontally into 2 even slices.

5. In a small bowl, stir the crème fraîche, Parmesan, egg yolk, truffle oil, and sugar together until combined. In another small bowl, stir the Dijon and horseradish together until combined. Lay the bread out on a work surface.

6. Spread one-quarter of the horseradish mustard on each of 4 slices of the bread and place a slice of pâté on top, followed by a slice of cheese, 2 sliced cornichons, and one-quarter of the arugula. Spread 1 tablespoon of the lingonberry preserves on each of the remaining bread slices and top the sandwiches with them.

7. Melt the butter in a large skillet over medium-low heat. Using a pastry brush, brush the tops of each sandwich with the crème fraîche mixture until lightly coated. Using a spatula, carefully transfer the sandwiches to the pan, crème fraîche side down. Cook until golden brown on the bottom, 4 to 5 minutes. Brush the tops of each sandwich with a light coating of the remaining crème fraîche mixture, then flip and continue cooking until the bottoms are golden brown, and the cheese is melting, 3 to 4 minutes more.

8. Slice the sandwiches on the diagonal and serve immediately.

2⅔ cups unbleached bread flour

2 teaspoons instant yeast

¾ teaspoon kosher salt

1½ cups whole milk, heated until lukewarm

1 tablespoon olive oil

2 teaspoons honey

¼ teaspoon baking soda

3 tablespoons warm water

2 tablespoons vegetable oil, plus more as needed

About ¼ cup fine cornmeal

MAKES 18 PIZZAS

ENGLISH MUFFIN PIZZAS

At some point after my first season of *Top Chef*, I decided that I wanted people to know me for more than just my occasional use of liquid nitrogen. When I was invited to appear on *Top Chef All-Stars*, I grew a beard and started baking bread at home. All kidding aside, I worked really hard on my own English muffin recipe. I love these so much that I want to open an English muffin pizza truck. Interested investors should contact me directly!

1. TO MAKE THE DOUGH: In a large bowl, whisk the flour, yeast, and salt together until combined. In a large liquid measuring cup or a small bowl, stir the milk, olive oil, and honey together until combined. While whisking, slowly pour the milk mixture into the flour mixture, whisking until the liquid is absorbed and spongy dough forms. Cover the bowl tightly with plastic wrap and refrigerate for at least 12 hours, or overnight.

2. Remove the dough from the refrigerator and let come to room temperature.

3. In a small bowl, stir the baking soda and warm water together until the baking soda dissolves. With a large rubber spatula, gently fold the soda mixture into the dough until just combined.

4. TO COOK THE MUFFINS: Heat the vegetable oil in a large skillet over medium heat. Grease four 4-inch English muffin ring molds with vegetable oil and dust the interiors with cornmeal, shaking out the excess. Place the molds in the pan and fill each one two-thirds full with dough. Sprinkle ½ teaspoon cornmeal over the top of each muffin, reduce the heat to low, and cook until the bottoms are golden brown, about 12 minutes. With a large spatula,

flip the muffins, in their molds, and cook for an additional 12 minutes. Using the spatula, transfer the muffins, still in the molds, to a rack; set the pan aside. Cool for 3 minutes, then remove the molds. Stand the muffins up on their sides to keep them from collapsing under their own weight, and let cool completely on the rack.

5. Meanwhile, heat the pan again over medium heat. Regrease the muffin molds and dust again with cornmeal. Place them in the skillet, fill them two-thirds with dough, and sprinkle with cornmeal, then reduce the heat to low, and cook as directed above. Let cool, and continue making muffins until the dough is used up.

6. To make the pizzas, preheat the broiler. Split the muffins and toast them lightly. Top with your choice of sauce and/or other ingredients and broil until the toppings are hot, the cheese is melted, and the edges are crisp. Or butter the muffins and top each with crisped slices of the braised bacon. Add a warm poached egg on each muffin and drizzle with Bear-naise with Brown Butter.

NOTE: *Store completely cooled muffins in an airtight bag at room temperature for up to 3 days or freeze them for up to 1 month.*

COUNTRY HAM,
RICOTTA CHEESE +
BRUSSELS SPROUTS

MORE MUFFIN PIZZA SUGGESTIONS

TOMATO SAUCE (PAGE 35) WITH PEPPERONI OR COOKED ITALIAN
CRUMBLED SAUSAGE + SHREDDED MOZZARELLA

SAUTÉED SHRIMP WITH SNAIL BUTTER (PAGE 46)

CRISPED PRESSURE-COOKER BRAISED BACON (PAGE 45) SLICES,
POACHED EGGS + BEAR-NAISE WITH BROWN BUTTER (PAGE 40)

GOAT CHEESE,
TRUFFLES + LEMON

TOMATO SAUCE
(PAGE 35), SLICED
BURRATA + TORN
FRESH BASIL LEAVES

8 ounces white pepper jack cheese, coarsely grated

1 small poblano pepper, roasted, peeled, seeded, and finely diced (see page 244)

1 small jalapeño, seeded and minced

¼ cup Aioli (page 24) or good-quality store-bought mayonnaise

1 tablespoon chopped fresh cilantro

Grated zest and juice of ½ lime

Kosher salt to taste

¼ cup crème fraîche or sour cream

2 tablespoons freshly grated Parmesan

1 large egg yolk

1 to 2 drops white truffle oil

½ teaspoon sugar

Eight ½-inch-thick slices brioche or Pullman sandwich white loaf

½ cup Gentleman's Chutney (page 51)

2 tablespoons unsalted butter

½ cup arugula for serving (optional)

MAKES 4 SANDWICHES

PIMENTO JACK CHEESE SANDWICHES

Like a lot of people who are transplants to the South, I had never had pimento cheese, the iconic, often bright-orange cheddar sandwich spread, before I moved to Atlanta. It seemed odd to me at first, but I've come to love it so much that I eat it for lunch almost every day. My version is part pimento cheese, part melty cheese dip, part Tex-Mex grilled cheese—and the secret ingredient that lends it a special earthiness is a drop or two of truffle oil.

1. In a medium bowl, stir the cheese, poblano, jalapeño, aioli, cilantro, lime zest and juice, and salt together until well combined. In a small bowl, whisk the crème fraîche, Parmesan, egg yolk, truffle oil, and sugar together until well combined.

2. Lay 4 of the bread slices on a work surface and spread one-quarter of the cheese mixture evenly over each slice. Spread 2 tablespoons of the relish on each of the 4 remaining slices of bread, place them on top of the cheese, and press down lightly.

3. Melt the butter in a large skillet over medium-low heat. With a pastry brush, spread a thin layer of the crème fraîche mixture on the top of each sandwich. With a spatula, transfer the sandwiches to the skillet, crème fraîche side down, and cook until golden brown on the bottom, 3 to 4 minutes. Lightly brush the tops of the sandwiches with the remaining crème fraîche mixture, flip them, and continue cooking until the bottoms are golden brown and the cheese is melted, 2 to 3 minutes more.

4. Let the sandwiches stand for 5 minutes to allow the cheese to set up. Lift the top slice and add the arugula. Slice the sandwiches in half and serve warm.

2.0 CHEESE WIZARD

To put a unique spin on your burger,
along with a light and airy texture,
substitute Cheese Wizard, a cheddar
cheese foam, for the cheese slice.

To make cheddar foam, put 2 cups heavy cream
and 4 ounces cheddar cheese, shredded, in a medium
saucepan and warm gently over medium-low heat,
stirring frequently, until the cheese is completely melted
and the mixture is smooth. Pour the cream into a pitcher
or bowl and refrigerate, covered, until cold.

When ready to dispense, whisk the cream
thoroughly to loosen it, then transfer the mixture to an
iSi siphon (see page 14) and charge with 2 charges. Let
the canister sit for 5 minutes, then shake it vigorously
before dispensing the foam on top of the hot burgers.

One 12-ounce piece boneless top round, coarsely chopped

One 12-ounce piece brisket, coarsely chopped

4 ounces beef fat, coarsely chopped

OR

2 pounds ground beef with a 75%/25% meat to fat ratio

¼ cup Korean BBQ spice mix blend, or your favorite BBQ seasoning

2 tablespoons kosher salt

2 teaspoons freshly ground black pepper

5 teaspoons vegetable oil

2 tablespoons unsalted butter

5 garlic cloves, smashed

5 sprigs fresh thyme

4 thick slices cheddar cheese

One 6-ounce piece chilled Pressure-Cooker Braised Bacon (page 45) for serving

English muffins, handmade (page 95) or store-bought, split and toasted

1 beefsteak or heirloom tomato, thinly sliced

½ to ¾ cup Candied Onions (page 48) for serving

MAKES 4 BURGERS

BURGERS WITH CANDIED ONIONS, BRAISED BACON + CHEDDAR

Since I own a gourmet burger chain, I tend to think that gives me the right to know what makes a good burger: different tastes and textures coming together harmoniously. To the beef's meaty flavor, I add salt from bacon, acidity from tomato, earthiness from onion, and a tang from cheddar cheese. If you can get your hands on some dry-aged beef fat or trim, it makes a world of difference. You can use any bun you like, but I'll take mine on a badass homemade English muffin—it's the absolute best finishing touch to this cheeseburger.

1. If using top round and brisket, in a large bowl, toss the meat, fat, and spice mix together to combine. Attach the medium-sized die to a meat grinder and grind the beef and fat, then transfer to a medium bowl and mix gently until evenly combined. If using ground beef, form the meat into 4 patties, about ¾ inch thick, and, with the handle of a wooden spoon, make an indentation in the middle of each patty. (This will prevent the burgers from shrinking into meatball shapes while cooking). Season the patties on both sides, using 1½ teaspoons salt and ½ teaspoon pepper for each one.

2. Heat 1 tablespoon of the olive oil in a large cast-iron skillet over high heat until smoking. Place the beef patties in the pan, immediately reduce the heat to medium-high, and cook for 4 minutes; do not press on the burgers so they retain their juices. With a spatula, carefully flip the

patties, and add the butter, garlic cloves, and thyme to the pan. Once the butter has melted, tip the pan and baste each burger a few times, spooning the hot butter over it. Continue to cook, basting often, until the burgers are well browned on the bottom and the meat is medium-rare, 5 to 6 minutes. Remove the burgers from the hot pan, top each with a slice of cheddar, and let rest for 5 minutes.

3. Meanwhile, to prepare the bacon: Heat the remaining 2 teaspoons oil in another large skillet over medium-high heat. Cut the chilled bacon into 8 thin slices and cook on both sides until crisp, 3 to 4 minutes per side. Drain on paper towels.

4. To build the burgers, put 2 slices of tomato on each muffin bottom, followed by a burger. Top each burger with 2 to 3 tablespoons candied onions, some bacon, and the top bun. Serve immediately.

FOR THE BRINE

10 cups water

5 tablespoons packed light brown sugar

5 tablespoons coarse salt

8 garlic cloves

12 juniper berries, crushed

8 whole cloves

1 tablespoon black peppercorns, cracked

1 tablespoon yellow mustard seeds

1 teaspoon allspice berries, crushed

1 bay leaf, crushed

¾ teaspoon red pepper flakes

1 beef brisket flat cut, fat cap intact (about 4 pounds)

FOR COOKING THE BRISKET

1 yellow onion, roughly chopped

1 carrot, roughly chopped

1 stalk celery, roughly chopped

FOR THE SANDWICHES

8 thick slices rye bread or pumpernickel-rye swirl

¼ cup Pastrami Mustard (page 27)

1 cup Brussels Kraut (page 126)

8 cornichons, sliced lengthwise

¼ cup Sauce Maria Rosa (page 34)

MAKES 4 SANDWICHES, WITH LEFTOVER MEAT

CORNED BEEF ON RYE WITH SAUCE MARIA ROSA + BRUSSELS KRAUT

Corned beef is about as blue collar as it gets. It's a fatty off-cut of meat that swims in salt and spices for over a week. It's masculine yet perfumed. Raw-looking but cooked forever. Growing up, my hippie parents did a lot of things that were "too adult" for kids that I won't mention, but one thing I could partake in was eating New York deli sandwiches on rye bread. It wasn't beer or whiskey or contraband, but eating corned beef on rye with spicy mustard seemed very adult to me.

1. TO BRINE THE BRISKET: In a small saucepan, combine 2 cups of the water with the brown sugar, salt, garlic, juniper, cloves, peppercorns, mustard seeds, allspice berries, bay leaf, and red pepper flakes and bring to a simmer, stirring to dissolve the sugar and salt. Remove from the heat and let cool.

2. Put the brisket in a heavy-duty gallon-sized resealable plastic bag or a large nonreactive container. Pour the cooled brine over it and add the remaining 8 cups water. Refrigerate the brisket in the brine for at least 12 hours, and up to 3 days.

3. TO COOK THE BRISKET: Put the onion, carrot, and celery into a stockpot. Remove the brisket from the brine, rinse well under cold water, and place it on top of the vegetables. Pour in enough water to cover, and bring the liquid to a boil. Cover, reduce the heat to maintain a gentle simmer, and cook until the brisket is fork-tender, about 4 hours. Remove the brisket from the pot and let cool slightly.

2.0 CORNED TONGUE

Cooking with offal meat is in vogue in chef circles these days. It's something I really enjoy, so instead of using the traditional brisket for the corned beef, I often opt for tongue, Not only do I like the idea of tasting something that could have tasted you, but I also think that tongue, with a texture that's a bit more relaxed and giving than roast beef, is a seriously undervalued cut of meat. It's almost magically soft.

To make corned tongue, substitute a 3- to 4-pound whole beef tongue for the brisket. The tongue needs to cure in the brine for a minimum of 5 days, and up to 8 (the longer, the better). Cook the tongue as described in step 3, simmering until a knife inserted into the thickest part meets no resistance, about 3 hours. Remove it from the liquid, and when it is cool enough to handle, peel off the skin and discard. The tongue can be very thinly sliced and used for the sandwiches. Leftovers can be made into corned beef hash, and they'll keep for up to 2 weeks, since the meat is preserved through brining.

4. TO MAKE THE SANDWICHES: Very thinly slice about 24 slices of the brisket (see note). Spread 1 tablespoon pastrami mustard on 4 of the bread slices. Pile about 6 slices of brisket on each slice, followed by ¼ cup Brussels kraut and some cornichon slices. Spread 1 tablespoon of the sauce on each remaining bread slice and top the sandwiches with them. Cut each sandwich in half diagonally and serve.

NOTE: Leftover brisket, once cooled, can be wrapped tightly in plastic wrap or stored in a resealable food storage bag with some of the cooking liquid and refrigerated for up to 5 days. Leftovers can be made into corned beef hash.

FOR THE PORK BELLY

One 1-pound slab rind-on smoked pork belly (or slab bacon)

Kosher salt and freshly ground black pepper to taste

2 tablespoons Dijon mustard

3 tablespoons packed light brown sugar

FOR THE SANDWICHES

2 teaspoons vegetable oil

Juice of ½ lime

1 avocado, halved, pitted, and sliced

Kosher salt and freshly ground black pepper to taste

8 sandwich-style croissants split in half, or alternatively, some good-quality white bread

¼ cup Smoked Aioli (page 25)

½ cup drained Pickled Radishes (page 54)

1 cup arugula leaves, watercress sprigs, or flat-leaf parsley

1 ripe peach, persimmon, or apple, halved, pitted, and sliced (optional)

PORK-BELLY SANDWICH

This sandwich started out as an idea for a reinvented BLT, when I was the chef at the restaurant Home in Atlanta. I wanted an intense salty bacon flavor, but instead of bacon, I use cured, smoked pork belly and slow-roast it in the oven; it is an interesting way to coax flavor and texture out of an unexpected source. Instead of the tomatoes that give the traditional BLT a bright acidity, I use tart pickled radishes. I add a few slices of fresh peaches when they're in season, as their sweetness adds another level of flavor and fun (persimmons are a nice alternative). Some people forget tomatoes are fruit—you can always play around and switch out a tomato for another slightly sweet, fleshy fruit (such as persimmon, peach, or apple).

1. TO COOK THE PORK BELLY: Preheat the oven to 325°F. Place a double layer of aluminum foil on a baking sheet and set the pork belly in the center fat side up. Season on both sides with salt and pepper and smear the Dijon evenly over the meat side (not the rind). Sprinkle the brown sugar evenly over the mustard and press so it adheres.

2. Wrap the pork tightly in the foil and roast for 3 hours. Let cool to room temperature.

3. Peel the rind off the pork belly and discard. Wrap the belly tightly in plastic wrap and chill thoroughly in the refrigerator, at least 2 hours and up to 5 days.

4. TO MAKE THE SANDWICHES: Unwrap the pork and slice it into 8 even slices. Heat the oil in a large nonstick skillet over medium-high heat. Add the pork and sear on both sides until crisp, about 1 minute per side. Drain on paper towels.

5. Sprinkle the lime juice over the avocado slices and season them lightly with salt and pepper.

6. Spread 1 tablespoon of the smoked aioli on 4 of the bread slices. Top the remaining 4 pieces of bread with 2 slices pork belly each, followed by some pickled radishes, one-quarter of the arugula leaves, and one-quarter of the avocado slices; top with several peach slices, if using. Put the top bread slices in place and serve immediately.

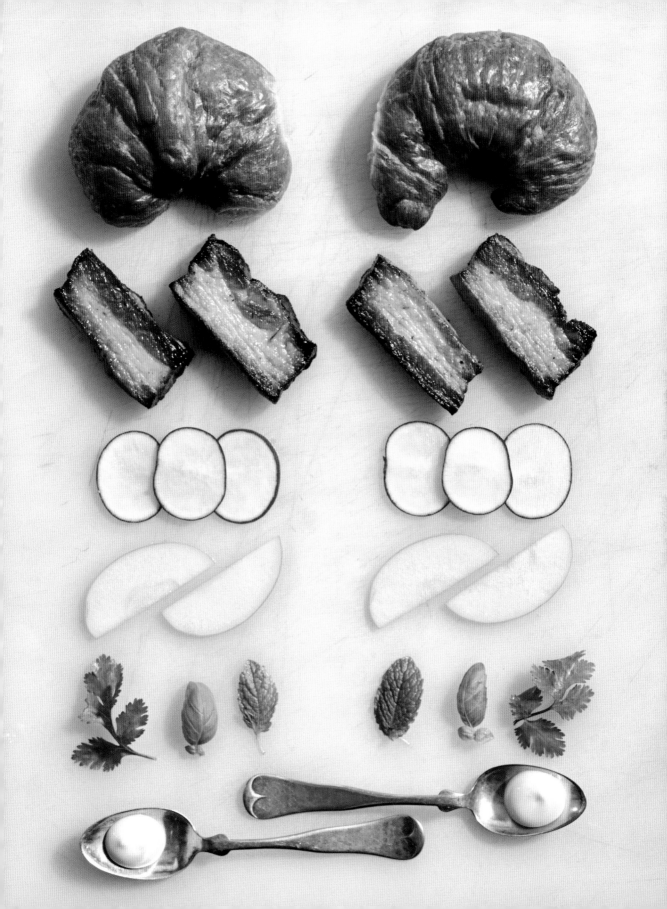

SNACKS, SIDES, SOUPS + SALADS

I spend a lot of the year on the road, cooking for live audiences at events around the world, from the Wisconsin Dells to Hong Kong. For these demos, I like to prepare hors d'oeuvres and finger foods, appetizers and single-serving soups, salads, and small dishes that people can sample on the spot, to get the flavor of my style in one bite. I'm often asked what's new, what's my next big step, what's in my hair (answer: equal parts duck fat and liquid nitrogen). My answer to the first question, whenever possible, is for them to taste what I'm cooking at that moment.

Often these one-bite dishes are miniature versions of appetizers or sides that might be part of any meal I serve. And, as with everything I cook, my goal is for them to be delicious, creative, and exciting. How can I take something as ubiquitous as Caesar salad and remix it? I make it smoky and powerfully flavored by seasoning it liberally with smoked paprika, hickory powder, and smoked sea salt. I reinvent Swedish meatballs so they are deeply savory by adding umami paste and using lamb, plus aromatic cumin and cardamom. To make what could be a tired beet salad look fresh and modern, I thinly shave licorice on top of it for a chewy bite.

The recipes in this chapter include some now overlooked but tried-and-true dishes. It's challenging to remix them creatively in a way that is still approachable and recognizable, but I live for that challenge. Some of the remixes here aren't that far removed from the classic versions, but others—an iceberg wedge salad turned into a thin disk resembling carpaccio, and gazpacho with a crispy frozen top courtesy of liquid nitrogen—are as creative as any of my main courses.

FL
OF MY
ONE

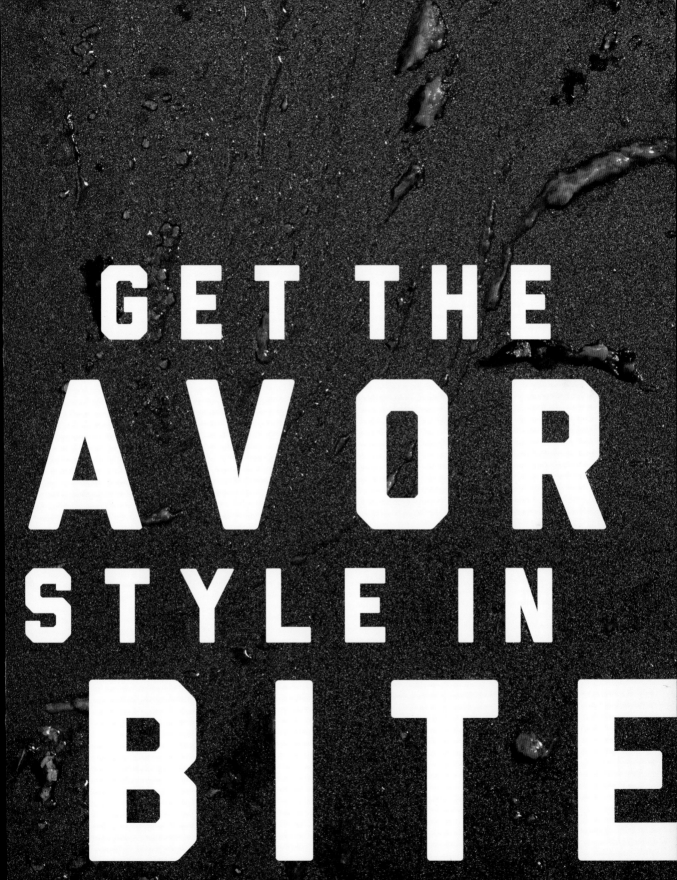

- 2 tablespoons olive oil
- 4 ounces pancetta, cut into ¼-inch dice
- 1 yellow onion, finely diced
- 2 stalks celery, diced
- 1 leek, white part only, finely diced and rinsed
- 2 sprigs fresh thyme
- 1 bay leaf
- Kosher salt and freshly ground black pepper to taste
- 8 ounces shucked fresh clams (about 20 medium cherry-stones), roughly chopped, and any clam liquor
- 8 ounces bottled clam juice
- 4 cups heavy cream
- 8 ounces small red potatoes, scrubbed and cut into eighths
- 24 small cockles, scrubbed
- Juice of ½ lemon

OPTIONAL GARNISHES

- Worcestershire sauce
- Hot sauce, such as Crystal
- Chopped fresh flat-leaf parsley
- Chopped fresh dill
- Oyster crackers or sourdough croutons

SERVES 6 TO 8

NEWER ENGLAND CLAM CHOWDER

Although I'm a native New Yorker, there is only one chowder for me—and it wears a Red Sox cap. My love for clams can be chalked up to my Long Island roots. To me, they are the ultimate soulful ingredient: They're not pristine, like lobster. They're gritty and tough-minded. They even come with their own built-in salt packet. But sorry, New York, in a soup, they're best with a cream base.

1. Heat the olive oil in a large saucepan over medium heat. Add the pancetta and cook until the fat is rendered and the pancetta is beginning to brown, about 10 minutes. Add the onion, celery, leeks, thyme sprigs, and bay leaf, season lightly with salt and pepper, and cook until the vegetables are softened, 6 to 8 minutes.

2. Meanwhile, put the clams and clam juice into a blender and puree.

3. Once the vegetables are softened, pour the pureed clams into the pan, along with the heavy cream, and bring to a simmer. Taste and adjust the seasoning with salt and pepper if necessary, and add the potatoes. Reduce the heat to medium-low and simmer for 5 minutes. Place the cockles on top of the simmering soup, cover the pan, and cook until the cockles have opened, about 10 minutes more. Remove the bay leaf and thyme sprigs and discard, along with any unopened cockles.

4. To serve, stir the lemon juice into the chowder and ladle into warm bowls. If desired, garnish each bowl with a few drops of Worcestershire sauce, some hot sauce, parsley, dill, and/or oyster crackers.

2.0 FRIED CLAM STRIPS

Fried clams are great. My first encounter with them was as a kid at White Castle, where my friends and I would get sliders with a large side of fried clams—I think they're better than fried potatoes. I maximize their deeply satisfying crunch by using them as a garnish for this creamy, classic soup.

To make fried clam strips: Drain 8 ounces fresh clam strips (about 1 cup) thoroughly in a strainer. Pour 1 cup cornmeal into a pie plate and season generously with kosher salt and freshly ground black pepper. Dredge the clams in the seasoned cornmeal, toss in a strainer to shake off any excess, and fry in batches in 350°F vegetable oil until golden brown, 1 to 2 minutes; transfer them to a medium bowl as they are done. Toss with 1 teaspoon finely grated lemon zest, 1 teaspoon fresh lemon juice, 2 teaspoons chopped fresh flat-leaf parsley, and 1 teaspoon chopped fresh dill. Season with salt and pepper to taste, and garnish each bowl of soup with 3 or 4 hot fried clam strips.

CANNED SOUPS

As a way to evoke the warm, homey feeling I had when my mom served me soup from a Campbell's can, I like to present my homemade soups in clean soup cans. It's also a little Warhol and pop art, a way to add whimsy to a meal. I've been serving "canned soups" in my restaurants for years. Here are three of my favorites.

SERVES 4 TO 6

CELERY ROOT SOUP

When most people first see celery root, they are like, "What the hell is that gnarly, dirty thing?" I say it's a humble, inexpensive, underappreciated, underused gem waiting to be discovered. Celery root, or celeriac, tastes like celery but is great as a substitute for starchy potatoes. You can slice and fry it for chips, but it also makes a great puree and therefore a great creamy soup.

4 tablespoons (½ stick) unsalted butter

2 large leeks, white and light green parts only, thinly sliced and rinsed

1 medium celery root (about 1½ pounds), peeled and cut into ½-inch pieces

1 yellow onion, chopped

Kosher salt and freshly ground white pepper to taste

4 cups Pressure-Cooker Chicken Stock (page 44) or store-bought low-sodium broth

4 cups heavy cream

1 tablespoon fresh thyme leaves

OPTIONAL GARNISHES

Toasted Herb Bread Crumbs (page 47) or croutons, with a drizzle of white truffle oil

Fresh lump crabmeat and fresh lime juice

Crumbled salt-and-vinegar potato chips

1. Melt 2 tablespoons of the butter in a large saucepan over medium heat. Add the leeks, celery root, and onion, season with salt and pepper, and cook until softened, about 10 minutes. Add the stock, cream, and thyme and bring to a simmer. Reduce the heat to medium-low and cook until the celery root is very soft, about 20 minutes.

2. Working in small batches, puree the soup in a blender, then pour through a fine-mesh strainer into a clean large saucepan and reheat it gently. Taste and adjust the salt and pepper if necessary. Whisk in the remaining 2 tablespoons butter until melted. Ladle the soup into warm bowls and top with one of the garnishes, if using.

CREAMED CORN SOUP

I call corncobs "bones" on my restaurant menus because, like meat cooked on the bone, cooking corn "on the bone" enhances its flavor. Save your corn bones to infuse milk, stock, or even an anglaise sauce. This approach is similar to the "nose to tail" movement; I call it "seed to stalk" cooking. The garnishes for the soup are very deliberate, though playful, suggestions: lobster adds richness, and the grape jelly distinctive bright sweetness; popcorn kernels and Cap'n Crunch add textural interest.

6 large ears sweet corn, husked

4 quarts heavy cream

2 tablespoons unsalted butter

1 yellow onion, chopped

2 stalks celery, diced

Kosher salt and freshly ground white pepper to taste

4 cups Pressure-Cooker Chicken Stock (page 44) or store-bought low-sodium broth

OPTIONAL GARNISHES

Cooked lobster meat, with a dollop of Concord grape jelly

Freshly popped popcorn

Cap'n Crunch cereal

1. Stand a corncob on end and, with a sharp knife, cut the kernels away from the cob; reserve the cob. Repeat with the remaining corn (you should have about 5 cups kernels).

2. Break or cut the cobs into pieces (about 2 inches long) and transfer them to a medium saucepan. Pour the cream over the corncobs and bring to a simmer over medium heat. Reduce the heat to medium-low, cover the pot, and cook for 10 minutes. Remove from the heat and let stand, covered, for 20 minutes.

3. Meanwhile, melt the butter in a large saucepan over medium heat. Add the onion and celery and cook until softened, about 5 minutes. Add the reserved corn kernels, season with salt and white pepper, and cook for 5 minutes. Pour in the chicken stock and bring to a simmer. Cook for 10 minutes, or until the liquid has reduced slightly.

4. Pour the corn-infused cream through a fine-mesh strainer into the saucepan with the corn kernels; discard the cobs. Return the soup to a simmer and cook for 5 minutes.

5. Working in small batches, puree the soup in a blender, then pour through a fine-mesh strainer into a clean large saucepan and reheat it gently. Taste and adjust the seasoning with salt and pepper if necessary. Ladle the soup into warm shallow bowls and top with one of the garnishes, if using.

SPANISH-STYLE BUTTERNUT SQUASH SOUP

Butternut squash soup is ubiquitous. It's the type of dish that as a young and restless chef I hated. Every hotel, local bistro, and amateur cook throws it together come early fall. But as I've matured, I realized it's because this soup is really delicious, plain and simple, and when you cook with that goal in mind, you are well on your way. As with most of my soups, I make them stand out with the garnish. I like a *lot of* crunchy and textural elements in my soup. A good soup, to me at least, can look a bit like a good bowl of cereal. Here, I crowd the silky butternut purée with chorizo to give this "girl next door" soup a little edge.

3 tablespoons unsalted butter

2 sprigs fresh sage

1 sprig fresh thyme

1 small sprig fresh rosemary

1 medium butternut squash (2½ to 3 pounds), halved lengthwise and seeded

Kosher salt and freshly ground black pepper to taste

1 yellow onion, chopped

2 stalks celery, diced

¼ cup amaretto

4 cups Pressure-Cooker Chicken Stock (page 44) or store-bought low-sodium broth

1 cup heavy cream

OPTIONAL GARNISHES

Crumbled cooked chorizo, a dollop of cranberry jelly, chopped fresh cilantro, and fresh lime juice

Toasted Herb Bread Crumbs (page 47) or croutons, with finely diced green apple

Dollops of crème fraîche, with a swirl of pomegranate molasses

1. Preheat the oven to 400°F. Line a baking sheet with aluminum foil and rub the foil with 1 tablespoon of the butter.

2. Lay the sage, thyme, and rosemary sprigs on the pan and set the squash halves cut side down on top of the herbs. Roast until the flesh is very soft, 40 to 45 minutes. Let stand until cool enough to handle.

3. With a large spoon, remove the squash flesh from the skin and transfer it to a medium bowl, along with any loose herb leaves on the pan.

4. Melt the remaining 2 tablespoons butter in a large saucepan over medium heat. Add the onion and celery, season with salt and pepper, and cook until softened, about 5 minutes. Add the amaretto to the pan, stir, and cook until it has mostly evaporated, 3 to 4 minutes.

5. Add the roasted squash to the pan, stir, and cook until hot. Pour in the chicken stock and cream, bring to a simmer, cover, and cook for 10 minutes.

6. Working in small batches, puree the soup in a blender until very smooth, then transfer to a clean large saucepan and reheat it gently. Taste and adjust the seasoning with salt and pepper if necessary and reheat to serve. Ladle the soup into warm bowls and top with one of the garnishes, if using.

1½ pounds green tomatoes, coarsely chopped

½ cup coarsely chopped fresh cilantro leaves and stems

½ red onion, coarsely chopped

1 small jalapeño, chopped

½ teaspoon ground coriander

½ teaspoon ground cumin

Juice of ½ lime, or more to taste

1 teaspoon kosher salt, or more to taste

Freshly ground black pepper to taste

½ teaspoon chicken or ham-flavored Sazón (optional; see page 191)

Tortilla chips, croutons, or chicharrones (fried pork rinds) for garnish (optional)

SERVES 4 TO 6

GREEN GAZPACHO

The difference between the flavor of a red tomato and that of a green one comes down to acidity. I'm not talking about green heirloom tomatoes; I'm talking about home-growns that remain unripe and green at the end of the season. They are tart-and-tangy gems, and they give this soup a flavor reminiscent of guacamole-meets-salsa, only lighter.

1. Put the tomatoes into a blender and puree. Add the cilantro, onion, jalapeño, coriander, cumin, lime juice, salt, pepper, and Sazón, if using, and puree until smooth. Add water 2 or 3 tablespoons at a time until the desired consistency is reached. Taste and adjust the seasoning with salt, pepper, and lime juice if necessary.

2. Serve the gazpacho in chilled bowls, garnished with tortilla chips, if you like.

2.0 FROZEN GREEN GAZPACHO

To ensure that the soup is stone cold when you serve it, a really neat thing to do is to freeze the top of it with liquid nitrogen. It also makes the soup look otherworldly—in a good way—like what people of the future might eat. I'm not condoning siphoning liquid nitrogen off a street corner in Manhattan, but one of my favorite ingredients is a bit more commonplace than you'd think. You can source your LN2 from an industrial gas supplier, a welder, or even a local university. Tell them you are doing a bathroom remodel with some light welding—trust me, telling Big Al from AirGas that you are using it to make gazpacho is going to be a tiresome conversation.

To freeze the surface of the soup, holding the canister with gloved hands, carefully pour ½ to 1 teaspoon liquid nitrogen directly onto the surface of the gazpacho in each bowl, freezing the top of the soup instantly. Be sure to allow the liquid nitrogen vapor to dissipate completely before serving.

½ cup Aioli (page 24) or good-quality store-bought mayonnaise

Juice of ½ lemon (about 2 tablespoons)

4 anchovies, drained

1 teaspoon smoked sea salt or kosher salt, or to taste

¼ teaspoon smoked hickory powder or 2 drops liquid smoke

¼ teaspoon pimentón

Freshly ground black pepper to taste

1 pound baby kale or 2 large romaine hearts, chopped into bite-sized pieces

½ cup Toasted Herb Bread Crumbs (page 47) or store-bought croutons

1 tablespoon capers, for garnish

A Parmesan cheese wedge for grating

SERVES 4

SMOKED CAESAR SALAD

Anchovies give Caesar salad its characteristic salty tang. The smoky flavors I add here—the smoked salt, hickory powder, and pimentón—serve to deepen the effect of the anchovy, to make the salad taste intensely savory, like the very best backyard barbecue version of itself.

1. Put the aioli, lemon juice, anchovies, salt, hickory powder, pimentón, and pepper into a blender and blend until smooth.

2. Put the greens in a large bowl, pour the dressing over the top, and toss until evenly coated.

3. To serve, divide the greens among four plates and season generously with pepper. Sprinkle the bread crumbs and capers over the greens, and grate fresh Parmesan over the salads at the table.

1 head iceberg lettuce, cored

½ cup shredded Pressure-Cooker Braised Bacon (page 45)

½ cup Buttermilk Herb Dressing (page 39)

½ avocado, halved, pitted, and cut into balls with a small melon baller or cut into small chunks

½ cup cherry tomatoes, halved

Kosher salt and freshly ground black pepper to taste

¼ cup crumbled blue cheese

3 scallions, sliced

2 tablespoons fresh tarragon leaves, torn (optional)

SERVES 4

ICEBERG CARPACCIO WITH BLUE CHEESE, BACON + AVOCADO

I'm being a bit of a wiseass here, as it's hardly uncommon to serve iceberg lettuce raw. But I do present it in the way that you would a dish of beef carpaccio: thinly sliced rounds arranged in the center of the plate, with the accompaniments and dressing on top.

1. Stand the lettuce head upright on a cutting board. With a sharp knife, cut four ½-inch-thick round slices from the center of the lettuce. Transfer the slices to four salad plates, and reserve the remaining lettuce for another use.

2. Cook the bacon in a small skillet over medium heat, stirring frequently, until crisped and warm, 3 to 4 minutes.

3. With a spoon, drizzle the dressing evenly over the lettuce slices. Scatter the bacon, avocado, and tomatoes evenly over the lettuce. Season each salad with salt and pepper. Scatter the blue cheese, scallions, and tarragon, if using, evenly over the plates and serve immediately.

2 pounds cherry
tomatoes, such as
Sweet 100s,
1 pound halved,
1 pound left whole

Kosher salt and
freshly ground
black pepper to
taste
Citrus Herb
Vinaigrette
(page 34)

½ cup drained
Pickled Celery
(page 54) or
2 small stalks
celery, thinly
sliced

½ cup Candied
Spiced Pecans
(page 49),
coarsely chopped
(or use plain
pecan or walnut
pieces)
½ cup crumbled blue
cheese

SERVES 4

SWEET CHERRY TOMATO SALAD WITH CITRUS HERB VINAIGRETTE, PICKLED CELERY + BLUE CHEESE *(page 107)*

The inspiration here was a tomato and mozzarella salad, but I wanted to roughen it up a bit. One of my chefs tossed together some pickled celery and walnuts from another dish, and this salad was born.

Arrange the tomatoes on a serving platter and season lightly with salt and pepper. Drizzle the dressing over the tomatoes and scatter the pickled celery, walnuts, and cheese over the top. Season again lightly with salt and pepper, if desired, and serve immediately.

6 small red beets
(about 1 pound),
tops removed

2 tablespoons red
wine vinegar

FOR THE DRESSING

1 tablespoon Dijon
mustard

2 teaspoons
champagne vinegar

1 teaspoon fresh
lime juice

1 teaspoon honey

1 teaspoon finely
grated fresh
ginger

1 garlic clove,
finely minced

¼ cup extra-virgin
olive oil

Kosher salt and
freshly ground
black pepper to
taste

¼ large ripe
cantaloupe, seeded
and rind removed

1 ripe avocado,
halved and pitted

Kosher salt and
freshly ground
black pepper to
taste

½ cup fresh
cilantro leaves
(optional)

¼ cup fresh mint
leaves, torn
(optional)

SERVES 4

RED BEET, CANTALOUPE + AVOCADO SALAD

A perfectly cooked beet has relatively the same texture as a piece of ripe cantaloupe, and both have the same toothsome, velvety texture as a slice of avocado. A composed salad like this one, in which the ingredients are arranged rather than tossed, is about balance. The focus here is on similar textures, but the flavors of the sweet melon, vegetal beets, and creamy avocado all complement each other. And the fresh cilantro leaves, champagne vinegar, and lime in the dressing bring a refreshing acidity to the mix.

1. Put the beets in a small saucepan, cover with water, and bring to a boil over medium-high heat. Add 1 tablespoon of the red wine vinegar, cover, and cook until a knife inserted into the center of a beet meets no resistance, about 45 minutes. With a slotted spoon, transfer the beets to a bowl.

2. When they are cool enough to handle (use gloves to prevent the beets from staining your hands), use a paper towel to rub the skin off the beets. Quarter the beets lengthwise, return to the bowl, and, while warm, drizzle with the remaining 1 tablespoon red wine vinegar.

3. Meanwhile, to make the dressing: In a small bowl, whisk the Dijon, champagne vinegar, lime juice, honey, ginger, and garlic together until combined. Whisking constantly, add the olive oil in a slow, steady stream, whisking until emulsified and thickened. Season with salt and pepper and whisk well.

4. Cut the cantaloupe into pieces the size of the beets and add to the beets. Drizzle one-quarter of the dressing over and toss gently.

5. Divide the beets and cantaloupe evenly among four salad plates. Using a small melon baller, scoop balls of the avocado and scatter over the plates. Drizzle more dressing over each plate and season each salad with salt and pepper. Sprinkle the cilantro leaves and mint, if using, evenly over the salads and serve immediately.

2.0 SHAVED LICORICE

If you are like me and love black jelly beans and black licorice, you know the power of anise, which lingers on the palate and, despite its bracing start, has an incredible sweet aftertaste. The three main components of this salad are all enhanced by the flavor of licorice.

Freeze 1 black licorice strip (it can be a Twizzler) until solid. Using a Microplane or other fine grater, shave one-quarter of the frozen licorice over each salad just before serving.

2 very ripe Hachiya or Fuyu persimmons, sliced crosswise into ¼-inch-thick slices

One 1-pound ball mozzarella di bufala or fresh cow's-milk mozzarella, thinly sliced

1 small white onion, very thinly sliced crosswise

¼ cup extra-virgin olive oil, or to taste

4 teaspoons aged balsamic vinegar, or to taste

Kosher salt and freshly ground black pepper to taste

½ cup fresh basil leaves, torn

SERVES 4

PERSIMMON CAPRESE

This dish is a straight-on remix of the classic Caprese salad of tomatoes and mozzarella cheese. My spin on it is a visual play on the original, and a case of mistaken identity. People forget that a tomato is actually a fruit, with some sweetness to it, and the persimmon is a fruit with strong vegetal notes. Use a creamy buffalo mozzarella if you can get it.

Arrange the slices of persimmon, mozzarella, and onion on four salad plates. Drizzle 1 tablespoon of the olive oil over each plate, followed by 1 teaspoon of the balsamic vinegar. Season with salt and pepper, sprinkle the basil leaves over the plates, and serve immediately.

¼ cup chopped pitted dates or dried cranberries

2 tablespoons sherry vinegar

6 cups wild arugula

¼ cup Balsamic Vinaigrette (page 33)

Kosher salt and freshly ground black pepper to taste

Juice of ¼ lemon

½ cup Candied Spiced Pecans (page 49), coarsely chopped

4 ounces feta cheese, crumbled

SERVES 4

ROCKET SALAD

I'm an Anglophile, in part from having a small amount of English roots, and in part from my love of English soccer. So I like to call arugula "rocket," like they do across the pond. A few years ago I discovered that growing your own rocket lettuce is easy. Throw down some seed, bury it, and walk away. It's a delicious weed. This is one of the dishes that I make after we've picked some homegrown rocket.

1. In a small bowl, pour the vinegar over the dried fruit and let stand for 10 minutes to plump.

2. Put the greens in a large salad bowl. Pour the fruit and their liquid over the arugula, then drizzle the vinaigrette over the top. Season lightly with salt and pepper. Squeeze the lemon over the greens and toss well to coat. Sprinkle the candied pecans and feta over the top and serve immediately.

BRUSSELS SPROUTS

BRUSSELS KRAUT

Preserving foods has become a do-it-yourself fad, which is good, because foods such as pickles, olives, and sauerkraut are delicious, healthy, and loaded with antioxidants. On a sandwich, not much beats the crunch and tang of sauerkraut, which I love to make with Brussels sprouts—not only because they are essentially tiny cabbages, but also because the name "Brussels kraut" makes me laugh. Hopefully your guests enjoy the play on words too.

1 pound Brussels sprouts, bottoms trimmed

1 cup cider vinegar

1 tablespoon caraway seeds

1. Bring a large pot of water to a boil and salt it generously. Fill a large bowl with ice water and set aside.

2. Meanwhile, with a sharp knife, cut the sprouts lengthwise into thin ribbons (what is called chiffonade). Drop the sprouts into the boiling water and blanch for 2 minutes, or until bright green and tender. Drain, drop the sprouts into the ice water, and let stand until cool, 8 to 10 minutes. Drain well in a colander, shaking off the excess water.

3. Transfer the sprouts to a nonreactive container. Stir in the cider vinegar and caraway seeds and cover. Refrigerate for at least 2 to 3 hours, stirring occasionally, before serving. (Brussels kraut can be stored in an airtight container in the refrigerator for up to 5 days.)

BRUSSELS SPROUTS SLAW

This slaw is a playful twist on the usual cabbage-and-mayo combo. Brussels sprouts have the same crunch as cabbage, but they're cuter and greener and more fun. What really makes the slaw, though, is the bright piquancy that comes from crisp apple, the pickle liquid, and lots of fresh herbs. And for those who aren't huge fans of Miracle Whip, it's just mayo with some sugar and vinegar, so feel free to make your own version.

Kosher salt

8 ounces Brussels sprouts, bottoms trimmed

1 Granny Smith apple

¼ cup Miracle Whip salad dressing

1 teaspoon liquid from a jar of bread-and-butter or sweet dill pickles

½ teaspoon yellow mustard seeds, toasted

1 teaspoon chopped fresh tarragon

1 teaspoon chopped fresh cilantro

1 teaspoon chopped fresh basil

Freshly ground black pepper to taste

1. Bring a large saucepan of water to a boil and salt it generously. Fill a medium bowl with ice water and set aside.

2. Drop the Brussels sprouts into the boiling water and blanch until bright green but still crisp, about 3 minutes. Using a slotted spoon, transfer the sprouts to the ice water and let stand until completely cool.

3. Drain the sprouts and remove the outer dark green leaves and reserve. Using a sharp knife, cut the sprouts lengthwise into thin ribbons (chiffonade). Put them in a medium bowl.

4. Core the apple, cut into thin matchsticks, and add to the shredded sprouts. In a small bowl, stir the Miracle Whip, pickle juice, mustard seeds, tarragon, cilantro, and basil together until combined. Add the dressing to the shredded sprouts and apples, season with salt and pepper, and toss well to combine.

5. To serve, line a small serving platter or shallow bowl with the reserved Brussels sprouts leaves and pile the slaw on top.

4 large globe
artichokes, stems
trimmed

1 cup Aioli (page
24) or good-
quality store-
bought mayonnaise

3 tablespoons
chopped fresh dill

2 tablespoons
drained capers,
chopped

1 teaspoon finely
grated lemon zest

2 teaspoons fresh
lemon juice

½ teaspoon smoked
sea salt

¼ teaspoon smoked
paprika

Hot sauce, such as
Tabasco or
Crystal, to taste

Freshly ground
black pepper to
taste

SERVES 4

CHARRED ARTICHOKES WITH SMOKY LEMON AIOLI

"What's your favorite vegetable?" is a question I always ask new cooks in my kitchen. There's no right answer, but a candidate's response reveals a lot about who he is and how he cooks. If it's onions, you're a nuts-and-bolts guy. Beets, you're probably a bit grungy. Artichoke is my favorite vegetable. I respect how it plays hard to get. All the work you put into prepping this vegetable is richly rewarded.

1. Set a steamer basket in a large pot with a lid, fill with 1 inch of water, and bring to a boil over medium-high heat. Set the artichokes stem end down in the basket, cover, and steam until a knife meets no resistance when it pierces the stem of an artichoke, 20 to 25 minutes. The artichokes can be served warm or slightly chilled.

2. Meanwhile, in a medium bowl, whisk the aioli, dill, capers, lemon zest and juice, sea salt, and paprika until well combined. Add the hot sauce and black pepper and stir.

3. To serve, arrange artichokes in four salad plates, and divide the aioli mixture among small bowls for dipping.

| 2 cups fresh English peas | 2 teaspoons kosher salt | ½ teaspoon freshly ground black pepper | 1 teaspoon sherry vinegar |

SERVES 4

MASHED SOUS VIDE ENGLISH PEAS

Cooking vegetables sous vide is both fun and convenient. It also all but ensures that you don't overcook them, so they retain their distinctive flavors and textures. When I serve peas with crunchy foods, I like them to be soft but not falling apart, and sous vide is the perfect method to make that happen. These are great with fish 'n' chips—just make the fish in the Fillet of Fish Sandwich (page 93) and cut into strips. For a proper English pub meal, give the vacuum bag a good pounding for "mushy peas." Pass it around the table and work off some stress!

1. Preheat the sous vide machine to 194°F. Put the peas, salt, pepper, and vinegar into a sous vide bag, spreading the peas in one layer, and vacuum-seal the bag. Immerse the peas in the water bath and cook for 20 minutes.

2. Remove the bag from the water bath and use your hands to mash the peas. Serve immediately.

2 pounds russet
(baking)
potatoes, peeled
and cut into
chunks

Kosher salt

½ cup heavy cream
or whole milk

8 tablespoons
(1 stick) cold
unsalted butter,
diced

½ teaspoon freshly
ground white
pepper, or to
taste

SERVES 4

SMOOTH MASHED POTATOES

This recipe is a conventional version of really smooth and creamy mashed
potatoes, but there's one thing about my technique that I'm adamant about:
using cold butter. When you whisk cold butter into a warm sauce, it makes
the emulsification stronger and keeps the sauce from breaking. Mashed spuds
won't separate, but the principle is the same: using cold butter promotes
the absolute smoothest texture.

1. Put the potatoes in a large saucepan and cover with
cold water. Salt the water generously and bring to a boil
over medium-high heat. Cook until the potatoes are very
soft, about 15 minutes. Drain and transfer to a large bowl.

2. Meanwhile, heat the cream in a small saucepan over
low heat.

3. Using a ricer or masher, mash the potatoes until
smooth. Add the cream a little at a time, stirring with a
rubber spatula. Add the butter a few tablespoons at a time,
stirring until completely melted before adding more. Add
the white pepper and season with salt to taste. Cover them
to keep warm, for up to 1 hour.

1.5 SMOOTHEST MASHED POTATOES

After the potatoes have gone through
the ricer, pass them through a tamis
or chinois. This is like pressing
your puree through a screen door
and produces an unbelievably smooth
texture.

FOR THE SPINACH

1 tablespoon olive oil, plus more for greasing the pan

1 small garlic clove, minced

1 small shallot, minced

1 whole star anise

2 pounds fresh spinach, trimmed and washed, sliced into thin ribbons

1 cup heavy cream

1 large egg

½ teaspoon kosher salt

Freshly ground black pepper to taste

FOR THE YORKSHIRE PUDDING

4 large eggs

¾ cup whole milk

1⅓ cups all-purpose flour

1½ teaspoons Pastrami Spices (page 50)

Pinch of kosher salt

2 tablespoons lard, beef fat, or bacon grease

2 tablespoons cold water

SERVES 6

NEW YORKSHIRE PUDDING WITH LICORICE-SPIKED CREAMED SPINACH

This is a modern spin on a classic New York-steakhouse dish. I make an assertive licorice-spiked creamed spinach and stuff it into traditional Yorkshire puddings seasoned with pastrami spices. This is an excellent side for grilled meat.

1. TO MAKE THE SPINACH: Preheat the oven to 325°F. Grease an 8-inch square baking dish with olive oil; set aside.

2. Heat the 1 tablespoon olive oil in a large skillet over medium heat. Add the garlic, shallot, and star anise and cook, stirring, until the garlic and shallot are softened, about 5 minutes. Add the spinach and, using tongs, toss in the hot pan until all of the spinach is just wilted, 2 to 3 minutes. Set a colander in the sink and pour in the spinach to drain. Discard the star anise.

3. In a large bowl, whisk the cream, egg, salt, and pepper together until combined. Using a large rubber spatula, firmly press on the spinach in the colander to remove excess moisture. Transfer the spinach to the cream mixture and stir well until combined.

4. Pour the spinach into the baking dish and bake until set in the center, about 30 minutes. Remove from the oven and cover tightly to keep warm. Raise the oven temperature to 400°F.

5. TO MAKE THE PUDDING: In a large bowl, whisk the eggs, milk, flour, pastrami spices, and salt together until combined. Put 1 teaspoon lard into each cup of a 6-cup jumbo muffin tin and transfer the pan to the oven. After 10 minutes, the fat should be smoking; remove the hot pan from the oven. Quickly whisk the cold water into the batter and fill each muffin cup one-third full with batter. Return the pan to the oven and bake until the puddings are puffed and golden brown, 30 to 35 minutes.

6. To serve, cut a 2-inch slit in the top of each pudding and carefully spoon about 1 cup of the creamed spinach inside the pudding. Serve immediately.

4 large russet (baking) potatoes (about 2 pounds), scrubbed

Olive oil for baking

¼ cup Snail Butter (page 46)

Kosher salt and freshly ground black pepper to taste

½ cup diced slow-roasted pork belly (see page 104)

½ cup grated sharp cheddar cheese

½ cup Mexican crema or sour cream

4 scallions, sliced

SERVES 4

PORK-BELLY-STUFFED BAKED POTATOES

At my restaurant HD1, I serve a dish called Pig in Sheets, which was inspired by the Jamaican beef patty. This is a more decadant, dressed-up version of a standard baked potato stuffed with bacon bits. It all comes down to the pork belly, which has a wonderful texture and meltiness to it. It's all the rage, of course, but for good reason.

1. Preheat the oven to 350°F. Rub the potatoes all over with oil and place on a baking sheet. Bake until the potatoes are soft and a knife meets no resistance when it pierces the center of a potato, about 1 hour. Remove the potatoes from the oven and let stand for 10 minutes.

2. With a knife, cut a slit down the top of each potato, and pull the potatoes open. Use a fork to fluff the potato flesh. Top each potato with 1 tablespoon snail butter and season well with salt and pepper. Top the potatoes with the diced pork belly, cheddar cheese, crema, and scallions and serve.

- 5 tablespoons olive oil, plus more if needed
- 1 small yellow onion, minced
- 2 garlic cloves, minced
- 1 teaspoon kosher salt, plus more to taste
- ½ teaspoon ground coriander
- ½ teaspoon ground cumin
- ½ teaspoon ground cardamom
- ¼ teaspoon freshly ground white pepper
- 1 teaspoon umami paste (see page 149) or anchovy paste
- 2 slices stale white sandwich bread, torn into small pieces
- 3 tablespoons whole milk
- 1½ pounds ground lamb
- 4 ounces pork fatback, finely minced
- 2 tablespoons chopped fresh flat-leaf parsley leaves
- 1 tablespoon chopped fresh chives
- 1 tablespoon chopped fresh dill
- Freshly ground black pepper to taste
- 3 tablespoons dry sherry
- ¾ cup plus 2 tablespoons Pressure-Cooker Chicken Stock (page 44) or store-bought low-sodium broth
- 1 teaspoon xanthan gum or cornstarch
- 1 to 2 tablespoons sherry vinegar
- 1 teaspoon finely grated lemon zest
- Lingonberry jam (from IKEA or elsewhere) for serving

SERVES 4 TO 6 (MAKES ABOUT 32 MEATBALLS)

SAVORY + AROMATIC SWEDISH MEATBALLS, KIND OF

This was the dish I took to my first elementary school "cultural awareness" event, because I thought it represented my background. I've since found out I'm Norwegian—not Swedish. No matter—I still love Swedish meatballs. But they've received a bad rap. My spiced-up version, accented by heady spices and piquant herbs, should change that.

1. Heat 2 tablespoons of the olive oil in a large nonstick skillet over medium heat. Add the onion, garlic, and salt and cook until the onions are softened, 4 to 5 minutes. Add the coriander, cumin, cardamom, and white pepper and cook, stirring, for another 2 minutes. Add the umami paste and stir well until combined. Transfer the mixture to a large bowl to cool completely.

2. Put the bread into a small bowl and pour the milk over it. Let stand until absorbed.

3. Pour the bread mixture into the cooled onion mixture and add the lamb and pork fat. Using a wooden spoon, mix the ingredients until roughly combined. Add the parsley, chives, and dill and season with salt and black pepper. Using your hands, mix the meat just until thoroughly combined. Be sure not to overmix. Form it into meatballs about 1½ inches in diameter.

[RECIPE CONTINUES]

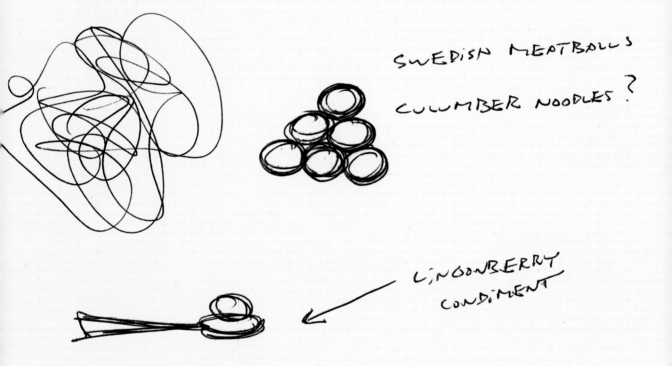

SWEDISH MEATBALLS

CUCUMBER NOODLES ?

LINGONBERRY
CONDIMENT

4. Heat the remaining 3 tablespoons olive oil in the same skillet over medium-high heat. Working in 2 batches and adding more oil if necessary, sear the meatballs lightly on all sides until just beginning to brown; transfer them to a large plate. Add the sherry to the skillet and scrape up any browned bits in the bottom of the pan. Cook until the liquid is nearly evaporated. Add the ¾ cup chicken stock and return the meatballs to the pan. Reduce the heat to medium-low, bring the liquid to a simmer, and cook until the meatballs are cooked through and the liquid is reduced slightly, about 5 minutes.

5. In a small bowl, whisk the xanthan gum and the remaining 2 tablespoons chicken stock together until combined. Push the meatballs to one side of the pan and whisk the xanthan gum mixture into the bubbling liquid. Stir the meatballs back into the center of the pan and cook until the sauce has thickened, about 3 minutes.

6. Taste the sauce and add sherry vinegar, salt, and/ or black pepper if necessary. Stir in the lemon zest, transfer the meatballs to a serving platter, and serve with the lingonberry jam on the side for dipping.

Kosher salt

1 cup baby carrots

4 ounces baby green beans, trimmed

6 ounces thin asparagus, trimmed

2 cups broccoli florets

12 small fingerling potatoes

3 tablespoons Balsamic Vinaigrette (page 33)

1 cup cherry tomatoes

½ English cucumber, sliced

2 tablespoons Pickling Brine (page 53)

1 cup Sri-Rancha (page 30)

8 radishes, halved, pickled, and drained (page 54)

½ celery root, peeled and cut into ¼-inch-thick matchsticks

SERVES 4

CRUDITÉS WITH SRI-RANCHA

This is my "farm-to-glass" dish, meaning that I take the freshest, ripest in-season veggies I can get my hands on and serve them with a fun dip. This easy appetizer makes a perfect start for a dinner party.

1. Bring a large pot of water to a rolling boil over high heat and salt it generously. Fill a large bowl with ice water and set aside. Put a large colander in the sink.

2. Drop the carrots into the boiling water and blanch until crisp-tender, 2 to 3 minutes. Using a strainer or slotted spoon, transfer them to the ice water and let stand until cool, then transfer to the colander to drain.

3. Blanch the remaining vegetables separately in the boiling water until crisp-tender, according to the following cooking times: the green beans for 1 minute, the asparagus for 1 minute, and the broccoli for 2 to 3 minutes. Cool in the ice water and drain.

4. Add the potatoes to the pot and cook until a fork easily pierces them, 8 to 10 minutes. Drain, transfer to a medium bowl, and drizzle 2 tablespoons of the vinaigrette over them. Let cool, tossing occasionally until the dressing is absorbed.

5. In a small bowl, toss the cherry tomatoes with the remaining vinaigrette. Put the cucumbers in another small bowl, drizzle the pickling brine over them, and let stand for 10 minutes.

6. To serve, fill a small glass bowl with the Sri-rancha and position it in the center of a large serving tray. Arrange the carrots, green beans, asparagus, broccoli, potatoes, tomatoes, cucumbers, radishes, and celery root around the bowl of dip. Serve, or cover and refrigerate until ready to serve.

Fresh Pasta Dough (Flavored Pastas: Squid Ink Pasta Dough, Saffron Pasta Dough, Parsley Pasta Dough) 144 | Spaghetti and Meatballs (Umami Paste) 148 | Spaghetti Carbonara (Chicken-Flavored Agar-Agar Noodles) 150 | Rigatoni alla Bolognese: Pressure-Cooker Bolognese 152 | **IMPASTAS:** MOROCCAN TUNA BOLOGNESE 154 | VEGETABLE LASAGNA 155 | POTATO "LINGUINE" WITH CONCH AND WHITE WINE (SPAGHETTI MADE FROM VEGETABLES) 157 | SQUID "LINGUINE" WITH SHRIMP 158 | ORECCHIETTE WITH SAUSAGE AND BROCCOLI RABE (GEODUCK CLAMS) 160 | BLACK SPAGHETTI WITH CRAB, UNI, AND CHILE OIL (CALABRIAN CHILE OIL AND BLACK GARLIC) 162 | BRAISED SQUID "CANNELLONI" 165 | Macaroni and Headcheese 166 | Sweet Potato Gnocchi with Kale, Sage, and Balsamic Brown Butter 169 | Fresh Ravioli: Corn and White Truffle Filling, Butternut Squash and Amaretto Filling, Fresh Ricotta with Chestnut Honey and Basil Filling, Oxtail-Marmalade Filling 170

PASTAS
+ IMPASTAS

Pasta is ripe for playful experimentation. At first glance, though, that may be hard to see. It seems so straightforward: Is there a more traditional comfort food than spaghetti and meatballs?

I have always wanted to be Italian. I grew up on Long Island in a community where many of our neighbors were Italian and, just like them, every Sunday we ate "pasta." But ours wasn't homemade like theirs. It was either spaghetti with Ragú sauce or out of a can. Now that I have my own family, I cook (better) pasta at home. It's the ultimate dinner for a busy weeknight, and I always use whatever we have in the fridge and pantry.

I learned how to make pasta during my training as a chef. One of the proudest moments of my career was when I was put in charge of making pasta at The French Laundry, chef Thomas Keller's revolutionary restaurant in California. The kitchen is in the front of the building and it has large windows through which I could see the hills of the vineyards and the incredible garden in the backyard. While I was there, guests would see me standing at that window making pasta at my station as they arrived. Working there was a real *moment* for me; it gave me an identity.

While the pursuit of perfection at The French Laundry shaped one way that I think about cooking pasta, an entirely different experience encouraged me to reconsider the form. A few years later I went to Atlanta to run a restaurant called Fishbone, but then it closed, and I went to Spain for six weeks— with the meager contents of my bank account and a backpack—to eat, travel, and think about what I wanted to do next. Spanish food was just coming into the spotlight and pushing the boundaries for creative food at the time, and I was particularly fascinated by chef Ferran Adrià, the mad scientist of modern cuisine whose legendary restaurant El Bulli was in Roses, in the mountainous region of northeast Catalonia. I took a train to Roses.

I was standing in front of Adrià's restaurant taking pictures when a man who looked like Latke from the television show *Taxi* walked up. It was the chef. In piecemeal Spanish, I told him I was a chef and would like to work with him. It just so happened that a young Hungarian chef had left the previous day, so the next thing I knew, I was in the kitchen wearing an apron, preparing rabbit brains while he made spaghetti out of Parmesan cheese. At that time, Adrià was in an Italian phase, and I soaked up all I could. I'd never seen a restaurant that operated that way: There was no flame or fire; all the cooking was by induction. It turned a lot of what I'd learned and knew on its head, and I liked it.

That's where my idea of an "impasta," a fun pasta imposter, was born: I saw Adrià making crab lasagna with lardo, and it struck a chord with me. What would happen if I tried to make pasta from something other than flour, water, and eggs? What if I added something other than salt to the pasta water, such as a splash of vinegar, a nub of bacon, or toasted garlic? It was the first time since culinary school that someone had turned my perspective upside down. It was a key moment in my growth as a chef.

I still cook pasta with both Keller and Adrià in mind, which is to say that I like the flexibility of being precise or experimental, depending on mood and circumstance. Sometimes I crave good old-fashioned spaghetti and meatballs, sometimes I like to remix the basic formula so a familiar favorite defies expectations and excites my guests. So here are pasta recipes to inspire your own creativity.

SPENCER BENNETT,
GRINDING WORKHORSE
+ ASPIRING ARTIST

2½ cups Italian
    "00" pasta flour,
    plus more for
    rolling

1 large egg
3 large egg yolks

½ cup water

Semolina flour for
dusting

MAKES 2 POUNDS

FRESH PASTA DOUGH

Making pasta by hand is one of the ultimate pleasures of cooking. There's
romance in creating something that's reliant on repetitive precision and
craft, on taking flour, eggs, and water and turning them into something
that doesn't much resemble their elements: a perfect handmade noodle. This
also happens to be a fun thing to do with kids in the kitchen.

1. Mound 2 cups of the pasta flour on a work surface
and make a deep well in the center. In a small bowl, whisk
the egg, yolks, and water together until combined and
pour it into the well. Using a fork, whisk the eggs around
the edges, gradually incorporating the flour. When the
mixture becomes too stiff to stir, knead it until it forms a
dough. Knead the remaining ½ cup flour into the dough
and continue kneading until it is very soft and smooth, 6 to
8 minutes. Wrap the dough tightly in plastic wrap and let
rest at room temperature for 20 minutes.

2. Cut the dough into 6 pieces and dust them lightly
with pasta flour. Working with one piece at a time and
keeping the remaining dough covered, flatten each piece of
dough to about ¼ inch thick and run it through the widest
setting on a pasta machine. Fold the dough in half and roll it
through again. Repeat 3 times, dusting the pasta sheet with
more flour if it gets sticky. Reduce the setting on the roller
by one notch and roll again. Fold the dough in half and
roll again on the same setting. Reduce the setting by one
notch and roll the pasta again. Continue rolling the dough,
reducing the setting by one notch each time, until you reach
the thinnest setting. Repeat with the rest of the dough.

3. Run the pasta strips through the cutter choice
(fettuccine, linguine) and arrange the cut pasta on a towel-
lined baking sheet. Sprinkle semolina flour over the pasta
and toss lightly to prevent sticking. Allow the pasta to air-dry
for 30 to 45 minutes before wrapping tightly in plastic wrap
and storing in the refrigerator. Fresh pasta will keep, tightly
wrapped, for up to 1 week in the refrigerator.

2.0 **FLAVORED PASTAS**

I like flavored pastas. The following
are three of my favorites. Squid ink has
a slightly metallic flavor that works great
with seafood. The saffron version imparts
depth to shellfish or poultry or veal. The
parsley adds a beautiful aesthetic to the
plate with its bright color.

SQUID INK PASTA DOUGH: Reduce the amount of
water to 6 tablespoons. Stir 1 tablespoon squid ink into
the water and proceed with the recipe as written.

SAFFRON PASTA DOUGH: In step 1, first heat the
water until hot, but not boiling, in the microwave. Add
1 teaspoon saffron threads and let stand until cool.
Pour the water through a fine-mesh strainer and discard
the saffron. Proceed with the recipe as written.

PARSLEY PASTA DOUGH: Add a pinch of salt to the
list of dry ingredients. Use 2 whole eggs (instead of 1 egg
and 3 egg yolks). In a blender, combine approximately
4 tablespoons parsley with 2 tablespoons water and puree.
Replace the water with the parsley puree. Proceed with the
recipe. (I like to make this one in sheets, above.)

IS THERE A MORE
COMFORT

TRADITIONAL
FOOD
THAN SPAGHETTI
AND MEATBALLS?

FOR THE MEATBALLS

3 tablespoons olive oil

1 yellow onion, finely chopped

2 cloves garlic, minced

4 anchovies, mashed

1 tablespoon chopped fresh flat-leaf parsley, plus more for garnish

2 teaspoons chopped fresh sage or ½ teaspoon dried

1 teaspoon kosher salt

½ teaspoon freshly ground black pepper

½ teaspoon red pepper flakes

½ cup whole milk

1 slice stale sourdough bread, roughly torn, about 1 cup

12 ounces ground veal

12 ounces ground pork

6 ounces lardo or pork fatback, finely chopped

3 cups Tomato Sauce (page 35)

Kosher salt

1 pound Fresh Pasta Dough (page 144), rolled out and cut into spaghetti or linguine, or store-bought dried spaghetti

1 ball fresh burrata or mozzarella (about 12 ounces), torn into small pieces

Freshly grated Parmesan cheese for serving

SERVES 4 TO 6

SPAGHETTI + MEATBALLS

We have two young kids, so we eat our fair share of pasta. We even have a tradition in the house when we make this recipe: Topless Spaghetti Night! It saves on laundry and is a hit with the kids. So draw the curtains, grab some Parm, and get cooking.

I. TO MAKE THE MEATBALLS: Heat 1 tablespoon of the olive oil in a large skillet over medium heat. Add the onion, garlic, anchovies, parsley, sage, salt, pepper, and red pepper flakes and cook until the onion is softened, about 5 minutes. Transfer to a bowl and refrigerate until cold.

2. Pour the milk over the bread in a small bowl and let soak for 1 minute.

3. In a large bowl, combine the veal, pork, and lardo. Mash the bread and milk together with your hands until it is a thick paste and add to the meat. Add the chilled onion-herb mixture and, using your hands, mix the ingredients well, but do not overwork. Wet your hands and roll the meat into balls about 2 inches in diameter and place them on a plate or baking sheet. Chill in the refrigerator for 10 to 15 minutes before cooking.

4. In a large deep skillet, heat the remaining 2 tablespoons olive oil over medium-high heat. Working in batches if necessary, cook the meatballs, turning occasionally, until lightly browned, 5 to 6 minutes. If you cooked them in batches, return all the meatballs to the pan, then add the tomato sauce and bring to a boil. Reduce the heat to maintain a gentle simmer, cover, and cook for 15 minutes.

5. Flip the meatballs, cover, and cook until the meatballs are cooked through, about 10 minutes more. (If the sauce gets too thick, add ¼ to ½ cup water to the pan.)

6. Meanwhile, bring a large pot of water to a boil and salt it generously. Add the spaghetti, stir, and cook until just al dente, 3 to 4 minutes for fresh, 8 to 9 minutes for dried. Drain the pasta in a colander and return it to the pot.

7. Carefully pour the meatballs and sauce over the spaghetti and, using tongs, toss the pasta until well coated in sauce. Divide the spaghetti and meatballs among shallow bowls or transfer it to a large serving platter. Sprinkle the burrata pieces over the top, garnish with Parmesan cheese, and serve.

2.0 UMAMI PASTE

Umami sounds like a Brazilian footballer or a supermodel, but it's really the flavor that makes your mouth water, which is just as cool. To add a more intense savory essence to this dish, substitute a tablespoon of one of my all-time favorite ingredients, umami paste, for the anchovies. It's a blend of pureed tomato, garlic, anchovy paste, black olives, balsamic vinegar, porcini mushrooms, Parmesan cheese, olive oil, and a little sugar and salt. I can't get enough of its flavor and I often incorporate it into my savory foods as a flavor booster, to enhance and intensify what's there already. Umami paste is available at gourmet grocery shops and from online food retailers—both Amazon and Dean & DeLuca (DeanDeLuca.com) sell a good-quality Italian umami paste called Taste No. 5.

I also sometimes use mashed anchovies in my tomato sauce, but you can substitute umami paste there too. Start with ¼ teaspoon and increase the amount to your personal liking. You can also add 1 teaspoon or so to meat marinades, soups, stews, and sauces.

1 tablespoon olive oil

8 ounces Pressure-Cooker Braised Bacon (page 45) or pancetta, diced

Kosher salt

1 pound Fresh Pasta Dough (page 144), rolled out and cut into spaghetti or store-bought dried spaghetti

½ cup grated Parmesan cheese, plus more for serving

2 to 3 teaspoons freshly ground black pepper, or to taste

4 large egg yolks (unbroken)

½ cup Toasted Herb Bread Crumbs (page 47)

¼ cup chopped fresh flat-leaf parsley for garnish (optional)

Cracked black pepper

SERVES 4

SPAGHETTI CARBONARA

Spaghetti carbonara is one of Italy's simplest delights. It's basically just noodles with bacon, egg, and Parmesan cheese. To make mine unique, I braise the pancetta, because I love to cook cured meats—it gives an incredibly luscious flavor and especially soft texture. To me, the braised bacon is what really makes this dish.

1. Heat the oil in a large skillet over medium heat. Add the bacon and cook, stirring occasionally, until browned and crisp, about 10 minutes. Keep warm over low heat.

2. Meanwhile, bring a large pot of water to a boil and salt it generously. Stir in the spaghetti and cook until al dente, 3 to 4 minutes for fresh, 8 to 9 minutes for dried. Reserve about ½ cup of the pasta cooking water and drain the spaghetti.

3. Immediately transfer the pasta to the skillet with the bacon. Add the Parmesan and a generous amount of pepper and, using tongs, very gently toss the pasta until coated in the fat and very hot. If the mixture seems dry, add some pasta water a little bit at a time.

4. To serve, divide the noodles among four warm shallow bowls. Place an egg yolk on top of each plate and garnish with a sprinkling of the bread crumbs, parsley, if using, more Parmesan, and a little cracked pepper. Serve immediately, instructing your diners to stir the egg yolk into the pasta.

2.0 CHICKEN-FLAVORED AGAR-AGAR NOODLES

A neat thing about agar-agar noodles is that you don't have to serve them cold as you would if they were made with regular gelatin; since agar-agar has a high flash point, you can heat and even reheat them without losing their shape. I use them in carbonara, combining agar-agar with chicken stock to make noodles. Agar-agar is sold at Whole Foods, Asian markets, and elsewhere.

To make the noodles, you need two things: 2 cups chicken stock and ¼ cup agar-agar. Line a 9½-×-13-inch baking pan with a double layer of plastic wrap and set aside. Heat half the chicken stock until very hot and pour it into a blender. Add the agar-agar and blend until smooth. Add the remaining stock, blend well, and let cool to room temperature.

Pour the mixture into the lined baking pan and refrigerate until firm. Bring a large pot of water to a boil. Invert the solidified chicken stock onto a cutting board and peel off the plastic. Cut the block lengthwise into ⅛-inch-wide ribbons. Reduce the water to a simmer, add the noodles, and stir very gently until they are hot, 20 to 30 seconds. Drain in a colander and gently shake to remove excess water. Toss with the braised bacon and Parmesan for "Chicken Carbonara."

Kosher salt

1 pound dried rigatoni, penne, or other short pasta

3 cups Pressure-Cooker Bolognese (recipe follows)

Freshly grated Parmesan cheese for serving

Chopped fresh basil and flat-leaf parsley for garnish (optional)

SERVES 4

RIGATONI ALLA BOLOGNESE *(page 141)*

If you're like me, you need a killer bolognese in your arsenal for potential deployment at any time. The trick to making one is to be simultaneously rustic and refined. My secret is the pressure cooker, which maximizes efficiency—you don't have to slave over your stove for hours, and you get an intensely flavorful sauce. But if you don't have one, or you enjoy the romance of a lazy Sunday spent stirring a pot and tasting the sauce for seasoning, obviously you can make sauce the old-fashioned way as well.

1. Bring a large pot of water to a boil and salt it generously. Add the pasta, stir, and cook until al dente, 8 to 10 minutes. Reserve about 1 cup of the cooking water and drain the pasta.

2. Meanwhile, heat the bolognese in a large deep skillet over medium-low heat until simmering.

3. Add the drained pasta to the simmering bolognese and toss well to coat, adding a little pasta cooking water to thin the sauce if necessary.

4. Divide the pasta among four warmed plates or pasta bowls and sprinkle Parmesan and fresh basil and parsley, if you like, over the top. Serve immediately.

PRESSURE-COOKER BOLOGNESE

3 tablespoons olive oil

1 pound boneless pork or veal shoulder, chopped into ½-inch pieces

1 pound sweet or spicy Italian bulk sausage

1 large yellow onion, finely chopped

2 carrots, finely diced

1 stalk celery, finely diced

6 garlic cloves, minced

1 bay leaf

Kosher salt and freshly ground black pepper to taste

2 tablespoons tomato paste

1 cup dry red wine

One 28-ounce can San Marzano tomatoes, crushed with your hands

20 fresh basil leaves

2 tablespoons balsamic vinegar, or more to taste

1. Heat the olive oil in a pressure cooker over medium-high heat. Add the pork and cook, stirring, until well browned, 5 to 6 minutes. Remove the meat from the pot with a slotted spoon and set aside. Add the sausage to the pot and cook, stirring, and breaking it up into very small clumps until browned, 4 to 5 minutes. Use the slotted spoon to remove the sausage and set aside with the pork.

2. Add the onion, carrots, and celery to the pot and cook, stirring, until very soft, about 5 minutes. Add the garlic and bay leaf, stir, and cook for 2 minutes more. Season the vegetables with salt and pepper, add the tomato paste, and stir until the paste begins to caramelize, 2 to 3 minutes.

3. Carefully pour the wine into the pot and bring to a simmer, scraping up any browned bits on the bottom of the pot. Cook until the liquid is reduced by half, 2 to 3 minutes. Add the crushed tomatoes, crushing more in the pot, return the browned meat and sausage to the pot, and stir well.

4. Attach the pressure cooker lid, reduce the heat to medium, and cook until the pot begins to hiss. Reduce the heat to medium-low and cook for 45 minutes. If the pot is not hissing, raise the temperature slightly until it does.

5. Remove the pot from the heat and let stand until the pressure has released and the lid unlocks. Remove the lid, return the pot to low heat, and simmer for 20 minutes, uncovered, to thicken the sauce. Stir in the basil and balsamic vinegar. Taste and adjust the seasoning with salt, pepper, and/or vinegar.

6. Allow the Bolognese to cool completely. Use right away or transfer to airtight containers and refrigerate for up to 1 week or freeze for up to 3 months.

Three 6- to 8-ounce tuna steaks

¼ cup extra-virgin olive oil

1 small yellow onion, finely chopped

1 carrot, finely minced

1 stalk celery, finely minced

2 garlic cloves, minced

1 tablespoon Moroccan spice blend or 1 teaspoon each ground coriander, cumin, and cinnamon

1 bay leaf

Kosher salt and freshly ground black pepper to taste

2 tablespoons tomato paste

¼ cup balsamic vinegar

½ cup dry sherry or red wine

2 cups Tomato Sauce (page 35)

½ cup pitted Picholine or other green olives, roughly chopped

2 teaspoons grated orange zest, plus more for garnish

1 pound Fresh Pasta Dough (page 144), rolled out and cut into linguine, or store-bought dried linguine

Juice of ½ lemon (about 2 tablespoons)

4 ounces feta cheese, crumbled, for garnishing

¼ cup mixed chopped fresh dill, parsley, and basil

SERVES 6 TO 8

MOROCCAN TUNA BOLOGNESE

My "impasta" version of Bolognese is all about tuna. Fresh tuna is bright red like beef, and has a meaty flavor and robust texture that mimics it—but it has the advantage of being healthier and tasting faintly of the sea. Tuna's clean flavor benefits from the warm, aromatic Moroccan spices, coriander and cumin, plus the salty feta cheese, parsley, basil, and fresh lemon juice. You can use leftover tuna (see the tuna loin recipe, page 225) or your favorite canned tuna stirred into the finished sauce. Think of this recipe as a "new school" tuna noodle casserole.

1. Grind or very finely mince 1 tuna steak. Cut the other 2 steaks into ½-inch chunks.

2. In a large deep heavy skillet, heat the olive oil over medium-high heat until rippling. Add the tuna and cook, breaking up the meat with a spoon and stirring vigorously until it's no longer pink and begins to brown, 2 to 3 minutes. Remove the tuna with a slotted spoon and set aside.

3. Add the onion, carrot, and celery to the pan and cook, stirring, until softened, about 5 minutes. Add the garlic, Moroccan spices, bay leaf, and salt and pepper, stir, and cook for 2 minutes to toast the spices. Add the tomato paste and cook and stir until it begins to caramelize, 2 to 3 minutes. Add the balsamic vinegar and sherry, scraping up any browned bits on the bottom of the pan.

4. Add the tomato sauce and cooked tuna and bring to a boil. Reduce the heat to maintain a simmer and cook until the sauce is very thick, 25 to 30 minutes.

5. Stir in the tuna chunks, green olives, and orange zest, cover, and cook for 10 minutes. Remove the lid, stir well, and taste and adjust the seasoning.

6. Meanwhile, bring a large pot of water to a boil and salt it generously. Add the linguine, stir, and cook until al dente, 3 to 4 minutes for fresh, 9 to 10 minutes for dried. Remove ½ cup of the cooking water and drain the pasta.

7. Add the pasta to the sauce, then add the lemon juice and half the feta and herbs. Toss the pasta with the sauce until well coated. If the sauce is very thick, add reserved pasta water 1 tablespoon at a time until loosened.

8. To serve, transfer the pasta to warm shallow bowls or a large platter. Sprinkle the remaining feta and herbs and some orange zest over the pasta and serve.

4 large zucchini (about 2 inches in diameter; about 2 pounds total)

6 tablespoons olive oil, plus more as needed

Kosher salt and freshly ground black pepper to taste

1 large eggplant (about 12 ounces), cut into ½-inch cubes

3 garlic cloves, chopped

One 28-ounce can San Marzano tomatoes, crushed with your hands

12 ounces fresh ricotta

1 cup freshly grated Parmesan cheese, plus (optional) more for serving

1 tablespoon chopped fresh basil or 1 teaspoon dried

1 tablespoon chopped fresh flat-leaf parsley or 1 teaspoon dried

1 teaspoon chopped fresh tarragon or ½ teaspoon dried

1 large egg, beaten

2 cups Tomato Sauce (page 34)

One 1-pound ball fresh mozzarella, torn into small pieces

IMPASTA

SERVES 6 TO 8

VEGETABLE LASAGNA

I've been making lasagna with vegetables, like the zucchini here, in place of the traditional noodles since I've been running restaurant kitchens. At my first Atlanta restaurant, Fishbone, we did an artichoke lasagna as a side dish, and since then I've enjoyed revisiting the theme. I love the way the vegetables are sturdy enough to handle the saucy richness of the other ingredients.

1. Using a Japanese mandoline, slice the zucchini lengthwise into ¼-inch-thick slices. Heat 2 tablespoons of the oil in a large skillet over medium heat. Working in batches, and adding more oil as necessary, cook the zucchini slices, turning once, until just softened, 2 to 3 minutes per side. Transfer to a paper-towel-lined baking sheet to drain. Season the slices lightly with salt and pepper.

2. Add the remaining ¼ cup oil to the skillet and heat over medium-high heat. Add the eggplant, season with salt and pepper, and cook, stirring, until the eggplant has softened but still holds its shape, 4 to 5 minutes. Add the garlic and toss for 1 minute. Add the tomatoes, season again with salt and pepper, and cook until most of the liquid has evaporated, 8 to 10 minutes. Remove from the heat and let cool.

3. Preheat the oven to 375°F. In a small bowl, stir the ricotta and ½ cup of the Parmesan together until combined. Season with salt and pepper, then add the basil, parsley, tarragon, and egg and stir well.

4. Grease a 2-quart baking dish. Spread ½ cup of the tomato sauce over the bottom. Arrange a layer of one-third of the zucchini slices on top. Spread ½ cup of the tomato sauce evenly over the zucchini. Add half the eggplant mixture and spread it evenly. With a spoon, drop half the ricotta mixture in small dollops over the eggplant. Sprinkle one-third of the mozzarella over the top. Spread another one-third of the zucchini slices over the top, followed by ½ cup tomato sauce and then the remaining eggplant mixture, the remaining ricotta, and another one-third of the mozzarella. Top with the remaining zucchini slices. Spread the rest of the sauce over the zucchini, being sure to cover it completely. Sprinkle the remaining ½ cup Parmesan over the top and scatter the remaining mozzarella over the lasagna.

5. Bake until bubbling and golden brown on top, about 45 minutes. Let stand for at least 15 minutes before slicing and serving, with additional Parmesan on the side, if desired.

- 3 large russet (baking) potatoes, peeled
- 1½ cups Pressure-Cooker Chicken Stock (page 44) or store-bought low-sodium broth
- 2 tablespoons unsalted butter

- 1 pound fresh conch, minced, or 1½ cups chopped shucked cherrystone or whole small white clams
- 1 tablespoon chopped fresh oregano

- ½ teaspoon finely minced jarred brined Calabrian chiles or red pepper flakes
- Kosher salt and freshly ground black pepper to taste

- ¼ cup dry white wine
- 3 tablespoons chopped fresh flat-leaf parsley
- Grated zest and juice of ½ lemon
- ½ cup Toasted Herb Bread Crumbs (page 47) for garnish

IMPASTA

SERVES 4

POTATO "LINGUINE" WITH CONCH + WHITE WINE

This recipe is most often requested by *Top Chef* fans. I made it during the Bahamas episode, when the challenge was to catch and cook our own conch. The other chefs went for traditional island flavors, such as pineapple, mango, and banana leaves. I took inspiration from my Long Island roots. Linguine in clam sauce inspires this dish, lending it elegance and Italian flavors. *Top Chef* judge (and Italian-American chef) Tom Colicchio mistook my ribbons of barely cooked potato for perfectly prepared pasta. I didn't win the challenge, but it made quite an impression.

1. Using a Japanese mandoline or a very sharp long knife, cut the potatoes lengthwise into long, thin sheets (as thin as possible—ideally, you should be able to see through them). Stack the slices a few at a time and cut them lengthwise into ¼-inch-wide ribbons.

2. Pour the chicken stock into a large skillet and bring to a simmer over medium-high heat. Add the potatoes and butter and cook until the potatoes begin to absorb the stock, about 4 minutes. Add the conch, oregano, and chiles and cook until the potatoes are al dente and most of the stock is absorbed, about 5 minutes. Season with salt and pepper.

3. Pour in the wine and toss the potatoes gently until it evaporates. Stir in the parsley.

4. Divide the "linguine" among four warmed shallow bowls. Squeeze some lemon juice over each bowl and top with a sprinkling of bread crumbs. Serve immediately.

2.0 SPAGHETTI MADE FROM VEGETABLES

My "impastas" fit the bill for gluten-free diners. And vegetable pasta is really fun to make.

The easiest way to do this is with 2 long, thin zucchini and 2 long, thin yellow squash, each about 6 ounces. Halve the vegetables lengthwise and, using a spoon, scrape out the seeds. Using a Japanese mandoline with a julienne blade, slice the vegetables lengthwise into long, thin ribbons. (You can also do this by hand with a long sharp knife; cut each vegetable in half, then cut lengthwise into ⅛-inch-thick slices. Stack a few of the slices at a time and slice lengthwise into ⅛-inch-wide ribbons.)

In a large skillet, heat 2 cups Tomato Sauce (page 35) or another favorite tomato sauce until simmering. Add the veggie ribbons and cook, stirring occasionally, until tender, about 5 minutes.

8 large squid bodies
(about 1 pound)

8 ounces shrimp
(any size),
peeled and
deveined

¼ cup Sicilian or
other extra-
virgin olive oil

4 garlic cloves,
chopped

½ teaspoon red
pepper flakes

1 teaspoon chopped
fresh rosemary,
plus more for
garnish

Grated zest and
juice of ½ lemon

Kosher salt

¼ teaspoon freshly
ground black
pepper, plus more
for garnish

¼ cup dry white wine

2 tablespoons
unsalted butter

1 tablespoon chile
oil (see page
162), plus more
for garnish

Maldon or gray sea
salt for garnish

IMPASTA

SERVES 4

SQUID "LINGUINE" WITH SHRIMP

This "impasta" version of shrimp scampi, both protein-packed and gluten-
free, relies on olive oil, lots of garlic, minced rosemary, black pepper,
and lemon juice to make an intensely flavorful dish with a subtly chewy,
textured bite. Don't be afraid to bust out the good olive oil for this
(like a strong, green grassy-flavored one), because you will taste it. Be
sure to have all of your ingredients ready to go before you begin cooking
this dish because it comes together very quickly.

1. Cut the squid bodies open down one side, rinse them, pat them dry, and lay them flat on a parchment-lined baking sheet. Place in the freezer for 15 minutes, or until very firm.

2. With a sharp knife, cut the squid lengthwise into ¼-inch-wide strips. Set aside.

3. Put the shrimp in a food processor and pulse until coarsely ground.

4. In a large skillet, heat the olive oil over high heat until rippling. Add the garlic and stir for 10 seconds, then immediately add the ground shrimp, red pepper flakes, rosemary, lemon zest and juice, a pinch of salt, and the black pepper. Stir vigorously to break up the shrimp, then toss the mixture until the shrimp is just cooked, about 2 minutes.

5. Add the white wine and stir until it has nearly evaporated. Add the butter and toss well until melted and combined. Remove from the heat, stir in the squid strips, and let stand for 2 minutes, or until the squid is just cooked. Stir in the chile oil, then taste and add more salt and pepper if necessary.

6. Divide the mixture among four heated shallow pasta bowls, and garnish each one with rosemary, black pepper, a drizzle of chile oil, and a sprinkling of Maldon salt. Serve immediately.

Kosher salt

1 bunch (about 12 ounces) broccoli rabe, ends trimmed

1 tablespoon olive oil

1 pound bulk spicy Italian sausage

½ teaspoon fennel seeds

Pinch of red pepper flakes, or as desired

1 pound dried orecchiette

2 tablespoons red wine vinegar

Grated zest and juice of ½ lemon

Freshly ground black pepper to taste

Freshly grated Parmesan cheese for serving

IMPASTA

SERVES 4

ORECCHIETTE WITH SAUSAGE + BROCCOLI RABE

I can't get enough of the interplay of sweet with sour, the way these two taste components enhance each other. The magic of putting sweet and sour together is something that the makers of SweeTarts candy figured out a long time ago. A more sophisticated and savory way to do it is here; this dish is a variation of a very traditional Italian pasta preparation in which the broccoli rabe is there for pleasant bitterness and bite, the sausage for sweetness, and the chile flakes for tingling heat. The geoduck clam variation (opposite) is a fun impasta version of this recipe.

1. Bring a large pot of water to a boil and salt it generously. Fill a large bowl with ice water and set aside. Drop the broccoli rabe into the boiling water and cook until bright green but still crisp-tender, about 2 minutes. Drain and immediately drop into the ice water to stop the cooking. Once the broccoli rabe is cold, drain well. Chop the stems and leaves into ½-inch pieces and cut the florets into larger chunks; leave smaller ones intact.

2. Heat the olive oil in a large skillet over medium-high heat. Add the sausage, fennel seeds, and red pepper flakes and cook, breaking the meat up with a spoon, until it is well browned, about 10 minutes. Using a large spoon, remove the excess fat from the pan and discard.

3. Meanwhile, bring a large pot of water to a boil and salt it generously. Stir in the orecchiette and cook until al dente. Reserve about ½ cup of the cooking water and drain the pasta.

4. Add the broccoli rabe to the sausage, raise the heat to high, and toss until very hot. Add the vinegar and cook, tossing, until it has nearly evaporated. Add the lemon zest and juice and toss. Taste and adjust the seasoning with salt and pepper. Add the cooked pasta and toss; if the mixture seems dry, add some of the pasta water a few tablespoons at a time.

5. Divide the pasta among four warm shallow bowls and sprinkle Parmesan generously over the top. Serve immediately.

2.0 GEODUCK CLAMS

I love clams and I always have. The geoduck (pronounced "gooey-duck") from the Pacific Northwest is a special favorite. Everyone giggles when they first see these odd-looking large clams, which have chewy necks and tender cylinders (or siphons). The meat itself resembles abalone. If you've never worked with geoduck clams, I encourage you to try them because their flavor is singularly sweet-salty and addictive.

You can replace the pasta in this recipe with 1 large geoduck clam (about 2 pounds), shelled and cut crosswise into ⅛-inch-thick coins (when preparing the clams, you'll notice, as I did one day, that the sliced geoduck resembles orecchiette). The clams need very little cooking, so when the sausage and broccoli rabe sauce is finished, remove it from the heat and stir in the cut clams. Cover the pan and let stand for 3 to 4 minutes. The heat from the pan will lightly cook the clams, and you'll find they are amazingly similar in texture to orecchiete. Geoducks are available at good fish markets around the country.

- 4 lobes uni (sea urchin roe)
- 2 tablespoons olive oil
- 1 small yellow onion, finely minced
- 3 garlic cloves, minced
- 1 jalapeño, seeded and chopped
- Kosher salt and freshly ground black pepper to taste
- 1 pound Fresh Squid Ink Pasta Dough (page 145), rolled out and cut into spaghetti
- 1 tablespoon Calabrian chile oil, plus (optional) more for garnish
- 8 ounces lump crabmeat, picked over for shells and cartilage
- 2 teaspoons grated lemon zest, plus more for garnish
- ¼ cup chopped mixed fresh flat-leaf parsley and basil, plus more for garnish
- ½ cup Toasted Herb Bread Crumbs (page 47) for garnish

IMPASTA

SERVES 4

BLACK SPAGHETTI WITH CRAB, UNI + CHILE OIL

"Ocean" is probably my favorite flavor. This dish came from my desire to marry Italian flavors with the essence of the sea in a bowl. The saltiness and freshness of the sea are present in the crab and uni; the comfort and simplicity of classic Italian food is in the homemade pasta; and the chile oil adds an extra intensity that makes this dish all mine—and now yours.

1. Put the uni in a mini food processor and puree until smooth. Transfer to a bowl and refrigerate.

2. In a large deep skillet, heat the oil over medium heat. Add the onion, garlic, and jalapeño and cook until softened and lightly browned, about 10 minutes. Season with salt and pepper and keep warm over low heat.

3. Meanwhile, bring a large pot of water to a boil and salt it generously. Add the spaghetti and cook until al dente, 3 to 4 minutes. Reserve about ½ cup of the pasta water, drain the pasta, and add to the skillet.

4. Drizzle the chile oil over the pasta, then add half the crabmeat, the lemon zest, the herb mixture, and half the uni puree. Using tongs, very gently toss the mixture to combine. Add a little of the pasta water 1 tablespoon at a time if the pasta seems dry. Taste and adjust the seasoning with salt and pepper.

5. To serve, divide the pasta among four warmed shallow bowls. Sprinkle the remaining crab over the pasta, followed by small dollops of the remaining uni. Garnish each bowl with a drizzle of chile oil, if desired, then scatter chopped herbs, the bread crumbs, and lemon zest over the top. Serve immediately.

1.5 CALABRIAN CHILE OIL

Calabrian hot chile oil is made with a paste of the small, fiery-hot chile peppers of the region. It is best used as a finishing condiment. Drizzle some over raw seafood or cooked pasta or green vegetables—or mix a little into your favorite mayo or sour cream. It can be found in specialty Italian markets and various online stores, including OliveOilOfTheWorld.com.

1.5 BLACK GARLIC

I'm fascinated with black foods, in part because they're
good-looking rarities. I love their glossy darkness and slick
sophistication, and the visual play of a black food against a
matte white plate. One of my favorites is black garlic. It's
essentially fermented garlic, and it is popular in South Korea.
It tastes like Chinese black beans but is fragrant like roasted
garlic. You can substitute it for the garlic in this recipe,
if you like—it gives the dish a nice funkiness, if you're into
that. Buy it in specialty stores or by mail-order from online
gourmet and exotic food vendors.

8 large squid with tentacles (4 inches long; about 1 pound total), cleaned

1 tablespoon olive oil

12 ounces fresh ground Mexican chorizo

½ yellow onion, finely chopped

2 garlic cloves, minced

2 ounces kale or mustard greens, stemmed and finely chopped

⅓ cup diced jarred piquillo or roasted red peppers

¼ cup golden or dark raisins

2 tablespoons capers, drained

1 teaspoon grated lemon zest, plus more for garnish

½ teaspoon kosher salt

Freshly ground black pepper to taste

3 tablespoons chopped fresh flat-leaf parsley, plus more for garnish

½ teaspoon saffron threads, soaked in 1 tablespoon warm water

3 cups Tomato Sauce (page 35)

Warm crusty bread for serving

IMPASTA

SERVES 4

BRAISED SQUID "CANNELLONI"

When you're mimicking a pasta, you want your dish to resemble the actual noodle you're imitating as much as possible. A squid body looks like a long tube of cannelloni. Although cannelloni is Italian, this dish is all about Spanish flavors: The stuffing relies on the delicious interplay of piquillo peppers with chorizo and saffron. Cooking squid slowly over low heat coaxes out its flavor while keeping it moist and tender.

1. Cut the tentacles off the squid and rinse them, along with the bodies. Drain and set aside.

2. In a large skillet, heat the oil over medium heat. Add the chorizo and cook, breaking it up with a spoon, until browned and cooked through, 6 to 8 minutes. Add the onion and garlic and cook, stirring, until softened, about 3 minutes. Add the kale and cook, stirring, until wilted, 2 to 3 minutes. Remove from the heat and add the peppers, raisins, capers, lemon zest, salt, and pepper and stir well. Let cool completely, then stir in the parsley.

3. Preheat the oven to 350°F. Stir the saffron, with its liquid, into the tomato sauce. Spread ½ cup of the sauce over the bottom of a 2-quart baking dish. With a small spoon, stuff the sausage mixture into the squid bodies and arrange them in the dish. Scatter the squid tentacles over the stuffed squid and pour the remaining tomato sauce over, making sure the squid bodies are covered.

4. Cover the dish tightly with aluminum foil and bake until the squid is tender, 45 to 60 minutes.

5. Sprinkle parsley and lemon zest over the top of the "cannelloni" and serve with warm crusty bread alongside.

4 tablespoons
(½ stick)
unsalted butter,
plus more for
greasing the
baking dish

½ head cauliflower,
cored

Kosher salt and
freshly ground
black pepper to
taste

1 tablespoon olive
oil

8 ounces headcheese
or mortadella,
cut into ½-inch
cubes

¼ cup all-purpose
flour

2 cups whole milk,
at room
temperature

2 cups shredded
mozzarella cheese
(about 8 ounces)

2 cups grated sharp
white cheddar
cheese (about
8 ounces)

¼ cup freshly
grated Parmesan
cheese

1 pound elbow
macaroni, cooked
until al dente and
drained

½ cup Toasted Herb
Bread Crumbs
(page 47) for
garnish

SERVES 6 TO 8

MACARONI + HEADCHEESE

This is everyone's favorite comfort food classic—macaroni and cheese—with
an unusual addition: headcheese, a classic terrine made of so-called "spare
parts," the head, tongue, and often the feet of a pig that's been purposed
for other, loftier pursuits. Europeans think nothing of eating headcheese
for breakfast every day, but it's a harder sell for Americans. I want to
show that it can be delicious—and what better vehicle than creamy, rich
mac 'n' cheese? In the béchamel sauce, I use pureed cauliflower, which is
healthier and has a divine texture, with its own vegetal richness.

1. Preheat the oven to 375°F. Butter a 2-quart baking
dish and set aside.

2. Bring a large pot of water to a boil. Add the cauliflower and cook until very soft, 12 to 15 minutes. Drain.

3. Puree the cauliflower in a food processor until very
smooth. Season with salt and pepper and set aside.

4. Heat the oil in a medium saucepan over medium
heat. Add the headcheese and cook, stirring occasionally,
until browned and crisp, 8 to 10 minutes. Drain on a paper-
towel-lined plate and let cool.

5. Melt the butter in the same saucepan over medium
heat. Whisk in the flour and let the mixture bubble for
1 to 2 minutes. Whisking constantly, gradually pour in the
milk and continue to whisk until the mixture begins to bubble
and thicken. Add ½ cup each of the mozzarella and cheddar
and 1 tablespoon of the Parmesan and whisk until smooth.
Taste and add salt if needed. Remove from the heat.

6. Put the macaroni in a large bowl. Add the cheese
sauce, cauliflower puree, crisped headcheese, ¾ cup each
of the mozzarella and cheddar, and half of the remaining
Parmesan cheese and stir until the pasta is well coated.
Pour the mixture into the baking dish. Mix the bread crumbs
with the remaining cheeses and scatter evenly over the top.

7. Set the baking dish on a baking sheet and bake
until bubbling and golden brown on top, 35 to 40 minutes.
Let stand for 15 minutes before serving.

- 2 sweet potatoes (about 1 pound)
- 1 to 1½ cups all-purpose flour, plus more for rolling
- 1 large egg, beaten
- 1 teaspoon kosher salt, plus more as needed

- Freshly ground black pepper to taste
- 1 tablespoon olive oil
- 2 ounces pancetta, finely diced
- ½ small white onion, finely diced

- 4 tablespoons (½ stick) unsalted butter
- 3 tablespoons aged balsamic vinegar
- 2 ounces kale, stemmed and cut into thin ribbons

- 1 teaspoon chopped fresh sage, plus whole leaves for garnish
- A Parmesan cheese wedge for shaving

SERVES 4 AS A MAIN COURSE, 6 TO 8 AS AN APPETIZER

SWEET POTATO GNOCCHI WITH KALE, SAGE + BALSAMIC BROWN BUTTER

This dish was inspired solely by the straightforward combination of earthy sweet potato with the natural richness of nuts and root vegetables. I use aged balsamic vinegar to showcase the flavor of that intense, marvelously aged Italian product. The sauce of balsamic and brown butter works really well with this rustic dish.

1. Preheat the oven to 400°F. Prick the sweet potatoes all over with a fork and put them on a baking sheet. Roast until completely soft, 1 to 1¼ hours. Let stand until cool enough to handle.

2. Halve the sweet potatoes and scrape the flesh into a large bowl. Refrigerate until cool.

3. Add 1 cup of the flour, the egg, salt, and pepper to taste to the sweet potatoes and mix until a soft dough forms. Turn out onto a well-floured work surface and knead gently until the dough is smooth and no longer sticky. (If it is still sticky, add a bit more flour and continue kneading.) Use a bench scraper to keep the dough from sticking and to release it from the work surface. Cut the dough into 6 portions and roll each portion into a long cylinder about ½ inch thick. Cut each one into ½-inch pieces and transfer to a baking sheet lined with a floured towel.

4. Bring a large pot of water to a boil and salt it generously.

5. Meanwhile, heat the oil in a large skillet over medium heat. Add the pancetta and cook until beginning to brown, about 5 minutes. Stir in the onions and cook until softened, 6 to 8 minutes. Transfer the mixture to a small bowl and set aside.

6. Melt the butter in the same skillet over medium-low heat and cook until the milk solids begin to turn brown and the butter gives off a nutty aroma. Immediately add the vinegar and swirl the pan to combine. Add the kale, stir, and add 1 to 2 tablespoons water to help the leaves wilt. Reduce the heat to low and keep warm.

7. Reduce the heat under the boiling water to maintain a simmer. Drop the gnocchi into the water and cook until they all float, 8 to 10 minutes. Drain the gnocchi and add to the balsamic brown butter, along with the reserved pancetta and onions. Sprinkle in the chopped sage, season with salt and pepper, and toss well to coat.

8. Divide the gnocchi among warm shallow bowls and, using a vegetable peeler, shave Parmesan strips over the top. Garnish with sage leaves and serve immediately.

2½ cups Italian "00" pasta flour, plus more as needed

4 large egg yolks

¼ cup whole milk

2 tablespoons olive oil

Semolina flour for dusting

Ravioli Filling (recipes follow)

1 egg, beaten

Kosher salt

Tomato Sauce (page 35), brown butter, or olive oil for serving

SERVES 4 TO 6

FRESH RAVIOLI

Ravioli is such a romantic food—there's something about discovering the surprise of what's inside that gets me every time. It was the first dish I made as a professional chef that really made me feel accomplished: "Not everyone can do this, and certainly not everyone can do this by hand," I thought as I patted myself on the back. I realize now that making ravioli is a process, to be sure, but it's quite simple. Ravioli is a favorite of my two young daughters.

1. Mound the pasta flour on a work surface and make a deep well in the center. In a small bowl, whisk the egg yolks, milk, and olive oil together until combined and pour it into the well. Using a fork, whisk the eggs around the edges, gradually incorporating the flour. When the mixture becomes too stiff to stir, knead it until it forms a firm dough. Continue kneading until very soft and smooth, 6 to 8 minutes. If the dough is sticky, add more flour 1 tablespoon at a time. Wrap the dough tightly in plastic wrap and let rest at room temperature for 20 minutes.

2. Cut the dough into 8 pieces and dust them lightly with semolina flour. Keeping the remaining dough covered as you work, flatten one piece of dough to about ¼ inch thick and run it through the widest setting on a pasta roller. Fold the dough in half and roll it through again. Repeat 3 times, dusting the pasta sheet with more flour if it gets sticky. Reduce the setting by one notch and roll again. Fold the dough in half and roll again on the same setting. Reduce the setting by one notch and roll the pasta again. Continue rolling the dough, reducing the setting by one notch each time, until you have reached the thinnest setting. Lay the pasta sheet on a work surface dusted with semolina flour and cover with a towel, then roll out the remaining dough.

3. Lay a pasta sheet on a work surface. Place tablespoons of the filling every 3 inches down the center of the sheet of dough. With a pastry brush, lightly brush beaten egg around each filling mound. Gently place another pasta sheet directly on top and press around the mounds of filling to seal. Using a ravioli cutter or sharp knife, cut the dough evenly between the mounds of filling into squares. Dust with semolina flour, transfer to a floured baking sheet, and cover with a towel. Repeat with the remaining dough sheets and filling.

4. Bring a large pot of water to a boil and salt it generously. Cook the ravioli in batches until the pasta is al dente, 6 to 8 minutes. Using a skimmer, transfer to a platter and cover with a clean towel while you cook the remaining ravioli.

5. Toss the ravioli with heated sauce, brown butter, or olive oil, and serve.

CORN + WHITE TRUFFLE FILLING

Corn and truffles are flavorful in the same deeply satisfying way. One is humble and the other is haute, but they belong together on a bright summer dinner plate. You could also use the corn milk for an avant-garde dish of cereal or for corn Popsicles.

4 ears sweet corn, husked

1 cup whole milk

4 ounces mascarpone cheese

½ teaspoon white truffle oil

Kosher salt to taste

¼ teaspoon freshly ground white pepper

Freshly grated nutmeg to taste

1. With a sharp chef's knife, cut the kernels from the corn cobs and transfer to a bowl. (You should have about 3 cups kernels.) With the back of the knife, scrape down each cob to extract as much liquid as possible, and add it to the kernels; set aside. Cut or break one of the cobs into small rounds and put in a saucepan.

2. Pour the milk over the corncob and bring to a simmer over medium heat. Cook for 5 minutes, then cover, turn off the heat, and let stand for 30 minutes.

3. Strain the milk into a clean saucepan. Add the corn kernels and liquid and bring to a simmer over medium-low heat. Cook, stirring frequently, for 15 to 20 minutes, until most of the liquid has evaporated. Transfer the mixture to a food processor and puree until very smooth. Transfer to a bowl and let stand until completely cool.

4. Fold the mascarpone into the corn puree. Add the truffle oil, salt, white pepper, and nutmeg and stir until combined. Taste and add salt and/or nutmeg if necessary. Cover and refrigerate until ready to use. (The filling will keep for up to 5 days.)

BUTTERNUT SQUASH + AMARETTO FILLING

I don't generally use the term "sexy" when it comes to food, but I find it appropriate in describing this combination. The squash's starchy sweetness is enhanced up by amaretto's strong nutty-almond essence. Make it on a cold winter's night for a loved one.

1 small butternut squash (about 1 pound), halved lengthwise and seeded

2 teaspoons olive oil

½ cup amaretto

4 ounces mascarpone or ricotta cheese

Kosher salt and freshly ground black pepper to taste

1. Preheat the oven to 400°F. Rub the cut sides of the squash with the olive oil and place the squash cut side down on a baking sheet. Roast until very soft, about 1 hour. Let stand until cool enough to handle.

2. Meanwhile, put the amaretto in a small saucepan and bring to a simmer over medium heat. Cook until the liquid is reduced to 2 tablespoons, about 10 minutes. Remove from the heat and cool completely.

3. With a large spoon, scoop the squash flesh into a large bowl. Let cool completely.

4. Fold the reduced amaretto and mascarpone into the squash until smooth. Season with salt and pepper and refrigerate until ready to use.

FRESH RICOTTA WITH CHESTNUT HONEY + BASIL FILLING

Ricotta takes on other flavors well, and the natural sweetness of honey and the brightness of basil make this filling perfect for spring. It's all about soft, milky textures. Play off that by garnishing the ravioli with some torn prosciutto or other salty charcuterie meat. Chestnut honey is available in gourmet and Italian groceries and at online food retailers such as Amazon.

1¼ pounds fresh ricotta

1 tablespoon very finely chopped fresh basil

1 tablespoon chestnut honey

½ teaspoon white truffle oil

Kosher salt and freshly ground black pepper to taste

1. Put the ricotta in a fine-mesh strainer set over a bowl and let stand for 30 minutes to drain.

2. Transfer the thickened cheese to a bowl and stir in the basil, honey, and truffle oil. Season with salt and pepper and refrigerate until ready to use.

OXTAIL-MARMALADE FILLING

Think of oxtail marmalade as an incredibly reduced, thick, rich beef
stew. The meat is falling-apart tender, giving the ravioli a hit of homey
intensity. Leftover filling, along with some of the braising liquid, can be
heated and tossed with cooked pasta, or served over creamy polenta or rice.
Or this filling is so good you might forgo the pasta and slather it on some
warm rye toast, with a good grating of horseradish.

3 pounds oxtails

Kosher salt and freshly ground black pepper to taste

All-purpose flour for dusting

2 tablespoons olive oil

1 small yellow onion, finely chopped

1 large carrot, very finely diced

1 stalk celery, very finely diced

2 garlic cloves, minced

2 tablespoons tomato paste

2 tablespoons sugar

2 large sprigs fresh thyme

1 bay leaf

1 cup dry red wine

2 cups store-bought low-sodium beef broth

1. Preheat the oven to 325°F. Season the oxtails generously with salt and pepper. Dust them lightly with flour just until coated. Heat the oil in a large Dutch oven over medium-high heat until rippling. Working in batches if necessary, sear the oxtails on all sides until golden brown; remove from the pot and set aside. Remove all but 1 tablespoon of the fat from the pot.

2. Add the onion, carrot, celery, and garlic to the pot, season with salt and pepper, and cook, stirring, until softened, about 5 minutes. Add the tomato paste and sugar and cook, stirring, until the tomato paste begins to caramelize, 3 to 4 minutes. Add the thyme, bay leaf, and red wine, scraping up any browned bits in the bottom of the pot, bring to a boil, and cook for 2 minutes. Add the beef broth, return the oxtails to the pot, nestling them into the liquid in an even layer, and bring the liquid to a simmer.

3. Cover the pot and transfer to the oven. Cook until the meat is very tender and falling from the bone, 2½ to 3 hours.

4. Remove the oxtails with a slotted spoon and set aside to cool. Strain the braising liquid; discard the bay leaf and thyme sprigs. (The braising liquid can be cooled to room temperature and refrigerated for another use.) Transfer the strained vegetables to a bowl.

5. Once the oxtails are cool enough to handle, using a fork or your fingers, pull the meat from the bones and finely shred it. Add to the reserved vegetables. Mix the meat and vegetables well, season lightly with salt and pepper, and moisten with 1 or 2 tablespoons of the braising liquid if the mixture seems dry. Refrigerate the filling until ready to use.

Lemon-Curd-and-Black-Pepper-Roasted Chicken (Waste Not, Want Not) 180 | Tandoori Fried Chicken 183 | Chicken Salad with Vadouvan Spice (Sous Vide Chicken; Homemade Vadouvan Spice Mix) 185 | Chicken Confit with Green Olives and Kumquats (Sous Vide Confit and Leftover Fats) 186 | Chicken Cutlets with Boiled Peanuts, Currants, and Brown Butter 188 | Arroz con Pollo (Sazón Packets) 191 | Quail Potpie 192 | Leftover-Chicken Terrine 195 | Fried-Chicken Fried Rice with Pork Belly and Toasted Garlic 196

BIRDS
IN HAND

Chicken is on nearly every restaurant menu and it's a go-to dinner for many families when they cook at home. Because it is so ubiquitous, it can sometimes be overlooked or considered boring. Also, I think part of the bad rap it gets is due to how easy it is to overcook it. I want home cooks to see chicken as I do: as a blank canvas ripe with potential for creativity.

I always offer chicken on my restaurant menus: perfect fried chicken (mine's a genre-bender of Southern technique combined with Indian spice), savory fried rice studded with sesame chicken, and chicken cutlets with boiled peanuts are just a few of my favorite recipes that I share in this chapter. Even at HD1, my restaurant devoted to gourmet hot dogs, we came up with a great preparation for chicken wings that we serve there; instead of the standard Buffalo-style variety, we coat wings with prepared lemon curd and lots of black and white pepper. I've turned that idea into a gorgeous, easy recipe for a whole roasted chicken—the ultimate comfort food, not to mention a cinch to throw in the oven when there's not a lot of time.

I also realize there are some tried-and-true favorites that don't necessarily need to be changed. My chicken salad is a straightforward preparation that gets a hit from vadouvan, a curry-based spice mix that's easy to make but can also be found in specialty markets. There is also an arroz con pollo, which was inspired by my wife's heritage, which is as close to traditional as my cooking gets.

Finally, there's nothing better than making a meal that you know will yield great leftovers. That's an opportunity to turn the original dish into something different and perhaps even more delicious the second time around—try my luxurious chicken terrine, made entirely from leftover roasted chicken, to see what I mean). I hope this chapter inspires and gives you a new appreciation for everyday birds.

PORK BELLY
FRENCH LENTILS
MICROWAVE APPLE P

CHICKEN THIGH
WHIPPED MAPLE
SOFT POLENTA

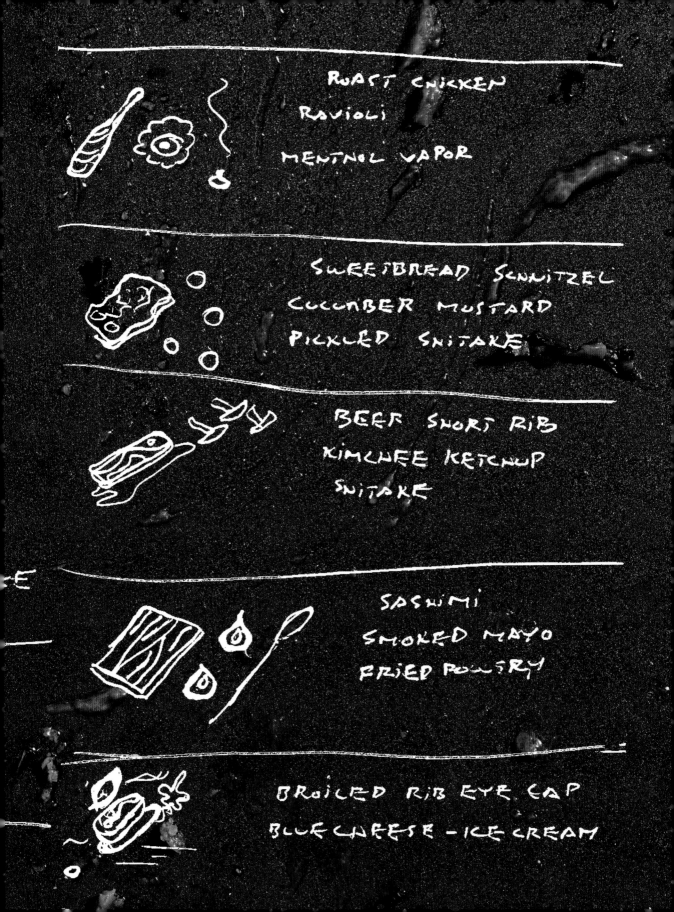

ROAST CHICKEN
RAVIOLI
MENTHOL VAPOR

SWEETBREAD SCHNITZEL
CUCUMBER MUSTARD
PICKLED SHITAKE

BEEF SHORT RIB
KIMCHEE KETCHUP
SHITAKE

SASHIMI
SMOKED MAYO
FRIED POULTRY

BROILED RIB EYE CAP
BLUE CHEESE - ICE CREAM

FOR THE BRINE

1 tablespoon black peppercorns

2 teaspoons Szechuan peppercorns (optional)

2 teaspoons coriander seeds

8 cups water

Scant 1 cup Kosher salt

1 fresh red Thai chile, sliced, or 1 teaspoon red pepper flakes

One 4- to 5-pound free-range chicken

For the Lemon Curd

4 large egg yolks

1/3 cup sugar

Grated zest and juice of 2 lemons

2 tablespoons unsalted butter, diced

1 tablespoon black peppercorns

1 teaspoon coriander seeds

1 teaspoon finely chopped fresh rosemary or 1/2 teaspoon dried

1 teaspoon finely chopped fresh sage or 1/2 teaspoon dried

1 tablespoon water

SERVES 4

LEMON-CURD-+-BLACK-PEPPER-ROASTED CHICKEN

Don't be afraid to take a good working formula and make it modern. The combination of zesty lemon and black pepper is classic, and an excellent way to perk up the mildness of chicken. Brining the chicken—submerging it in a salty solution—makes the meat moist and tender. I never miss an opportunity to get some extra flavor in there too: I make a spicy brine with peppercorns and chiles that adds subtle heat to the chicken before it's even cooked (the brine can be saved in the fridge for up to a week and used for other poultry as many times as you like). If you don't want to make lemon curd, use 1/2 cup store-bought curd mixed with 2 tablespoons water.

1. TO BRINE THE CHICKEN: Put the black peppercorns, Szechuan peppercorns, if using, and coriander seeds into a saucepan and toast over medium-low heat, swirling the pan, until fragrant, 2 to 3 minutes. Add 2 cups of the water and the salt, raise the heat to medium-high, and stir until the salt is completely dissolved. Remove from the heat and add the remaining 6 cups water and the chile. Let cool to room temperature.

2. Rinse the chicken well under cold water. Transfer to a tall narrow plastic container just large enough to hold it. Pour the brine over the chicken and adjust the bird if necessary so it is completely immersed. Refrigerate for at least 2 to 3 hours, or preferably overnight.

3. TO MAKE THE LEMON CURD: Meanwhile, in a medium saucepan, whisk the egg yolks, sugar, and lemon zest and juice until combined. Put the pan over low heat and stir constantly with a wooden spoon until the mixture is very thick and hot, but just below a simmer, about 15 minutes. Remove from the heat and whisk in the butter a little at a time until smooth. Using a rubber spatula, press the mixture through a fine-mesh strainer set over a small bowl to remove the zest. Cover and let stand until cool or refrigerate if not using right away.

[RECIPE CONTINUES]

4. Position a rack in a roasting pan. Remove the chicken from the brine and rinse well under cold running water. Pat the chicken completely dry with paper towels and set it on the rack in the pan. Let the chicken come to room temperature, 20 to 30 minutes.

5. Preheat the oven to 450°F. Coarsely crush the black peppercorns and coriander seeds with a mortar and pestle or on a cutting board with the bottom of a small pan. Transfer to a small bowl and stir in the rosemary and sage. Add three-quarters of the spice mixture to the lemon curd, along with the water, and stir to combine.

6. Pat the chicken again with paper towels to make sure it is completely dry. Gently loosen the skin by sliding your fingers between the breast and skin and working them down to the thighs and drumsticks. Spoon half the lemon curd under the breast skin and use your hands to spread the curd evenly under the loosened skin all the way to the legs. With kitchen twine, tie the legs together tightly. Brush the remaining curd evenly over the surface of the chicken, coating the whole bird. Sprinkle the remaining spice mix evenly over the chicken. Return to the rack in the pan and pour 1 cup of water into the pan.

7. Roast the chicken for 30 minutes. Reduce the heat to 325°F and continue roasting until the chicken is golden brown and the juices run clear when the thigh is pierced, 1½ to 1¾ hours. Add water ½ cup at a time to the pan if it starts to dry out. Let the chicken stand for 10 to 15 minutes before carving.

1.5 WASTE NOT, WANT NOT

The best leftovers from roasting a chicken are often overlooked. Everyone knows about using the meat for things like chicken salad, but you can also salvage all of the flavors from the cooking process. It's simple: when your chicken is done, pour the liquid from the roasting pan into a container and chill in the refrigerator overnight. The mixture will separate into fat and liquid, both of which could make one of your next meals memorable. Use the solid fat the next day to cook a piece of fish in, and use the juices in a vinaigrette or for a quick sauce or to simmer vegetables. The carcass of the bird can also be picked clean to make a quick pressed terrine (page 195) and the bones can be made into a dynamite pressure-cooker stock. A simple roast chicken and all its elements represent what honest, respectful cooking is all about: maximizing flavor, wasting nothing.

8 cups water

Scant 1 cup kosher salt, plus more as needed

2 tablespoons packed light brown sugar

6 tablespoons store-bought tandoori spice blend

One 5- to 6-pound free-range chicken

2 cups plain whole-milk Greek yogurt

¼ cup raspberry or cider vinegar

Peanut or vegetable oil for deep-frying

2 cups all-purpose flour

1 teaspoon freshly ground white pepper

Freshly ground black pepper to taste

2 tablespoons chopped fresh cilantro (optional)

2 tablespoons chopped fresh flat-leaf parsley (optional)

2 limes, cut into wedges

Bottled Pepper Vinegar (page 41) for serving (optional)

SERVES 6 TO 8

TANDOORI FRIED CHICKEN

Why mess with something as traditional as Southern fried chicken? Because this recipe makes a great dish even better. It's not too far a stretch, either. Southern fried chicken is often marinated in buttermilk, and tandoori chicken is marinated in yogurt, so there's a natural similarity between the two. Sometimes that's all I'm looking for when trying to reinvent a dish: finding that one ingredient that bridges the gap, and then my mind races off to create a new remix. I serve this with pepper vinegar. Want to make your own? Steep some hot peppers in a jar of good old white vinegar.

1. Heat 2 cups of the water in a small saucepan over medium-high heat. Add the salt, sugar, and 2 tablespoons of the tandoori spices and stir until completely dissolved. Remove from the heat and pour into a large bowl or nonreactive container. Add the remaining 6 cups water and let cool to room temperature.

2. Cut the chicken into 8 pieces, then cut the breasts crosswise through the bone into 3 equal pieces each. Add the chicken pieces to the brine and refrigerate for 1 hour to 2 hours.

3. Drain the chicken. (The brine can be stored in the refrigerator and reused for other poultry for up to 1 week.) In a large bowl, whisk the yogurt, vinegar, and 2 tablespoons of the tandoori spices until combined. Add the chicken pieces, tossing well to coat and making sure they are completely covered. Refrigerate for at least 3 hours, or, preferably, overnight.

4. When ready to fry the chicken, remove it from the refrigerator and let stand for at least 30 minutes to come to room temperature. Fill a large pot with 3 inches of oil and attach a deep-fry thermometer to the side of the pot. Heat the oil over medium-high heat to 325°F.

5. In a large bowl, mix the flour, white pepper, black pepper, and the remaining 2 tablespoons tandoori spices until combined. Remove the chicken from the bowl, shake or brush the excess yogurt back into the bowl, and dredge the chicken in the flour, shaking off the excess. Dip the floured pieces in the yogurt again, coating completely, then shake off the excess, return the pieces to the flour, and dredge well; shake off the excess. Working in two batches if necessary, fry the chicken, turning often and adjusting the heat to maintain the oil temperature at 325° to 350°F, until golden brown and cooked through; the white meat will take 10 to 12 minutes, the dark meat 13 to 15 minutes. The juices should run clear when the thickest part of the meat is pierced with a knife, and an instant-read thermometer inserted should read between 160° and 165°F. If cooking the chicken in batches, keep the first batch warm in a 200°F oven on a rack set over a baking sheet. Sprinkle the chicken with salt while still hot.

6. To serve, sprinkle the cilantro and parsley, if using, over the chicken, and pass the lime wedges for squeezing over the chicken at the table. Serve with the pepper vinegar on the side, if desired.

2.0 SOUS VIDE CHICKEN

A chicken breast should be the first thing a novice cooks sous vide. It will convert you, because it produces a chicken breast that is opaque all the way through without any of the striations—and, even better, without the ligneous texture of an overcooked chicken breast. What you get is a perfectly cooked, superjuicy piece of meat. It makes the most amazing chicken salad.

To prepare chicken breasts sous vide, preheat the sous vide machine to 144°F. Put chicken breasts in a sous vide bag, along with ½ teaspoon vegetable oil, a sprinkle of kosher salt, and a pinch of freshly ground white pepper. Massage the breasts to distribute the seasonings and oil. Vacuum-seal the bag and immerse in the water bath for 45 minutes to 1 hour. Remove the bag and cool to room temperature before proceeding as directed with this or any other recipe.

4 boneless, skinless chicken breast halves (7 to 8 ounces each)

2 cups Pressure-Cooker Chicken Stock (page 44) or store-bought low-sodium broth

½ cup Aioli (page 24) or good-quality store-bought mayonnaise

1 tablespoon ground vadouvan spice mix (below)

Kosher salt and freshly ground black pepper to taste

½ cup fresh cilantro leaves

Pickled Celery (page 54; optional)

1 lime, cut into wedges, for garnish

MAKES ABOUT 4 CUPS

CHICKEN SALAD WITH VADOUVAN SPICE

The important thing about chicken salad is to keep it moist; cooked chicken can become dry quite easily, so you need a really good mayonnaise to hold it together. I love making my own (see page 24), but I don't always have time, and when that happens I'm a Duke's guy. Duke's is a pleasantly acidic Southern brand, originally out of Greenville, South Carolina, and now available throughout the Southeast (and at DukesMayo.com). Whatever kind of mayonnaise you use, mix in some vadouvan spice, a traditional South Indian curry-flavored mix.

1. Put the chicken breasts and stock in a saucepan and heat over medium-low heat until the liquid just begins to simmer, then cook until the chicken is just cooked through, 3 to 4 minutes. (Remove one of the breasts and cut into the thickest part to check the doneness; it should be just opaque, with no pink remaining.) Remove the chicken from the stock (reserve for another use), cover, and let cool to room temperature.

2. Chop or tear the chicken into small bite-sized pieces and transfer to a medium bowl. Add the aioli, vadouvan spices, and salt and pepper and fold gently until well combined. Add the cilantro leaves and stir to combine.

3. Serve the chicken salad with the pickled celery mixed in, if you like, or on the side, and a wedge of fresh lime.

2.0 HOMEMADE VADOUVAN SPICE MIX

Vadouvan spice mix originated in South India in the French settlement called Pondicherry (which is why you can sometimes find it referred to as "French curry" or "French masala"), and there are many variations now used in cuisines around the world. It is usually made from roasted onions, garlic, curry leaves, cardamom, cumin, fennel, fenugreek, cayenne, and other spices. Dried vadouvan spice blends are available online or in specialty or Indian markets.

To make your own to use in this recipe, stir 2 teaspoons mild curry powder, ½ teaspoon garlic powder, and ½ teaspoon ground fennel together until combined.

FOR THE DRY CURE

1 cup kosher salt

2 whole star anise, finely crushed with the side of a knife

1 teaspoon freshly ground black pepper

1 teaspoon fresh thyme leaves or ½ teaspoon dried

1 teaspoon finely grated orange zest or dried orange peel

½ teaspoon dried lavender flowers (optional)

8 large bone-in, skin-on chicken thighs (about 2 pounds), patted dry

FOR THE CONFIT

2 cups vegetable or canola oil, or as needed

4 sprigs fresh thyme or ½ teaspoon dried thyme

2 whole star anise

1 teaspoon black peppercorns

1 teaspoon dried lavender flowers (optional)

½ cup all-purpose flour

Freshly ground black pepper to taste

FOR THE SAUCE

1½ teaspoons yellow mustard seeds

¼ cup sugar

¼ cup water

18 kumquats, thinly sliced and seeded, or 1 small tangerine, peeled and finely chopped, any seeds removed

½ cup coarsely chopped pitted green olives, such as Picholine or Cerignola

Kosher salt and freshly ground black pepper to taste

SERVES 4

CHICKEN CONFIT WITH GREEN OLIVES + KUMQUATS

To "confit" something means to preserve it in its own fat, which is a technique that rural French people used for hundreds of years to keep their families fed through the winter. The seasonings in the cure are aggressive, with salt, pepper, star anise, thyme, and orange zest, ensuring a super-tender, moist, succulent, and incredibly satisfying result.

1. TO CURE THE CHICKEN: In a small bowl, stir the salt, star anise, pepper, thyme, orange zest, and lavender, if using, together until combined. Sprinkle one-third of the mixture into the bottom of a baking dish just large enough to hold the thighs in a single layer. Lay the thighs close together on the spice mixture and sprinkle the remaining spice mixture over them. Using your hands, pack the spices onto the thighs so the meat is completely covered. Lay a smaller pan or a plate that fits inside the pan over the chicken and weight it with heavy cans or a pot. Refrigerate for 2 hours.

2. TO MAKE THE CONFIT: Preheat the oven to 300°F. Rinse the chicken thighs thoroughly under cold water and pat them dry with paper towels. Transfer them skin side up to a straight-sided ovenproof skillet or small roasting pan just large enough to hold them in a single layer. Pour enough oil into the skillet to just cover the thighs. Add the thyme, star anise, peppercorns, and lavender, if using.

3. Place the pan over low heat and warm the oil until hot to the touch, then transfer the pan to the oven. Cook until the meat is very tender (a knife should meet no resistance when the center of a thigh is pierced). With a slotted spoon, remove the thighs, draining off the excess oil, and transfer them to a baking sheet, skin side up.

1.5 SOUS VIDE CONFIT + LEFTOVER FATS

People think that cooking sous vide is only about precision, but its convenience and cost efficiency lend it beautifully to making confit. Using 1 tablespoon of fat instead of submerging a duck or chicken leg in a few quarts of fat makes economic sense, and the method reduces the cooking time by half. The oil used to make the confit can also be reused; the flavor accumulates and intensifies as more meat fats are introduced to it every time you use it. Simply let the oil cool completely, then strain it through a fine-mesh strainer and store it in an airtight container in the refrigerator for up to 1 month, using it as often as you like.

4. Put the flour into a shallow dish and season generously with pepper. Pour 2 tablespoons of the confit oil into a medium skillet and heat over medium heat. Using tongs, dip the skin side of each chicken thigh into the flour, shake off the excess, and transfer to the skillet, skin side down. Cook until the skin is crisp and golden brown, 5 to 6 minutes. Remove the thighs from the skillet and cover to keep warm until ready to serve.

5. TO MAKE THE SAUCE: Meanwhile, put the mustard seeds in a small saucepan and toast them over medium-low heat, swirling the pan, until fragrant, 2 to 3 minutes. Add the sugar and water and bring to a simmer. Add the kumquats, stir, and cook until the mixture is bubbling and the kumquats are beginning to break down, about 5 minutes. Stir in the olives and season with salt and pepper.

6. To serve, divide the thighs among four serving plates and a spoon of the sauce over the top.

4 boneless, skinless chicken breast halves (about 8 ounces each)

Kosher salt and freshly ground black pepper to taste

2 large eggs

1 teaspoon Dijon mustard

Hot sauce, such as Crystal, to taste

1 cup all-purpose flour

1 tablespoon chopped fresh flat-leaf parsley or 1½ teaspoons dried

2 teaspoons chopped fresh sage or 1 teaspoon dried

1 teaspoon chopped fresh rosemary or ½ teaspoon dried

¼ cup olive oil, or as needed

3 tablespoons sherry vinegar

¼ cup dried currants

1 small white onion, finely diced

2 garlic cloves, chopped

½ cup shelled Pressure-Cooker Boiled Peanuts (page 89) or store-bought roasted or boiled peanuts

2 tablespoons drained capers

Juice of ½ lemon

2 tablespoons unsalted butter, diced

Fresh flat-leaf parsley leaves for garnish (optional)

Fresh dill for garnish (optional)

SERVES 4

CHICKEN CUTLETS WITH BOILED PEANUTS, CURRANTS + BROWN BUTTER

I have blue-collar roots; I consider myself a grinder at heart. So is a cutlet. A fillet is upscale; a cutlet is what everyone eats for dinner. This is one of my all-time favorite preparations for it. It's basically Southern-style schnitzel, garnished with a little salsa of currants, capers, boiled peanuts, and some chicken pan juice.

1. Preheat the oven to 250°F. Set a cooling rack on a baking sheet and set aside.

2. With a very sharp long knife, cut each chicken breast half into 3 flat, thin pieces by holding the knife horizontally and slicing the breast lengthwise on a very sharp bias. Season the chicken lightly with salt and pepper.

3. In a pie plate, whisk the eggs, Dijon, and hot sauce together until combined. In another pie plate or a shallow dish, mix the flour, parsley, sage, and rosemary until combined. Season generously with salt and pepper. Dredge all of the chicken pieces in the seasoned flour,

shaking off the excess. Working with a few pieces at time, dip the floured chicken pieces into the egg wash, let excess drip off, and then dredge again in the flour, shaking off the excess. Then put on a plate.

4. Heat the olive oil in a large nonstick skillet over medium-high heat until rippling. Add half of the breaded chicken and cook until golden, turning once, 3 to 4 minutes per side. Transfer to the rack-lined baking sheet and keep warm in the oven. Add more oil to the pan if necessary and repeat with the remaining chicken.

5. Meanwhile, pour the sherry vinegar over the currants in a small bowl.

6. Drain all but 1 tablespoon of the oil from the skillet. Add the onion and garlic to the pan and cook over medium heat until softened, 4 to 5 minutes. Add the currant mixture and cook, scraping the pan to remove any browned bits on the bottom. Add the boiled peanuts and cook, stirring, until hot. Remove the pan from the heat and stir in the capers and lemon juice. Add the butter and toss until well combined; taste and adjust the seasoning with salt and pepper.

7. To serve, put 3 chicken cutlets on each of four plates and spoon the peanut-caper salsa over the top. Garnish with parsley leaves and/or dill, if using, and serve immediately.

8 bone-in, skin-on chicken thighs (about 2 pounds), rinsed and patted dry

Kosher salt and freshly ground black pepper to taste

3 tablespoons olive oil

1 yellow onion, finely chopped

1 green bell pepper, cored, seeded, and chopped

3 jarred piquillo peppers, sealed and chopped, or 1 red bell pepper, cored, seeded, and chopped

3 garlic cloves, chopped

2 Roma (plum) tomatoes, halved, seeded, and chopped

½ teaspoon ground Espelette pepper, cayenne pepper, or hot paprika

2 bay leaves

2 tablespoons tomato paste

1 cup basmati rice

1 small packet (1¼ teaspoons) Sazón seasoning

½ teaspoon saffron threads

3 cups Pressure-Cooker Chicken Stock (page 44) or store-bought low-sodium broth

Hot sauce, such as Crystal, to taste

2 tablespoons chopped fresh cilantro

2 tablespoons chopped fresh flat-leaf parsley

1 cup plain whole-milk yogurt for serving

Lime zest (optional)

SERVES 4

ARROZ CON POLLO

My wife, Jazmin, is of Honduran descent. When you walk into her mother's house, everything is Latin-inspired, especially the cooking. This dish is a Latin staple, and because Jazmin likes it so much, arroz con pollo has become a staple for us. You can throw in half a bag of frozen peas toward the end to up the nutritional content. We serve it with a bottle of hot sauce on the table and a bowl of yogurt.

1. Season the chicken on both sides with salt and pepper. In a large straight-sided skillet, heat the oil over medium-high heat until rippling. Sear the chicken thighs, turning once, until golden brown, 8 to 10 minutes per side. Transfer to a plate and set aside.

2. Drain half the oil from the pan and return the pan to the heat. Add the onion, bell pepper, piquillos, garlic, tomatoes, Espelette, and bay leaves and cook, stirring, until the onion begins to brown, 6 to 8 minutes. Stir in the tomato paste and cook, stirring, until it begins to caramelize, 3 to 4 minutes.

3. Add the rice, Sazón, and saffron and cook, stirring, for 2 to 3 minutes. Pour in the chicken stock, season with salt, pepper, and hot sauce, stir, and bring to a boil. Reduce the heat to maintain a simmer and nestle the chicken thighs skin side up in the rice. (Try not to submerge the skin, so it stays crisp as the rice cooks.) Cook, partially covered, until the rice has absorbed the liquid and the chicken is cooked through, 25 to 30 minutes. If the chicken skin is not crisp, place the pan under a hot broiler until the chicken is crispy and golden brown on top.

4. To serve, remove the bay leaves, sprinkle the cilantro and parsley over the rice, and gently stir to incorporate. Serve directly from the pan, with the yogurt sprinkled with lime zest and the bottle of hot sauce on the side.

1.5 SAZÓN PACKETS

I embrace certain store-bought "prepared foods," such as Sazón. It's all about umami, or monosodium glutamate (MSG). Sazón mixes are packets of dried seasoned salt sold in supermarkets (Goya is the most familiar brand) and are used in Latin American cooking. The general ingredients are equal parts ground coriander, cumin, paprika, garlic powder, and salt—a great flavor punch. You can make it at home, but I typically use the prepared version.

4 cups Pressure-Cooker Chicken Stock (page 44) or store-bought low-sodium broth

1 teaspoon black peppercorns

1 bay leaf

4 fresh quail (about 1½ pounds each)

8 ounces baby red potatoes, scrubbed and quartered

1 bunch (6 to 8) baby carrots, halved lengthwise, or 2 large carrots, sliced

2 turnips (about 12 ounces), trimmed, peeled, cut lengthwise into 8 wedges each, and then halved crosswise

6 tablespoons (¾ stick) unsalted butter

½ cup all-purpose flour, plus more for rolling

½ teaspoon freshly ground white pepper

Kosher salt and freshly ground black pepper to taste

1 cup fresh or frozen peas

¼ cup chopped fresh flat-leaf parsley or 2 teaspoons dried

1 tablespoon fresh thyme leaves or 1½ teaspoons dried'

1 large egg, beaten, for egg wash

One 8-ounce sheet frozen puff pastry (9½ × 9½ inches), thawed according to the package instructions

SERVES 8 TO 10

QUAIL POTPIE

There is nothing homier than a chicken potpie. But if you want to put a different spin on it, make it with quail. The meat of these small plump birds has a sweet, gamy-nutty flavor that's stronger than that of chicken and really elevates this dish from its humble origins. If you can't get quail, you can substitute 2 large bone-in, skin-on chicken breasts (about 1½ pounds total) and 6 boneless, skinless chicken thighs (about 1 pound total) for them.

1. Put the chicken stock, peppercorns, and bay leaf in a large saucepan and place over medium-low heat. Rinse the quail and add them to the pan. Heat until the liquid begins to gently simmer, then cover the pan, reduce the heat to low, and cook for 15 to 20 minutes, until the quail are completely cooked through, with no traces of pink in the meat. With a slotted spoon, remove the quail and set aside to cool.

2. Pour the stock through a fine-mesh strainer, discard the spices, and return the broth to the saucepan. When the quail are cool enough to handle, remove the skin and discard. Pull the meat from the bones, dice, and reserve.

3. Preheat the oven to 400°F. Put a 3-quart rectangular baking dish on a baking sheet and set aside.

4. Return the broth to a gentle simmer over medium heat. Add the potatoes and cook until they begin to soften,

3 to 4 minutes. Add the carrots and turnips, return the liquid to a simmer, cover, and cook for 5 minutes. With the slotted spoon, transfer the vegetables to a medium bowl. Keep the broth warm over low heat.

5. In another large saucepan or a deep skillet, melt the butter over medium heat. Sprinkle in the flour and whisk well until smooth, then continue whisking until the mixture is bubbling, 1 to 2 minutes. Whisking constantly, gradually add the warm stock a little at a time, whisking until completely incorporated. Cook, whisking occasionally, until the sauce is bubbling and very thick, 2 to 3 minutes. Remove from the heat.

6. Stir the white pepper into the sauce, taste, and adjust the seasoning with salt and black pepper. Gently stir in the diced quail, potatoes, carrots, turnips, peas, parsley, and thyme until well combined. Transfer the mixture to the baking dish.

7. Lightly dust a work surface and a rolling pin with flour and roll the puff pastry sheet to a rectangle, about 1 inch larger than the baking dish. Brush the edges of the dish with the egg wash. Lay the pastry sheet over the dish and press it against the edges so it adheres. Trim the excess pastry, if desired. Brush the top of the pastry well with egg wash and cut 3 or 4 slashes in it with a sharp knife to allow steam to escape.

8. Bake until the pastry is golden brown and the filling is bubbling, about 40 minutes. Let stand for 15 to 20 minutes before serving family-style.

Carcass of a
    roasted chicken
    (home-roasted or
    store-bought),
    with its juices
    and drippings
    (see page 182)

FOR SERVING

Thin slices
    baguette or
    crackers

Whole-grain mustard
Smoked Aioli
    (page 25)

Cornichons

LEFTOVER-CHICKEN TERRINE

Calling this "pressed leftovers" would be underselling its appeal, but that's exactly what it is. This terrine is a perfect example of what to do with the leftover bits and pieces and juices of a roasted chicken. Whether you roasted the bird at home or bought a rotisserie chicken at the grocery store, what's important in making this terrine is being scrupulous about getting every scrap of meat from the carcass. Take the extra time and care to strip the bones completely, and you will reap the rewards of your efforts in a luxuriously flavored, rich, soft, and savory terrine.

1. Remove every piece of meat, skin, and fat you can from the chicken bones, using a paring knife if necessary. Discard any cartilage or tendons. Tear the meat into small pieces and transfer to a small, straight-sided, widemouthed jar or a small clean can.

2. Pour the melted roasting juices and drippings over the meat. This next step is crucial for binding the terrine together. Wrap the bottom of a small, unopened, heavy can that just fits inside the jar in plastic wrap or parchment paper and very firmly press down on the mixture to compress it. Leave the can inside the jar and transfer it to the refrigerator. Weight the smaller can with another heavy object or plate. The more weight you put on top, the more firmly the terrine will set. Chill for at least 2 to 3 hours, or, preferably, overnight.

3. To unmold, remove the smaller can and weight, invert the jar onto a small plate, and tap the bottom until the terrine releases itself. Serve with baguette slices, mustard, aioli, and cornichons on the side.

3 tablespoons
toasted sesame
oil

¼ cup diced pork
belly or pancetta

3 garlic cloves,
minced

2 tablespoons
grated fresh
ginger

6 scallions, sliced

2 tablespoons soy
sauce

1 large egg, beaten

2 cups cooked brown
rice

1½ to 2 cups
chopped or pulled
leftover fried
chicken (including
the skin and
crunchy coating)

3 tablespoons
chopped fresh
cilantro

Hot sauce, such as
Sriracha or
Crystal, to taste

SERVES 4

FRIED-CHICKEN FRIED RICE WITH PORK BELLY + TOASTED GARLIC

This is a leftovers classic if ever there was one, a great catchall for the extra box of steamed rice from Chinese takeout and the few remaining pieces of crunchy fried chicken left from a picnic. What brings them together is the depth of the sauce, with the brightness and subtle heat of ginger, the freshness of cilantro, and the intensity of garlic and soy sauce combined with the sesame oil.

1. Heat 2 tablespoons of the oil in a wok or large nonstick skillet over medium heat. Add the pork belly and cook, stirring frequently, until crisp, 6 to 8 minutes. Add the garlic, half of the ginger, and half of the scallions and cook, stirring constantly, until softened, 2 to 3 minutes.

2. Whisk 1 tablespoon of the soy sauce into the egg. Stirring vigorously, add the egg to the skillet and cook, stirring, until the egg begins to set, about 30 seconds. Add the rice and chicken and toss or stir until very hot, 3 to 4 minutes. Remove the pan from the heat, add the remaining ginger, scallions, and 1 tablespoon soy sauce and toss well to combine. Stir in the cilantro.

3. To serve, drizzle the remaining tablespoon of sesame oil over the top of the rice, along with a few dashes of hot sauce.

FINS, SHELLS + SCALES

ELI
KIRHSTEIN,
GENIUS,
ANTAGONIST
+ FRIEND

My new dream restaurant is an upscale fish-and-chips shop. I have a special relationship with fish and seafood: Everything in this category is pretty much a favorite of mine. If I had to make a choice, I would trade all of the other proteins for seafood.

Sure, this affinity began in my Filet-O-Fish days, but it runs deeper than that. After I'd kicked around in restaurant kitchens and then graduated from the Culinary Institute of America, I was offered a fellowship there and put to work in the fish kitchen. While the average student would cut two whole salmon a day, I cut three hundred, including all the fish for the CIA restaurants. I could also order any kind of fish that I wanted to teach the students about. I took full advantage of that: I had monkfish with intact livers, whole eels, all manner of exotica that swam and interested me. I learned how to tell by smell when a fish was amazingly fresh or just a day or two old, as well as the best methods of preparing flatfish, streaky fish, and chunky-textured fish. The knowledge I gathered from working with fish in such an intense, day-in, day-out way stayed with me: On *Top Chef All-Stars* we had a challenge led by the world-famous chef and fish specialist Eric Ripert of Manhattan's Le Bernardin. We were charged with cutting a whole cod and a whole flounder in nine minutes. I knew right away that 90 percent of my competitors probably couldn't do it, but I could, and I did! There's a certain amount of bravado in working with fish in a restaurant kitchen. And because of its precious nature, only the truly skilled get to touch it.

At home, I cook a lot of fish, but I'm not raiding a restaurant kitchen for prime halibut fillets to bring home; I tend to buy my fish at Whole Foods, as many of you probably do. Recently I read a study that said that although Americans know fish is good for them and that they should eat more of it, they are still reluctant to cook it. I get that: Even with all my experience cooking fish, I still screw it up sometimes. What I can do is teach you ways that will make cooking fish much easier—with reliably tasty results. All you really need is some good fish, a hot pan, butter, a few paper towels, and some solid techniques that I'm excited to share. I also like to keep current on the sustainability of heavily fished species. Check out the Monterey Bay Aquarium Seafood Watch's website to see which fish are at a critical population; try to eat only those listed as best choices.

MALTED
BARLEY
PANNA COTTA

— CRANBERRY

SALMON WITH AVOCADO
DILL — CANDIED HORSERADISH

FOR THE HORSERADISH CREAM

½ cup crème fraîche

2 tablespoons prepared horseradish

FOR THE VINEGAR SAUCE

1 small shallot, finely minced

¼ cup seasoned rice vinegar

1 teaspoon ground turmeric

1 teaspoon Sriracha hot sauce

1 tablespoon finely minced fresh cilantro stems

1 tablespoon finely minced fresh dill stems

¼ teaspoon freshly ground black pepper

12 small fresh coldwater oysters, such as Hog Island (Pacific Northwest) or Beau Soleil (North Atlantic), scrubbed

SERVES 4

BEAUTIFUL RAW OYSTERS WITH HORSERADISH CREAM + VINEGAR SAUCE

This dish is the equivalent of a beautiful model dressed down in a T-shirt and jeans. It's about letting simple beauty shine, and consists of nothing more than fresh, cold raw oysters with a bracing, piquant cream accompanied by a vinegar sauce I brighten with shallots, fresh herbs, and a dash of hot sauce: refreshing.

1. TO MAKE THE HORSERADISH CREAM: In a small bowl, stir the crème fraîche and horseradish together until combined. Pour into a small fine-mesh strainer set over a bowl to drain and refrigerate until ready to serve.

2. TO MAKE THE VINEGAR SAUCE: Put the shallot in a small bowl and pour the vinegar over it. Let stand for at least 15 and up to 30 minutes. Meanwhile, toast the turmeric in a small skillet over medium-low heat, shaking the pan, until fragrant, 2 to 3 minutes. Add the shallot mixture, along with the Sriracha and cilantro and dill stems, then add the pepper and stir well to combine. Refrigerate until chilled, or for up to 3 days.

3. When ready to serve the oysters, transfer the horseradish cream to a small bowl. Cover a large platter with crushed ice. Using an oyster knife, carefully open the oysters, then remove and discard the top shells. Use the knife to cut the muscle attaching each oyster to the bottom shell, taking care not to spill any liquid in the shell, and place them on the bed of ice. Serve immediately, with the horseradish cream and vinegar sauce on the side.

2.0 OYSTERS WITH HORSERADISH PEARLS

I refer to this presentation of raw oysters as "oysters and pearls" in homage to one of my mentors, Thomas Keller, who makes a very different dish with the same name. When you get a canister of liquid nitrogen for the first time, it's like getting a new toy (though of course you must be careful with it). And the first time my cooks and I played with it, we dropped all sorts of things into it to see what would happen. One of my tests was to drop a little bit of the horseradish cream into the canister. Like Dippin' Dots ice cream sold in ballparks across America, the horseradish cream froze into perfect spheres that looked almost like caviar. I get a lot of questions about how to make faux caviar or faux pearls from liquid nitrogen, and I'm happy to say it's a very simple process.

Put ½ cup crème fraîche and 2 tablespoons prepared horseradish into a blender and mix on high for 1 to 2 minutes until very smooth. With a rubber spatula, press the mixture through a fine-mesh strainer set over a small bowl, then transfer the mixture to a squeeze bottle. Gently squeeze the bottle over a small amount of liquid nitrogen in a metal dish, letting the droplets fall directly into it. Use a metal spoon to scoop the frozen balls out of it and immediately transfer them to a container and plate in the freezer until ready to use. Serve the oysters on the half shell with a drizzle of the vinegar sauce and a small spoonful of horseradish pearls on top of each one.

2 tablespoons olive oil

1 small yellow onion, minced

2 garlic cloves, minced

1 fresh red Thai chile or ½ small jalapeño, sliced

2 pounds small clams, such as cockles or littlenecks, scrubbed

¾ cup ginger beer

FOR THE TEXAS TOAST

4 slices Texas toast or four 1-inch-thick slices sourdough bread

2 tablespoons Snail Butter (page 46) or unsalted butter, softened

2 tablespoons unsalted butter

4 scallions, green parts only, sliced

½ cup chopped fresh flat-leaf parsley

SERVES 4

CLAMS STEAMED IN GINGER BEER WITH TEXAS TOAST

Sometimes the key to cooking with spontaneity is to open your mind and your pantry. The idea for this dish came about when I had one of my favorite ingredients, fresh clams, and no real plan for how to cook them. I realized that almost everyone has a can of soda in the pantry or fridge—and what is soda, after all, but a carbonated fortified sauce? Steaming clams in lager is nothing new, but if you do it in ginger ale or ginger beer (any citrus-flavored soda works too), you add a little sweetness and body to the cooking broth. In fact, it creates such a flavorful broth that you'll want some Texas Toast on the side to sop it up.

1. Heat the oil in a stockpot or Dutch oven over medium heat. Add the onion and garlic and cook until softened, 4 to 5 minutes. Stir in the chile and cook for 1 minute. Add the clams and ginger beer, raise the heat to high, cover, and cook until the clams open, about 5 minutes.

2. Meanwhile, to make the toast: Toast the bread in a toaster or under the broiler until golden brown on both sides. Keep warm until ready to serve.

3. Discard any clams that have not opened. Stir the butter, scallions, and parsley into the cooking liquid and mix until well combined.

4. To serve, divide the clams and their liquid among four bowls. Spread the snail butter evenly on the warm toast and serve alongside.

FOR THE CLAMS

2 tablespoons olive oil

3 garlic cloves, chopped

1 tablespoon fresh thyme leaves or 1 teaspoon dried

½ cup dry white wine

12 large clams, such as cherry-stones, scrubbed

FOR THE STUFFING

4 ounces pancetta, finely chopped

1 small yellow onion, finely chopped

3 slices stale white bread, toasted and torn into small pieces (about 2½ cups)

1 tablespoon chopped fresh oregano (optional)

¼ cup freshly grated pecorino cheese

Kosher salt and freshly ground black pepper to taste

FOR SERVING

2 tablespoons rendered beef, chicken, or duck fat or steak juices (optional)

¼ cup Snail Butter (page 46; optional)

SERVES 4 OR 5

CLAMS STUFFED WITH PANCETTA

The Rat Pack-era classic clams casino is a retro treat, clams on the half shell topped with oregano, lemon, and bread crumbs. I've always loved it, but I also think it can easily be made more vibrant. One way to do this is to drizzle a little melted beef fat or steak juice over the top of the clams. It's a small, unexpected touch that adds a burst of intense flavor.

1. TO COOK THE CLAMS: Heat the oil in a stockpot or Dutch oven over medium heat. Add the garlic and thyme and cook until the garlic is softened, 3 to 4 minutes. Add the wine and clams, cover, raise the heat to high, and cook until the clams open, about 5 minutes. With a slotted spoon, remove the clams from the broth (discard any that have not opened) and let stand until cool enough to handle.

2. Open the clams fully and, with a paring knife, remove the clam meat from the shells; reserve 16 of the largest shells. Coarsely chop the clams and set aside, along with the cooking liquid. Put the reserved clam shells on a baking sheet.

3. TO MAKE THE STUFFING: Preheat the oven to 375°F. Put the pancetta in a large skillet and cook over medium heat until the fat is rendered and the meat is beginning to crisp, 6 to 8 minutes. Add the onion and cook until softened, about 4 minutes. Transfer the mixture to a large bowl, add the chopped clams and bread, and toss until combined. Add ½ cup of the clam cooking liquid and stir; add more liquid 2 tablespoons at a time until the mixture is well moistened, but not soggy. Stir in the oregano, if using, and pecorino, season with salt and pepper, and mix well.

4. Mound the stuffing evenly into 12 clam shells (there may be enough filling to fill up to 16). If using the beef fat, drizzle about ½ teaspoon over each clam. Bake until golden brown, 25 to 30 minutes. Let stand for 10 minutes before serving.

5. To serve, put 3 (or 4) clams each on four small plates and put about 1 teaspoon snail butter, if using, on top of each clam. Serve immediately.

2.0 CLAMS STUFFED WITH BEEF MARROW

You can take the concept of clams-with-beef-juice a little bit further by adding some bone marrow to the stuffing, along with the aromatics and bread crumbs. Think of ingredients like foie gras or bone marrow as alternatives to butter—or as butter of the gods. Bone marrow is incredibly rich in flavor, and its velvety texture makes it melt in your mouth.

Preheat the oven to 375°F. Put 4 center-cut beef marrow bones, about 3 inches long, in a small baking dish, standing them upright, and roast in the oven until the marrow is soft and beginning to separate from the bones, about 30 minutes. Let cool slightly before using a small spoon to scoop the marrow from the bones. Coarsely chop the marrow, and stir ½ cup of it into the clam stuffing before filling the shells and baking as directed. Any leftover marrow can be stored in the refrigerator and added to pasta or simply spread on toast points with mustard.

1 pound fresh jumbo lump or Dungeness crabmeat, picked over for shells and cartilage but left in large chunks

¼ cup Smoked Aioli (page 25) or good-quality store-bought mayonnaise

1 tablespoon Dijon mustard

2 teaspoons chopped fresh dill

2 teaspoons chopped fresh flat-leaf parsley

2 teaspoons chopped fresh chives

½ teaspoon kosher salt

½ cup all-purpose flour

¼ cup clarified butter (page 45), melted

2 tablespoons unsalted butter

1 cup Brussels Sprouts Slaw (page 127) for serving

SERVES 4

CRAB CAKES WITH BRUSSELS SPROUTS SLAW

I like a classic crab cake—not too much filler, not too wet inside, just crabmeat lightly bound. What makes a crab cake special is its rich decadence. The traditional accompaniments of crunchy coleslaw (mine is, naturally, unconventional) and tangy mustard sauce balance the luxuriousness of the crab with crunch and acidity.

1. Line a small plate with plastic wrap. Put the crabmeat in a medium bowl. In a small bowl, stir the aioli, mustard, dill, parsley, chives, and salt together until combined. Add the mixture to the crab and, using a large rubber spatula, fold gently to incorporate the dressing without breaking up the crab. Divide the mixture into four equal portions. Gently form each portion into a cake shape about 1 inch thick and transfer to the lined plate. Cover and refrigerate for at least 30 minutes, and as long as overnight.

2. To cook the crab cakes, pour the flour into a pie plate. Gently dip each cake lightly in the flour. Heat the clarified butter in a medium nonstick skillet over medium heat. Add the cakes and cook until golden on the bottom, 3 to 4 minutes. Very gently flip them with a small spatula and continue cooking for 2 to 3 minutes. Add the 2 tablespoons butter to the pan and, once it has melted, use a large spoon to baste the cakes with butter, tilting the pan if necessary to scoop it up. Continue to cook until the cakes are brown on the bottom. Drain on paper towels.

3. To serve, place the crab cakes on four small plates. Top each with ¼ cup Brussels sprouts slaw.

2.0　MUSTARD CAVIAR

You can make "mustard caviar," essentially bright yellow dots of bracing mustard seeds, to add an explosion of sweet, sour, and earthy flavor to these crab cakes. The candied mustard seeds look like fish eggs, so there's an obvious connection to pairing it with seafood. But the caviar works just as well on say, a pulled pork sandwich.

To make mustard caviar, put 2 tablespoons yellow mustard seeds in a small skillet and toast over medium-low heat, swirling the pan occasionally, until fragrant and just beginning to pop, 3 to 4 minutes. Meanwhile, stir ¼ cup sugar and ¼ cup water together in a small bowl. Pour the mixture into the skillet, stir well, and cook until the mustard seeds are swollen, the sugar dissolves, and the liquid is reduced and syrupy, 2 to 3 minutes. Remove from the heat and let cool to room temperature. Store in an airtight container in the refrigerator for up to 6 weeks.

OTHER THINGS TO DO WITH LIQUID NITROGEN

MAKE INCREDIBLY SMOOTH ICE CREAM OR SORBET

GRIND INGREDIENTS SUPERFINE BY "NITRO MILLING" IN A BLENDER

USE TO DROP THE TEMPERATURE OF ANYTHING. LIKE A STOCK THAT NEEDS TO BE CHILLED.

FREEZE ALCOHOL

POUR INTO AN UNOCCUPIED SWIMMING POOL. STAND BACK. AND WATCH.

FREEZE UNDERWEAR OR CHEFS' KNIVES IN SOLID BLOCKS OF WATER

1.5 LIQUID-NITROGEN MILLING

My friend and acclaimed Charleston chef Sean Brock makes a great version of shrimp and grits by freezing some shrimp in liquid nitrogen, grinding them frozen into pieces, and folding them into hot grits. It's a great idea, and if you're so inclined, go for it!

12 head-on large prawns or jumbo Black Tiger shrimp (plus 1 for the sauce—see below)

3 tablespoons olive oil

2 garlic cloves, chopped

1 tablespoon chopped fresh flat-leaf parsley, plus (optional) more for garnish

1 teaspoon chopped fresh sage, plus more for garnish

1 teaspoon chopped fresh rosemary, plus more for garnish

1 teaspoon finely grated lemon zest

1 teaspoon kosher salt

¼ teaspoon freshly ground black pepper

FOR THE SAUCE

1 tablespoon olive oil

2 ounces pancetta, finely diced

1 large prawn or jumbo Black Tiger shrimp, shelled, deveined, and finely minced

2 anchovies, mashed, or ½ teaspoon anchovy paste

½ teaspoon red pepper flakes

1 cup Tomato Sauce (page 35)

Kosher salt and freshly ground black pepper to taste

FOR THE POLENTA

2 cups whole milk

2 cups Pressure-Cooker Chicken Stock (page 44) or store-bought low-sodium broth

1 teaspoon kosher salt, or more to taste

1 cup instant polenta

3 tablespoons unsalted butter

½ teaspoon white truffle oil (optional)

SERVES 4

PRAWNS 'N' POLENTA

The inspiration for this dish is shrimp 'n' grits, which I first encountered when I moved to Atlanta from New York. This one is a riff on the classic with what might be deemed "Yankee" ingredients. I substitute prawns for the shrimp and polenta for the grits. Sacrilege? Not if it tastes good.

1. Put the 12 prawns in a bowl or large resealable plastic bag, add the oil, garlic, parsley, sage, rosemary, lemon zest, salt, and pepper, and mix until well coated. Cover, or seal the bag, and refrigerate for at least 30 minutes, and up to 2 hours.

2. MEANWHILE, TO MAKE THE SAUCE: Heat the oil in a medium skillet over medium heat. Add the pancetta and cook until just crisp, about 5 minutes. Add the minced prawn, anchovies, and red pepper flakes and cook, stirring to break up the prawn, until the anchovies are dissolved, 2 to 3 minutes. Add the tomato sauce and bring to a simmer. Reduce the heat to medium-low and simmer until the sauce is very thick, about 20 minutes. Taste and adjust the seasoning with salt and pepper if necessary. Keep warm over very low heat until ready to serve.

3. TO MAKE THE POLENTA: Bring the milk, stock, and salt to a simmer in a large saucepan over medium heat. Whisking constantly, slowly pour in the polenta in a slow, steady stream, then whisk until very smooth. Cook, whisking, until the polenta begins to bubble and get very thick, 2 to 3 minutes. Stir in the butter and truffle oil, if using. Taste for seasoning and add salt if necessary. Cover to keep warm.

4. TO COOK THE PRAWNS: Heat a cast-iron grill pan over medium-high heat. Remove the prawns from the marinade, shaking off the excess oil, and grill, turning once, until just cooked through, 2 to 3 minutes per side.

5. To serve, divide the polenta among four large plates. Place 3 prawns on the polenta on each plate, and drizzle the sauce over the top. Sprinkle with the chopped herbs and serve immediately.

2 tablespoons white vinegar

1 teaspoon black peppercorns

1 bay leaf

1 live lobster (about 1½ pounds)

⅓ cup Aioli (page 24) or good-quality store-bought mayonnaise

2 teaspoons Old Bay seasoning

½ teaspoon fish sauce

½ teaspoon Sriracha hot sauce

Kosher salt and freshly ground black pepper to taste

½ cup drained Pickled Celery (page 54) or 2 stalks celery, sliced

¼ cup finely diced Vidalia or other sweet white onion

¼ cup finely chopped fresh cilantro stems

12 fresh basil leaves, minced

3 sprigs fresh tarragon, leaves removed and minced

4 New England-style hot dog buns

2 tablespoons unsalted butter, melted

1 teaspoon Mustard Caviar (page 212)

SERVES 4

LOBSTER ROLLS WITH OLD BAYONNAISE

Every Christmas, my wife's extended family in Boston sends a few live lobsters our way. I'm usually put in charge of killing and cooking them. I like to use them for classic lobster rolls, dressed with homemade mayo spiked with Old Bay seasoning, Sriracha, and fish sauce and served in New England-style buns (top-split hot dog buns, toasted on both sides). It's an unpretentious way to enjoy a precious food.

1. Fill a large stockpot with water, add the vinegar, peppercorns, and bay leaf, and bring to a boil over medium-high heat.

2. Lay the lobster on a stable cutting board. Place one hand on the tail and hold it flat against the board. With the other hand, place the tip of a large sharp knife about 1 inch behind the eyes, where the body meets the tail, with the blade facing the head and, in one quick motion, plunge the tip of the knife straight down through the head and bring the blade down to the board to kill the lobster instantly. Reduce the heat under the boiling water to maintain a simmer, drop the lobster into the water, cover, and cook gently until the shell is bright red, 12 to 15 minutes.

3. While the lobster cooks, fill a large bowl with ice water. Drop the cooked lobster into the ice water and let stand until completely cool; drain. Twist the tail and claws from the lobster. Using kitchen shears, cut the shells open and remove the meat. (The body and shells can be frozen for use in stocks, soups, etc.) Coarsely chop the meat and transfer it to a medium bowl.

4. In a small bowl, stir the aioli, Old Bay, fish sauce, Sriracha, and salt and pepper together until combined. Add the dressing to the lobster and toss gently to combine. Add the celery, onion, cilantro stems, basil, and tarragon and toss gently to mix. Taste and adjust the seasoning with salt and pepper if necessary.

5. Heat a large skillet over medium-low heat. Brush both flat sides of the hot dog buns with the melted butter and place them flat side down in the skillet. Toast, turning once, until light golden brown on both sides, about 5 minutes total.

6. To serve, divide the lobster mixture into 4 portions and fill the toasted rolls with it. Garnish with mustard caviar and serve immediately.

2.0 LOBSTER SOUS VIDE

Sous vide is simply the best way to avoid squandering expensive lobster. This method guarantees a consistently cooked, thoroughly tender piece of meat that you can then very quickly grill or poach for lobster rolls.

Preheat the sous vide machine to 126.5°F. Meanwhile, bring a large stockpot of water to a boil and add 2 tablespoons white vinegar. Fill a large bowl with ice water and set aside. Kill the lobster as instructed on page 216 and twist off the tail and claws. Drop the claws and tail into the boiling water and cook for 2 minutes. Immediately transfer them to the ice water and let stand until completely cool. Use kitchen shears to remove the meat from the shells. Transfer the lobster meat to a vacuum-seal bag, add a pinch of kosher salt and ½ teaspoon unsalted butter, and seal. Immerse in the water bath and cook for 13 to 15 minutes. Remove the meat from the bag, let stand until cool, chop, then proceed with the recipe.

Four 6-ounce
center-cut cod
fillet with skin

Kosher salt and
freshly ground
black pepper to
taste

3 tablespoons
clarified butter
(see page 45)

2 sprigs fresh
thyme

2 garlic cloves,
smashed

2 tablespoons
unsalted butter

1 cup fresh apple
cider

¼ teaspoon white
truffle oil

Smooth Mashed
Potatoes (page
132) for serving

2 tablespoons
toasted almonds
for garnish
(optional)

2 tablespoons
capers for
garnish
(optional)

SERVES 4

PAN-ROASTED COD WITH MASHED POTATOES + CIDER SYRUP

I like the meatiness and versatility of cod, and I've been making
variations on this recipe for years. My favorite version is this one, an
elegant dish that isn't overdesigned or complicated. It doesn't need any
vegetables beyond the very smooth mashed potatoes, and it comes off as
particularly masculine, like steak 'n' potatoes, without having any overtly
"manly" ingredients. The syrup is made from ingredients I already have
around the house. If you take some nice apple cider and reduce the hell out
of it, you'll have a sauce with an intensely concentrated flavor that goes
great with the cod.

1. Pat the fish dry with paper towels and season well on
all sides with salt and pepper. Put the clarified butter, thyme,
and garlic in a large skillet and heat over medium-high heat
until the butter is rippling. Add the fish skin side down and
cook until the skin is crisp, 4 to 5 minutes. Flip the fish and
add the 2 tablespoons butter to the pan. Once the butter
is melted, use a large spoon to baste the cod with butter,
tilting the pan if necessary, and continue cooking until
the fish is opaque throughout and skin is very crisp, 3 to
4 minutes more. Drain on paper towels.

2. Meanwhile, bring the apple cider to a simmer in a
small saucepan over medium heat and cook until thick and
syrupy and reduced to about ¼ cup, about 10 minutes.
Remove from the heat and let cool briefly, then stir in the
truffle oil.

3. Divide the cod among four warm plates and spoon
the mashed potatoes alongside. Drizzle the cider syrup
over the fish. Garnish with the almonds and capers, if using,
and serve.

TUNA,
THE OTHER **OTHER** WHITE MEAT

Here I take three traditional steak-house favorites—steak frites, prime rib, and steak au poivre—and remix the dishes. I've got the same big ol' slab of meat, but mine's fish: bright red tuna, with a meaty flavor and toothsome texture that resembles steak but is lighter and fresher. The tuna is served rare in all three dishes, and you can really sink your teeth into it. For the full-on remix, I serve the prime rib with Pork-Belly-Stuffed Baked Potatoes (page 134). The fourth dish here, Tuna Tartare with Sunny-Side Up Eggs, was inspired by Sotohiro Kosugi, who for ten years ran an excellent sushi restaurant in Atlanta and is now the toast of Manhattan at Soto, a tiny, incredible sushi bar.

SERVES 4

TUNA STEAK FRITES

I like to cook certain fish the way I cook meat. And with tuna's obvious visual similarity to red meat, this dish even looks like steak. It's an easy fish to grill or baste in a pan. It's forgiving, and happens to work well with two of life's greatest joys: French fries and red wine!

One 2-pound piece center-cut sashimi-grade tuna loin

Kosher salt and freshly ground black pepper to taste

3 tablespoons clarified butter (see page 45)

1 sprig fresh rosemary (optional)

1 sprig fresh thyme (optional)

2 garlic cloves, smashed

2 tablespoons unsalted butter

French Fries (page 85) for serving

Season the tuna loin generously on all sides with salt and pepper. Put the clarified butter, rosemary and thyme, if using, and garlic in a medium skillet and heat over high heat until the butter is rippling. Push the herbs to the side, if using, and add the tuna loin. Sear the tuna on all four sides for 2 minutes; when turning it to the last side, add the 2 tablespoons butter and, once it is melted, use a large spoon to baste the surface of the tuna loin, tipping the pan if necessary to scoop up the butter. Transfer the tuna to a cutting board and let rest for 2 to 3 minutes before slicing. Using a very sharp knife, cut the tuna crosswise into 4 even steaks. The edges will be seared but the tuna will be rare in the center. Serve the steaks with the hot French fries.

TUNA FILLET AU POIVRE

The only way to make this more classic is to serve it under a silver dome.

One 3-pound piece center-cut sashimi-grade tuna loin

1 tablespoon kosher salt, or more to taste

3 tablespoons tricolor peppercorns (black, white, and pink), coarsely crushed

2 tablespoons all-purpose flour

2 tablespoons olive oil or clarified butter (see page 45)

¼ cup whiskey

½ cup Pressure-Cooker Chicken Stock (page 44) or store-bought low-sodium broth

2 tablespoons unsalted butter, diced

French Fries (page 85) for serving

1. Trim the edges and corners of the tuna loin with a sharp knife to give it a rounded shape, like a beef tenderloin. (Reserve the trimmings for tartare or another use.) Cut the tuna into 4 equal medallions. Mix the salt, peppercorns, and flour on a large plate. Press the medallions into the pepper mixture, turning to coat evenly on all sides and pressing the mixture into the tuna.

2. Heat the oil in a medium skillet over medium-high heat until rippling. Add the tuna steaks and sear on one side for 1 minute. Flip the steaks and sear on the opposite side for 1 minute. Transfer to a plate and cover to keep warm. Reduce the heat to medium.

3. Pull the pan briefly away from the heat and add the whiskey. Return the pan to the heat and carefully tip it slightly to ignite the alcohol. (If you have an electric stove, use a long lighter or match to ignite the liquor.) Allow the flame to burn out, then add the chicken stock, bring to a simmer, and cook until reduced by half, 3 to 4 minutes. Remove from the heat and whisk in the butter until melted and smooth. Taste and add salt if necessary.

4. Serve the tuna fillets with the warm French fries on the side and the peppercorn sauce poured over the top.

TUNA PRIME RIB

Pull this off at your next summer barbecue, and they will be talking about it for years.

One 2-pound piece center-cut sashimi-grade tuna loin	Olive oil Kosher salt to taste	3 tablespoons Hab Spice (page 50) or store-bought steak seasoning, such as Montreal brand	4 Pork-Belly-Stuffed Baked Potatoes (page 134) for serving

1. Preheat the oven to 450°F. Rub the entire surface of the tuna with oil and season evenly with salt. Pour the steak seasoning onto a large plate and press the tuna into the spices, turning to coat the surface evenly. Transfer the tuna to a small roasting pan or baking dish and roast for 20 minutes.

2. To serve, use an electric knife to cut the roasted loin crosswise into ½-inch-thick slices. The edges will be cooked but the center will still be rare. Let stand for 10 minutes before slicing. Transfer to four serving plates and put a baked potato on each plate.

TUNA TARTARE WITH SUNNY-SIDE UP EGGS

I love the temperature contrasts here: ice-cold tartare and warm gushing yolk. Feel free to substitute another fish, such as hamachi, or even some chilled raw beef or lamb. Any of these would be amazing.

1 pound sushi-grade tuna, finely diced

1 small crisp pear, such as Asian or Anjou, peeled, cored, and cut into very small dice

2 teaspoons finely grated fresh ginger

1 garlic clove, finely minced

4 scallions, finely chopped

2 tablespoons toasted pine nuts

½ teaspoon toasted sesame oil

½ teaspoon Asian chile sauce, such as sambal

Kosher salt and freshly ground black pepper to taste

1 tablespoon unsalted butter

4 large eggs

12 to 16 thin slices baguette, toasted, for serving

1. Put the tuna, pear, ginger, garlic, scallions, pine nuts, sesame oil, and chile sauce in a medium bowl and stir well to combine. Taste and add salt and pepper as needed. Cover and refrigerate for up to 1 hour until ready to serve.

2. Melt the butter in a medium nonstick skillet over medium heat. Fry the eggs until the whites are completely set but the yolks are still runny, 3 to 4 minutes. Season the eggs with salt and pepper.

3. To serve, divide the tartare among four salad plates and press it with the back of a spoon into a thin, even layer. Lay a warm fried egg in the center of each plate and serve with toasted baguette slices.

- 1 cup ground pork
- 1 tablespoon chopped scallion
- 1 garlic clove, shaved on a mandoline
- 1 tablespoon shaved (on a mandoline) peeled fresh ginger

- 2 tablespoons soy sauce
- 1 sheet Fresh Pasta Dough (page 144), cut into twenty-four 1-inch squares
- 2 large eggs, beaten, for egg wash

- 1 cup water
- 1 cup fish sauce
- 1 cup sugar
- Kosher salt
- 1 tablespoon unsalted butter

- 8 large sea scallops
- Extra-virgin olive oil for drizzling
- Fresh basil, cilantro, and mint with lime juice (optional)

SERVES 4

SCALLOPS WITH PORK TORTELLONI + FISH SAUCE CARAMEL

Here's a cultural mash-up that's not much of a stretch when you think about it. Dumplings? Ravioli? It's all the same thing. A somewhat traditional Asian filling of ground pork and scallion with the slippery Italian pasta and Vietnamese caramel sauce—this is a poster child for what's right with fusion.

1. In a small bowl, mix the pork, scallion, garlic, ginger, and soy sauce together until thoroughly combined. Lay the pasta squares out on a clean dry work surface. Spoon about ½ tablespoon of the pork mixture onto the center of each pasta square. One at a time, brush the edges of each square with egg wash and fold the dough over to make a triangle shape. Brush the two opposite points of the triangle with egg wash and press together to make the tortelloni shape.

2. In a small saucepan, combine the water, fish sauce, and sugar and cook over low heat, stirring constantly, until thickened. Reduce the heat to the lowest setting to keep warm; if the caramel starts to thicken too much, remove from the heat.

3. Meanwhile, bring a large pot of water to a boil and salt it generously.

4. Heat the butter in a sauté pan or skillet over medium heat. When it begins to foam, add the scallops and sear for 2 minutes on each side, until golden brown. Remove from the heat and let rest.

5. Cook the tortelloni pasta in the boiling water for 2 minutes; drain.

6. To serve, arrange 6 tortelloni on each of four plates and drizzle with olive oil. Add 2 scallops to each plate and drizzle the fish sauce caramel around the plates. If using, garnish with herb–lime juice mixture.

1 cup Spanish chorizo, diced

½ cup barbecue sauce

8 tablespoons unsalted butter, softened

½ cup chopped fresh flat-leaf parsley

Zest and juice of 1 lemon

2 tablespoons freshly ground black pepper

1 tablespoon kosher salt

8 large oysters (preferably Blue Points)

¼ cup herb bread crumbs (see page 47)

1 green apple, small diced (and kept in acidulated water, such as water with a drop of lemon juice, to keep from browning)

SERVES 8

BARBECUE BROILED OYSTERS WITH CHORIZO + GREEN APPLE

I was never really into cooked oysters, because I thought oysters were perfect raw, until I made this version. The barbecue sauce gives the dish the acidity and sweetness to complement the oceanic flavor of the oysters. The chorizo adds spice and punch while the apple gives it brightness and a fresh crunch.

1. In a sauté pan over medium heat, cook the chorizo until evenly browned. Spoon in the barbecue sauce and stir. Remove the pan from the heat and let cool.

2. In a small bowl, mix the butter, parsley, lemon zest and juice, black pepper, and salt, until evenly incorporated. Cover and refrigerate until cool.

3. Run the oysters under cold water and scrub the shells of any mud or dirt. Place an oyster cup side down on a cutting board with the point (hinge) facing you. With a folded towel or thick glove, hold down the oyster. Using an oyster knife, insert the blade through the hinge, angling it down the cup, then twist to pry the hinge open. Run the blade between the shells, rotating the oyster when you

get to the top, and then coming back down the other side. Be careful not to impale the meat. The shell should now separate. Remove the oyster from the shell. Strain the liquid and set it aside. Shuck the remaining oysters.

4. Preheat a grill or broiler.

5. Place the oyster shells in a pan just big enough to hold them and add an oyster to each shell. Spoon 1 tablespoon chorizo mixture and 1 teaspoon butter mixture over each oyster. Then sprinkle 1 tablespoon bread crumbs over the top. Place the pan on a grill or in the broiler until the butter is melted and the oysters are slightly cooked.

6. Remove from the heat and garnish with the diced green apple.

Roast Beef Tenderloin with Jerusalem Artichokes 237 | Grilled Rib Eye with Spiced Corn on the Cob (Sous Vide Steak) 238 | Beef Goulash (Dropping Acid) 241 | Pan-Seared Spiced Pork Chops with Microwave Applesauce 242 | Pork Shoulder Cooked in Green Chiles 244 | Lamb Ribs in a Chipotle-Malt Reduction 246 | Lamb Shanks Braised in Root Beer 248 | Brisket with Coriander, Black Pepper, and Brown Sugar 250 | Salisbury Steak 253 | Steak Tartare 254 | Pork-Belly "Chop" with Giant White Bean Ragout 257

MEAT

Even though I had been cooking for many years, it wasn't until I was battling for the title of Top Chef in Puerto Rico that I truly came to respect meat. We were at a traditional Sunday pig roast, enjoying the music and festivities. There was an entire village dancing, drinking, and partying. And at the center of everything was this amazing whole hog slowly turning over a wood fire. At first I thought we were just taking part in a community dinner, but it was more than that. Historically, throughout the Caribbean, pig roasts are a celebration of sustenance and survival. They are an expression of happiness and gratitude in its most basic form. The pig—nearly every part of the whole beast—feeds an entire village, sustaining the inhabitants and serving to nourish their morale. Not having grown up on a farm or ever really questioning where my next meal was coming from, I was struck by the villagers' appreciation.

That humid day, even though I was distracted by the stress of the cooking competition, I began to appreciate meat in a way I never had before.

These days, whole-animal cookery, and, in particular, the use of offal, is a cool trend. It takes knowledge and skill to cook a beef heart, and courage to put it on a menu. But sometimes it's done for the wrong reasons, for shock value. I do believe that we should use as much of the animal as we can, primarily because it will provide a great, satisfying meal. For cooking at home, I'm not going to suggest sourcing obscure cuts of meat or slaughtering whole animals. But I do encourage you to look at value. Some of the following recipes use popular cuts like rib-eye steaks or pork chops, but you'll also find other delicious, economical options like lamb ribs, beef cheeks, and marrow bones.

One of the best techniques for cooking tougher cuts of meat, like pork shoulder, is braising. Such

recipes have longer cooking times, but they aren't difficult or even time-consuming to prepare. Most of the work is done before you let something simmer or cook at a low temperature for a long time. And while that is happening, you can do other things—if you're like me, maybe snowboard down a mountain or go for a long run on a drizzly day. Trust me, these recipes, such as lamb shanks braised in root beer, are easy. One of my favorite aspects of food that is cooked slowly is that this method produces flavors that you can keep for another use. Save the juices, fat, and drippings from whatever you cook, and you'll build a stockpile of awesome things like clarified brisket fat and lamb stock. Sear your next steak in that fat, and suddenly you are doing things in your home kitchen that the best restaurant chefs do: saving and stacking flavors to make your food more delicious and exciting.

You'll also find recipes with shorter cooking times. A great way to cook a piece of meat is to sear it in a pan. Along with high-quality meat, you'll need solid cooking technique. Start by seasoning the meat aggressively (meat needs more salt than seafood does), and dry your meat with a few pats of a towel before cooking. Get your pan really hot before adding the meat (when it's just barely started to smoke, it's ready), then reduce the heat so the meat cooks properly on the first side. After you turn the meat over, add a generous pat of butter (or rendered fat) and maybe some garlic and/or herbs, then spoon that sizzling pool of butter over your meat again and again to baste it (like it's at a spa getting a brown-butter-and-herb treatment).

This all may sound silly, almost romantic, but it's what matters most to me when it comes to meat cookery: honoring the process, maybe like your ancestors did somewhere long ago.

One 2-pound
center-cut beef
tenderloin roast,
tied

Kosher salt and
freshly ground
black pepper to
taste

3 tablespoons
clarified butter
(see page 45)

2 sprigs fresh
thyme

1 sprig fresh
rosemary

2 garlic cloves,
smashed

1 tablespoon
unsalted butter

1 pound Jerusalem
artichokes,
scrubbed and
broken into small
pieces (skin
left on)

SERVES 4

ROAST BEEF TENDERLOIN
WITH JERUSALEM ARTICHOKES

While "meat and potatoes" is one of the most basic meals, I often crave
this simple but delicious combination. I keep it fairly classic, replacing
the starchiness of potatoes with the subtlety of Jerusalem artichokes for a
nice, light change. It's just as comforting and far from basic.

1. Remove the beef from the refrigerator at least 20 minutes before cooking. Preheat the oven to 350°F.

2. Pat the beef dry with paper towels and season it well on all sides with salt and pepper. Put the clarified butter, thyme, rosemary, and garlic in a large ovenproof skillet and heat over medium-high heat until the butter is rippling. Push the herbs to the side of the pan and sear the meat on all sides until deep golden brown. Add the 1 tablespoon butter to the pan. Once it is melted, tilt the pan slightly and use a large spoon to baste the meat several times with the hot butter. (If the garlic is getting too brown, remove it.)

3. Scatter the Jerusalem artichokes around the meat. Transfer the pan to the oven and roast, basting the meat several times with the butter, until an instant-read thermometer inserted into the center of the roast reads 130°F, 20 to 25 minutes, for medium-rare. Transfer the roast to a cutting board and let stand for 10 to 15 minutes before carving. Use a slotted spoon to remove the artichokes from the pan and transfer to a serving bowl; season them with salt and pepper.

4. Using an electric knife, carve the beef into slices or medallions. Serve with the artichokes on the side.

4 bone-in rib-eye steaks (about 1 pound each)

Kosher salt and freshly ground black pepper

2 tablespoons Hab Spice (page 50) or store-bought steak seasoning, such as Montreal brand

FOR THE CHILE CORN

¼ cup Mexican crema or sour cream, at room temperature

2 tablespoons unsalted butter, softened

¼ cup finely chopped fresh cilantro

1 garlic clove, finely minced

1 teaspoon togarashi (Japanese chile pepper blend) or ¼ teaspoon cayenne pepper plus ¾ teaspoon chili powder

4 ears sweet corn in the husk

Kosher salt and freshly ground black pepper to taste

SERVES 4

GRILLED RIB EYE WITH SPICED CORN ON THE COB

Who doesn't love a simple steak served with corn on the cob? My version is meant to be an instant classic for your backyard, cooked over an open wood fire. I took my inspiration from classic steak sauces and from the addictive Mexican-style corn sold in the husk at street fairs across the country.

1. Remove the steaks from the refrigerator and let stand for 30 minutes to come to room temperature. Preheat a gas grill to high or prepare a charcoal grill with a very hot fire (if you hold your hand 6 inches from the coals, you should have to pull it away in less than 3 seconds).

2. Season the steaks well on both sides with salt and pepper and the steak seasoning. Grill until charred on the first side, about 6 minutes. Turn and grill until charred on the second side and an instant-read thermometer inserted horizontally through the side of the steak reads 130°F, about 4 minutes. (The meat will continue cooking after you remove it from the grill and will rise to around 135°F, medium-rare.) Transfer to a platter and let rest. If using a charcoal grill, spread out the coals or use the cooler side of the grill. Reduce the heat under the grill to medium.

3. Meanwhile, to make the chile corn: In a small bowl, stir the crema, butter, cilantro, garlic, and togorashi together until combined. Pull back the husks from the corn and remove the silks. Using a pastry brush, coat each ear with the crema mixture and season lightly with salt and pepper. Close the husks and cook, turning frequently, until the corn is bright yellow and tender, about 10 minutes.

4. Transfer the steaks to four large plates, pull back the husks on the corn, and serve immediately.

2.0 SOUS VIDE STEAK

Cooking steaks on the grill is a great idea for entertaining—but it can get problematic when you're simultaneously socializing and manning the grill. To get around that, I cook steaks sous vide before people come over, to get perfectly moist, tender meat. Then I can sear the steaks quickly on a hot grill without having to worry. Better steak, better conversation.

To cook the steaks sous vide, preheat the sous vide machine to 137°F. Season the steaks lightly with salt and pepper, put each one in a sous vide bag, and seal. Immerse the bags in the water bath and cook for at least 3 hours, no longer than 4 hours. They will be a perfect medium-rare. Remove the steaks from the water bath, remove the bags, and pat dry. Sprinkle the steak seasoning evenly on both sides of each steak. Grill on a hot grill, turning once, until grill marks appear and the bone is charred, 2 to 3 minutes per side. Transfer to a plate, cover, and let rest for 10 minutes before serving.

4 large meaty beef back ribs (6 to 8 inches long) or 8 short ribs

Kosher salt and freshly ground black pepper to taste

½ cup all-purpose flour

3 tablespoons olive oil

3 yellow onions, halved lengthwise and sliced

1 bay leaf

¼ cup sweet Hungarian paprika, plus more for garnish

2 tablespoons caraway seeds, crushed, plus toasted whole seeds for garnish

One 28-ounce can whole peeled San Marzano tomatoes, crushed

2 to 3 tablespoons aged balsamic vinegar, to taste

¼ cup chopped fresh flat-leaf parsley leaves for garnish (optional)

Smooth Mashed Potatoes (page 132) for serving

SERVES 4

BEEF GOULASH

This is a dish I made on *Top Chef All-Stars* when chef Wolfgang Puck was a judge. Puck is Austrian, and my challenge was to prepare what I thought he would choose for his last meal. It had to be goulash, which I was not particularly familiar with. All I knew, really, was that it contained caraway, paprika, and onions. I had to imagine the rest of its components. I knew that balsamic vinegar—the key to this goulash's tang—was not a traditional ingredient, but the addition made the dish better, more flavorful, and brightly intense, and it was picked as the winner.

1. Preheat the oven to 325°F. Season the ribs well on all sides with salt and pepper. Put the flour into a pie plate, season with salt and pepper, and mix well. Dredge the ribs in the flour, coating completely and shaking off the excess. Heat the oil in a large Dutch oven (large enough to hold the ribs lying down) over medium-high heat. Sear the ribs until golden brown on all sides. Transfer to a plate.

2. Add the onions, bay leaf, paprika, and crushed caraway seeds to the pot, season with salt and pepper, and cook, stirring frequently, until the onions are beginning to turn golden, 12 to 15 minutes. Add the tomatoes and stir until well combined.

3. Set the ribs on top of the onions, rounded sides down, and pour in any accumulated juices from the plate. Bring to a simmer, cover, and transfer to the oven. Cook, turning the ribs over halfway through the cooking time, until the meat is very tender and falling from the bones, 2 to 2½ hours. Remove the ribs from the pot and cover to keep warm.

4. Taste the goulash and season with salt and pepper if necessary. Stir in the balsamic vinegar. To serve, divide the goulash among four shallow bowls and set a rib on top of each serving. Garnish with a sprinkling of toasted caraway seeds, paprika, and chopped parsley, if using Serve immediately, with the mashed potatoes.

1.5 DROPPING ACID

It's all about acidity. Young cooks think cooking is about salt, but acidity gives food punch and depth. What tastes better? Fried shrimp or fried shrimp with a squirt of lemon? Salad greens or greens tossed in vinaigrette? Always, always think about adding a drop of vinegar or citrus to finish a dish!

1 teaspoon fennel seeds

1 teaspoon coriander seeds

1 whole star anise

A 2-inch piece cinnamon stick

4 double-cut bone-in pork chops (12 to 16 ounces each)

Kosher salt and freshly ground black pepper to taste

3 tablespoons clarified butter (see page 45)

3 thin slices fresh ginger, smashed with the side of a knife

2 garlic cloves, smashed

2 sprigs fresh thyme

2 sprigs fresh sage

1 sprig fresh rosemary

2 tablespoons unsalted butter

2 Granny Smith apples, peeled, cored, and roughly chopped

SERVES 4

PAN-SEARED SPICED PORK CHOPS WITH MICROWAVE APPLESAUCE

Some cooks steer clear of pork chops, especially double-cut ones, because they can dry out so easily. This version is anything but dry. I baste the chops continually with clarified butter while they cook, add herbs and a little butter to the pan toward the end of the cooking time, then spoon the liquid over the meat. The microwave is a great tool for a creative chef: The applesauce is made from nothing but apples, and the nutrients aren't boiled out of the fruit. Macaroni and Headcheese (page 166) is an excellent side-dish choice if you want to round out the meal.

1. Preheat the oven to 400°F. Put the fennel and coriander seeds, star anise, and cinnamon stick in a small skillet and toast over medium-low heat, swirling the pan, until fragrant, 2 to 3 minutes. Transfer the spices to a mortar and pestle or spice grinder, and grind or pulse until coarsely ground. Or put the spices on a cutting board and smash with the bottom of a pan.

2. Season the pork on both sides with salt and pepper and rub the spice mixture evenly over the surface of the chops. Let stand for 10 minutes at room temperature.

3. Put the clarified butter, ginger, garlic, thyme, sage, and rosemary in a very large skillet and heat over medium-high heat until the butter is rippling. Move the herbs to the side of the pan, add 2 of the chops, and sear until golden on the first side, about 4 minutes. Flip the chops and cook until light golden on the second side, 3 to 4 minutes. Remove the chops to a plate and sear the remaining 2 chops on both sides.

4. Put the reserved chops into the skillet and add the 2 tablespoons butter to the pan. When it melts, baste the chops with the butter, using a large spoon, then transfer the pan to the oven. Roast, basting the chops several times, until an instant-read thermometer inserted into the thickest part of the chops reads 145°F, 20 to 25 minutes. Remove the pan from the oven and let stand for 10 minutes before serving. The pork will continue to cook and the temperature will rise to around 150°F, for medium.

5. Meanwhile, put the apples in a medium micro-wavable bowl (glass is best), add 1 tablespoon water, and cook on high in the microwave for 4 to 5 minutes, until very soft. Mash the apples with a fork or potato masher until smooth.

6. Serve the chops with the applesauce on the side.

6 large poblano peppers (about 2 pounds)

2 pounds tomatillos, husked and washed

1 boneless pork shoulder (about 5 pounds), cut into 6 equal pieces

Kosher salt and freshly ground black pepper to taste

½ cup all-purpose flour

3 tablespoons olive oil

1 yellow onion, coarsely chopped

2 large carrots, coarsely chopped

2 stalk celery, chopped

3 garlic cloves, chopped

1 tablespoon tomato paste

1 cinnamon stick

1 teaspoon coriander seeds

1 teaspoon cumin seeds

½ teaspoon whole cloves

1 bay leaf

2 cups Pressure-Cooker Chicken Stock (page 44) or store-bought low-sodium broth

Chopped fresh cilantro for garnish

4 lime wedges for serving

SERVES 4

PORK SHOULDER COOKED IN GREEN CHILES

Pork shoulder is arguably the most versatile inexpensive cut of meat there is. I use it for terrines, pâtés, hot dogs, and sandwiches. This is essentially a grown-up version of a homey dish. I strain and reduce the green chile sauce so it becomes a highly flavorful, thick glaze that coats the chunks of pork.

1. Using tongs, roast the poblano peppers over the flame of a gas burner, turning occasionally, until blackened on all sides. Or put them on a baking sheet and roast under the broiler, turning as necessary, until blackened on all sides. Let cool.

2. With a paring knife, remove the cores, seeds, and skin from the peppers and discard. Transfer the peppers to a food processor and pulse until coarsely chopped. Transfer to a bowl and set aside.

3. Heat a large cast-iron skillet or griddle over medium-high heat. Place the tomatillos on it and cook, turning frequently, until they are blackened on all sides and softened but still hold their shape, about 15 minutes. Transfer the tomatillos to the food processor bowl and pulse until coarsely chopped. Add to the bowl with the peppers and set aside.

4. Preheat the oven to 325°F. Season the pork all over with salt and pepper. Pour the flour into a pie plate, season with salt and pepper, and mix well. Dredge the pieces of pork in the seasoned flour, coating them and shaking off the excess. Heat the olive oil in a large Dutch oven over medium-high heat until rippling. Sear the pork, in batches if necessary, turning frequently, until golden brown on all sides, 2 to 3 minutes per side. Transfer to a plate or baking sheet and drain off the excess fat from the pot.

PORK SHOULDER
+
GREEN CHILI

5. Add the onion, carrots, celery, and garlic to the pot, season with salt and pepper, and cook, stirring frequently, until softened, about 5 minutes. Add the tomato paste, cinnamon stick, coriander seeds, cumin seeds, cloves, and bay leaf and cook, stirring often, until the tomato paste begins to caramelize, 2 to 3 minutes. Add the poblanos and tomatillos, and stir well.

6. Pour in the chicken stock and add the pork pieces, along with any accumulated juices. Cook until the liquid begins to simmer, then cover and transfer the pot to the oven. Bake until the meat is tender and easily shreds with a fork, 2 to 2½ hours.

7. With a slotted spoon, transfer the pork to a plate and cover to keep warm. Strain the cooking liquid through a fine-mesh strainer into a clean saucepan, pressing on the solids in the strainer with a rubber spatula to release as much liquid as possible; discard the solids. Bring the liquid to a simmer over medium heat and cook until reduced by one-quarter, about 10 minutes.

8. Serve the pork in shallow bowls with the sauce ladled over the top and garnished with chopped cilantro and the lime wedges.

2 full racks Denver-cut lamb ribs

Kosher salt and freshly ground black pepper to taste

1½ cups Pressure-Cooker Chicken Stock (page 44) or low-sodium store-bought broth

One 12-ounce bottle malt beverage, such as Goya Malta, or malt liquor, such as Olde English

½ cup honey

¼ cup low-sodium soy sauce

2 dried chipotle morita chiles or 1 canned chipotle in adobo

One 2-inch piece fresh ginger, not peeled, sliced into coins

4 scallions, sliced, for garnish (optional)

1 teaspoon toasted sesame seeds for garnish (optional)

SERVES 4 TO 6

LAMB RIBS IN A CHIPOTLE-MALT REDUCTION

When I was growing up on Long Island, among our neighbors was a family from Haiti. Their son, Ralph, could jump over a standing ten-speed bicycle and would often drink Malta, the sweet molasses-tasting soda found in Mexican groceries. I was never sure if the two were connected (but I digress). I always loved the deep molasses-caramel notes of this malt drink and use it here in a chipotle-Malta reduction. You may have to ask the butcher to order the lamb ribs (the cross-cut of the lamb breast). You could also substitute pork ribs in a pinch, but I love lamb ribs for their strong flavor, which stands up to the sauce.

1. Preheat the oven to 325°F. Season the ribs on both sides with salt and pepper. In a large roasting pan, mix the chicken stock, malt beverage, honey, soy sauce, chipotles, and ginger together until well combined. Set the ribs curved side up in the pan and transfer to the oven. Roast for 1 hour.

2. Flip the ribs and continue roasting until the meat is very tender and a knife meets no resistance when inserted between the ribs, 2½ to 3 hours. Check the pan occasionally, and if it is dry, add water ½ cup at a time.

3. Remove the pan from the oven. The liquid should be thick and syrupy. If not, put the pan over medium heat and simmer until the liquid is very thick. Brush the ribs with the sauce to glaze and keep warm until ready to serve.

4. To serve, transfer the rib racks to a cutting board. Cut into individual ribs and place on a serving platter. Brush them again lightly with some of the sauce. Sprinkle the scallions and sesame seeds, if using, over the top. Strain any extra sauce, pour into a bowl, and serve alongside the ribs.

4 lamb shanks (2½ to 3 pounds total)

Kosher salt and freshly ground black pepper to taste

⅓ cup all-purpose flour

3 tablespoons olive oil

1 small yellow onion, chopped

1 large carrot, chopped

1 stalk celery, chopped

2 garlic cloves, chopped

2 teaspoons tomato paste

One 12-ounce bottle root beer

3 cups Pressure-Cooker Chicken Stock (page 44) or store-bought low-sodium broth

6 fresh flat-leaf parsley stems, plus ¼ cup chopped parsley, for garnish

1 sprig fresh rosemary

1 bay leaf

SERVES 4

LAMB SHANKS BRAISED IN ROOT BEER

The first braise I ever made in cooking school was with lamb shanks, and soon afterward my roommate started calling me Richy Braise because I loved the technique so much. It's a great way to break down inexpensive, tough cuts of meat and turn them into meltingly soft delights. And it's almost impossible to mess up once you know how to do it. The sugary soda makes the cooking liquid sweeter and more intense.

1. Preheat the oven to 325°F. Season the shanks all over with salt and pepper. Pour the flour into a pie plate, season with salt and pepper, and mix well. Dredge the shanks in the seasoned flour, coating them and shaking off the excess. Heat the olive oil in a large Dutch oven over medium-high heat. Sear the shanks, turning frequently, until golden brown on all sides. Transfer to a plate or baking sheet and drain off all but 2 tablespoons fat from the pot.

2. Reduce the heat to medium, add the onion, carrot, celery, and garlic, and cook, stirring frequently, until softened, about 5 minutes. Add the tomato paste and cook, stirring often, until it begins to caramelize, 2 to 3 minutes.

3. Add the root beer, chicken stock, parsley stems, rosemary, bay leaf, and lamb shanks, along with any accumulated juices, and cook until the liquid begins to simmer. Cover, transfer the pot to the oven, and braise until the meat is tender and falling from the bone, 2 to 2½ hours.

4. Transfer the lamb to a platter and cover to keep warm. Remove the parsley stems, rosemary, and bay leaf and discard. Set the pot over medium heat and simmer until the cooking liquid is reduced and thickened, about 20 minutes.

5. Serve the lamb shanks in shallow bowls with the sauce poured over the top. Garnish with chopped parsley.

LAMB SHANK

RB

ROOT BEER
REDUX

One 3- to 4-pound brisket, fatty end

¼ cup coriander seeds, crushed in a mortar or under a pan

2 tablespoons kosher salt

2 tablespoons freshly ground black pepper

2 teaspoons pimentón

1 tablespoon cayenne pepper

¼ cup vegetable oil

¾ cup packed brown sugar

⅓ cup yellow mustard

Smooth Mashed Potatoes (page 132) for serving

SERVES 6 TO 10

BRISKET WITH CORIANDER, BLACK PEPPER + BROWN SUGAR

Brisket, a humble and inexpensive cut, is special. This dish fuses the Jewish delicatessen with the soulful South, two cherished food traditions. It is one of my go-to recipes for easy entertaining or large events. Its texture is melting, it's a guaranteed crowd-pleaser, and the "pastrami spices" (coriander, salt, pepper, and cayenne), mixed with brown sugar and mustard, guarantee instant familiarity and comfort. Don't be put off by the long cooking time; this is a great dish to pop into the oven before you go to bed. Serve it with Smooth Mashed Potatoes. Slice leftovers to make an amazing sandwich with Smoked Aioli (page 25).

1. Rinse the brisket under cold water and pat dry with paper towels. Season with the coriander, salt, black pepper, paprika, and cayenne pepper.

2. Heat the oil in a roasting pan over medium-high heat until just smoking. Sear the brisket, turning occasionally, until browned on all sides. Remove it to a platter to cool, covered, about 20 minutes.

3. Meanwhile, arrange 2 long overlapping sheets of aluminum foil that are large enough to envelop the brisket on a work surface.

4. Preheat the oven to 300°F. In a small bowl, mix the brown sugar and mustard to make a paste. Rub the brisket with the paste and place atop the foil sheets, making sure to get every last bit of the paste. Tightly wrap the brisket in the foil so that no mustard paste can escape.

5. Place the brisket on a roasting rack set in a roasting pan and cook for 10 hours. A paring knife should pierce the meat with ease. Let cool slightly.

6. Unwrap the brisket, slice, and serve with the mashed potatoes. Leftover brisket can be wrapped tightly in plastic wrap and stored in the refrigerator for up to 1 week.

WARNING: IF YOU START IT EARLY IN THE DAY SO IT COMES OUT IN THE LATE AFTERNOON, **IT MAY RUIN DINNER.** BECAUSE IT'S **IRRESISTIBLE** WHEN IT COMES TO SNACKING.

3 tablespoons olive oil

2 onions, diced

1 carrot, diced

1 stalk celery, diced

1 clove garlic, minced

5 pounds ground beef

Kosher salt and freshly ground pepper to taste

1 large egg

2 tablespoons Worcestershire sauce

¼ cup panko bread crumbs

Bones from an 8-bone lamb or beef rack, with a small amount of meat left on the rack

2 tablespoons transglutaminase (such as Activa GS)

Caul fat

SERVES 6

SALISBURY STEAK

Salisbury steak is made by combining minced beef with other ingredients and shaping it to look like a steak. In my version, the meat is actually a steak on the bone using caul fat and transglutaminase. Caul fat is a thin membrane covering a pig's intestines. It's a common ingredient in classical French cooking and holds meats together nicely, then melts away in the cooking process, adding moisture and flavor. Transglutaminase ("meat glue") is a naturally occurring enzyme that bonds proteins together. I use it to make meat adhere to a bone, thus creating my Salisbury steak. You can get caul fat at most butchers or grocery stores, and you can find transglutaminase through several online retailers.

1. Heat 1 tablespoon of the olive oil in a sauté pan over medium heat. Add the onions, carrots, celery, and garlic and cook until translucent. Set aside to cool.

2. In a large bowl, combine the cooled vegetables and the ground beef. Season with salt and pepper, add the egg, Worcestershire sauce, and panko, and mix thoroughly. Cover and let stand for 30 minutes (to hydrate the panko).

3. Lay a sheet of plastic wrap on a work surface. Place the meat on the wrap, shape into a cylinder slightly smaller than a hockey puck on its end, and roll up in the plastic. Place in the freezer until slightly firm, approximately 1 hour.

4. Lightly dust the meaty side of the rack bones with the transglutaminase. Remove the beef from the plastic wrap and press the rack onto the cylinder. Let sit bone side up for 30 minutes to bond thoroughly.

5. Preheat a sous vide machine to 152°F. Carefully wrap the whole "rack" in caul fat to hold it together. Put the rack in a sous vide bag and vacuum-seal the bag. Immerse in the water bath for 1 hour.

6. Remove the bag from the water bath and remove the rack from the bag. Heat the remaining 2 tablespoons olive oil in a sauté pan over medium-high heat. Add the rack meat side down and brown the meat. Remove from the heat and let rest for 5 minutes.

7. Slice the rack into chops and serve.

- 4 ounces beef filet (or high-quality ground beef)
- 2 ounces Asian pear, diced
- 2 tablespoons finely diced onion
- 2 garlic cloves, minced

- 1 teaspoon Sambal
- 2 scallions, minced
- 1 tablespoon sesame oil
- 1 tablespoon capers
- 1 tablespoon pine nuts, toasted

- 1 tablespoon minced fresh flat-leaf parsley
- Zest and juice of ½ lemon
- Kosher salt and freshly ground pepper to taste

- 4 egg yolks (from very fresh eggs)
- ¼ cup fresh arugula leaves
- Extra-virgin olive oil to taste

SERVES 4

STEAK TARTARE

This version is inspired by a classic Korean dish. The Asian pear, which is cut larger than the meat, provides a great crunch, and because of the vegetal tone to its flavor, it's not too sweet. The pine nuts provide depth and that somewhat chewy texture that they are all about. But don't think this is a ballet sort of combination. There's nothing gentle about this dish. Use a lot of garlic and punch up the Sambal to your desired heat level. This is supposed to be a full-impact dish.

1. With a sharp knife on a clean cutting board (or pulsing in a food processor), mince the beef aggressively. It should look like raw hamburger. Transfer the minced meat to a bowl and refrigerate until cold, approximately 30 minutes.

2. When you remove the bowl from the refrigerator, make sure your hands are very clean and the meat is cold. Using your hands, mix the pear, onion, garlic, Sambal, scallions, sesame oil, capers, pine nuts, parsley, lemon zest and juice, and salt and pepper into the meat.

3. Divide the tartare among four plates in an unassuming way. There's no need to use a ring mold! Using a spoon, place 1 egg yolk on top of each tartare.

4. In a bowl, dress the arugula leaves with olive oil and salt and pepper, and then let them fall where they may over each of the plates.

FOR THE PORK-BELLY "CHOP"

Four 6-ounce pieces of pork belly

3 tablespoons pink salt

2 cups kosher salt

½ cup light brown sugar

Sprig of thyme

4 pork rib bones

2 cups Pork BBQ Sauce (page 35), heated

FOR THE GIANT WHITE BEAN RAGOUT

1 tablespoon olive oil

1 small onion, diced

1 shallot, diced

1 red bell pepper, diced

1 clove garlic, minced

¼ cup raisins

3 cups large white beans, cooked

2 tablespoons unsalted butter

Zest and juice of 1 lemon

¼ cup chopped fresh flat-leaf parsley

Kosher salt and freshly ground black pepper to taste

SERVES 4

PORK-BELLY "CHOP" WITH GIANT WHITE BEAN RAGOUT

While essentially pork and beans, this dish is as close to art as I think I can get. Past the abstraction lies reason: The bone gives the often jiggly nature of pork-belly structure, and also makes this dish more portable for any sort of walk-around dinner party. Giant white beans are one of my favorites because they have a creamier texture than most beans. Beyond that I like their name.

1. TO COOK THE PORK BELLY: In a large resealable bag, mix the pork belly with the pink and kosher salts and sugar. Refrigerate the sealed bag and allow to cure for 6 to 8 hours.

2. Remove the pork from the bag and discard the salted-sugar mixture. Rinse the mixture off the pork belly and pat dry with a paper towel. Place the pork into a sous vide bag with the thyme sprig, and seal on high pressure to remove air from the bag. Place in a circulating water bath at 180°F for 12 hours. Remove the bag from the water bath and shock it (to stop the cooking) by plunging it into a bowl of ice water.

3. TO MAKE THE BEAN RAGOUT: In a large sauté pan over medium-low heat, heat the oil for a few seconds. Add the onion, shallot, bell pepper, and garlic and sweat the vegetables until they are translucent. Add the raisins and beans and allow to heat through. Add the butter, lemon zest and juice, and parsley. Season with salt and pepper, and remove from the heat.

4. TO FINISH THE DISH: Remove the pork belly from the sous vide bag. Reserve the residual fat and gelatinized liquid from the bag for another use.

5. Preheat the oven to 400°F. In a sauté pan over medium heat, sear the pork until evenly browned on all sides. Place the pan in the oven until the pork is warmed through, about 10 minutes. (It has already been cooked through in the water bath.)

6. Insert the small end of the rib bone in between the layer of fat and the layer of meat for each piece of belly, being careful not to damage the look of the belly "chop." Stand each rib chop on a plate, with about ¾ cup of bean ragout. Generously pour BBQ sauce over each piece of pork and serve immediately.

SWEETNESS

In many restaurants, the pastry kitchen is more rigid than the savory kitchen when it comes to following recipes, and I think that is the way a lot of home cooks treat making desserts as well. People worry that going off-recipe might result in a disaster, but there's no reason you can't be creative with desserts. (I once made white chocolate–wasabi sauce on national television—and people ate it and liked it!)

In my restaurants, we serve ice creams made using liquid nitrogen. People often assume that they have some molecular gastronomical provenance, but the truth is that they came about when I was trying to figure out a way to make ice cream without spending $4,000 on a professional ice cream machine. It didn't hurt that the supercold temperature of the nitrogen freezes the ice cream base so fast that the ice crystals are supersmall in comparison to ice cream made with the traditional method for making a much creamier mouth-feel. The reason I still serve these ice creams today, besides their incredible texture, is that the presentation is great, and makes a simple treat into something special. This holds true for making ice cream at home (see Dry Ice Cream, page 277): my technique is easy, and it will really impress your guests.

What I want from dessert is a way to end a meal in an unpredictable way. Dessert is not a requirement—it's an additional delicious note—but it can add a bit of fun to any meal. In my first season of *Top Chef*, I made a dish I called Banana Scallops, where I cut up bananas, coated them with brown sugar, and seared them to give them a crunchy brûléed exterior. They looked just like scallops, and I served them with banana guacamole and chocolate ice cream. Sound like dessert to you? It did to me! Dessert is an excellent place to remix some old favorites, like chocolate cake (see Black-Olive Chocolate Cake on page 267, which is especially moist and has a rich flavor and beautiful glossy-black color). Don't be scared to try new things—you might just find your own Banana Scallops.

STICKY TOFFEE
PUDDING

WHISKEY

ANDREA
LITVIN.
EVIL PASTRY
MASTERMIND

FOR THE PUDDING

1 cup chopped pitted Medjool dates

1¼ cups water

¼ cup brewed espresso

1 teaspoon baking soda

4 tablespoons (½ stick) unsalted butter, softened, plus more for greasing the pan

¾ cup packed dark brown sugar

3 tablespoons sorghum syrup or molasses

3 large eggs, beaten

1 cup all-purpose flour

FOR THE SAUCE

1 cup sugar

¼ cup Scotch whiskey

1½ cups heavy cream, warmed

8 tablespoons (1 stick) unsalted butter, diced

SERVES 6

STICKY PUDDING WITH SCOTCH SAUCE

Inspired by my love for all things British and the English pudding tradition, this is probably my most classic dessert. It's great after a meal of big, bold flavors, when you want to continue the decadent theme. I like to reduce flavors to reveal their deepest, syrupy nature (see the root beer in my lamb braise, page 248, and the cider syrup in my cod, page 220), and this dessert is a perfect example. The dates add a natural sweetness—and, of course, they're incredibly sticky.

1. TO MAKE THE PUDDING: Put the dates, water, and espresso in a small saucepan and bring to a boil over medium-high heat. Turn off the heat, stir in the baking soda, and let stand for 2 hours.

2. Preheat the oven to 350°F. Grease a 6-cup nonstick jumbo muffin tin with butter. Set it into a large deep baking dish.

3. In the bowl of a standing mixer fitted with the paddle attachment, cream the butter and brown sugar on medium speed until light and fluffy, about 5 minutes. Add the sorghum syrup and mix well. Drain the soaked dates and add them to the butter mixture, mixing on low speed until incorporated. Add the eggs and mix until incorporated. Remove the bowl from the mixer stand and, with a large rubber spatula, fold the flour into the date mixture until just combined. Divide the batter among muffin cups.

4. Pour enough hot water into the baking dish to come halfway up the sides of the muffin tin. Bake until the puddings are set and spring back when touched in the center, about 30 minutes. Remove from the oven and let stand until the water in the baking dish is cool, but the puddings remain warm.

5. MEANWHILE, TO MAKE THE SAUCE: Put the sugar and Scotch into a medium saucepan and stir to moisten the sugar. Set the pan over medium heat and cook, without stirring, until the caramel turns dark amber. Very carefully pour in the cream (it will bubble up) and cook, whisking gently, until very smooth and any bits of caramel have dissolved. Remove from the heat and whisk in the butter a little at a time, whisking until melted and combined each time before adding more.

6. Run a knife around each pudding. Place a large cutting board or platter over the pan and invert the pan and board; lift off the pan. Arrange the puddings on dessert plates. Serve the puddings warm, with the Scotch sauce drizzled over the top.

FOR THE CRUST

1¼ cups all-purpose flour, plus more for dusting

1 teaspoon sugar

½ teaspoon salt

8 tablespoons (1 stick) cold unsalted butter, diced

2 to 3 tablespoons ice water

FOR THE FILLING

½ cup packed fresh bread crumbs

2 tablespoons packed light brown sugar

½ cup chopped pecans

4 pitted dates, finely minced

1 cup Lyle's Golden Syrup

3 large eggs

½ teaspoon ground ginger

¼ teaspoon table salt

Buttermilk-Ginger Frozen Yogurt (page 274) for serving

SERVES 6 TO 8

PECAN TREACLE TART

This is a cross between treacle tart, an English sweet born in the eighteenth century that's made with golden cane syrup, and a classic Southern pecan pie. Here is another example of two dishes that share some commonality. The inverted sugar is the bridge between the two. I use Lyle's Golden Syrup, not high-fructose corn syrup: it's better, and the empty Lyle's tin makes a nice loose-change holder. Tangy Buttermilk-Ginger Frozen Yogurt pairs well with the sweet tart.

1. TO MAKE THE CRUST: Put the flour, sugar, and salt in a food processor and pulse until combined. Add the butter and pulse until small pea-sized crumbs form. While pulsing, add the ice water 1 tablespoon at a time until the dough begins to hold together. Turn the dough out onto a lightly floured surface and knead gently until it holds together. Press into a flat disk, wrap tightly in plastic wrap, and refrigerate for at least 1 hour, or up to 3 days.

2. Preheat the oven to 350°F. Dust a work surface lightly with flour and, using a floured rolling pin, roll the dough into a 12-inch circle. Transfer it to a 10-inch fluted tart pan with a removable bottom and press the dough into the bottom and up the sides of the pan. Trim the excess dough. Transfer the pan to a baking sheet and bake for 10 minutes, or until set. Remove from the oven and let cool. (Leave the oven on).

3. TO MAKE THE FILLING: In a small bowl, stir the bread crumbs, brown sugar, pecans, and dates together until combined. In a medium bowl, whisk the golden syrup, eggs, ginger, and salt together until well combined. Add the bread crumb mixture and fold together until combined. Pour into the cooled tart shell. Bake until the crust is golden, the filling is set, and a toothpick inserted in the center of the pie comes out clean, 40 to 45 minutes. Cool completely on a rack before slicing.

4. Remove the pan sides, cut the tart into slices, and serve with the frozen yogurt on the side.

8 tablespoons (1 stick) unsalted butter, softened, plus more for greasing the pan

½ cup sugar

½ vanilla bean, split, seeds scraped out and reserved, or 1 teaspoon vanilla extract

2 large eggs, at room temperature

1 cup all-purpose flour

¾ cup yellow cornmeal

½ teaspoon kosher salt

½ teaspoon baking powder

½ cup buttermilk or plain yogurt, at room temperature

Sweet Tea Ice Cream (page 275) for serving

SERVES 6 TO 8

CORN BREAD WITH SWEET TEA ICE CREAM

Nothing says the South like corn bread and sweet tea. Here I riff on the combo with a not-too-sweet dessert. I'm not the biggest fan of sweet tea as a drink, but I sure do love it as an ice cream.

1. Preheat the oven to 350°F. Butter an 8-inch square baking pan.

2. In the bowl of a standing mixer fitted with the paddle attachment, cream the butter and sugar together on medium speed until lightened, 3 to 4 minutes. Add the vanilla. Add the eggs one at a time, beating well and scraping down the sides of the bowl with a rubber spatula after each addition.

3. In a small bowl, whisk the flour, cornmeal, salt, and baking powder together until combined. With the mixer on low speed, add half the flour mixture to the creamed butter and mix until combined. Add the buttermilk and mix again. Scrape down the bowl, then add the remaining flour mixture and mix on low until just incorporated.

4. Spread the batter evenly in the prepared pan. Bake until the corn bread is beginning to turn golden, the top is firm to the touch, and a toothpick inserted in the center comes out clean, 20 to 25 minutes. Let cool for at least 10 minutes.

5. Cut the corn bread into 6 or 8 squares and serve warm with the ice cream on the side.

8 tablespoons (1 stick) unsalted butter, plus more for greasing the pan	4 ounces bitter-sweet chocolate (70% cocoa solids), chopped	2 large eggs, at room temperature	1 tablespoon natural cocoa powder, plus more for garnish
¼ cup all-purpose flour, plus more for the pan	2 tablespoons very finely minced pitted Kalamata olives	4 large egg whites, at room temperature ⅓ cup sugar	Whipped crème fraîche and chopped fresh cherries for garnish

SERVES 6

BLACK-OLIVE CHOCOLATE CAKE

This is like a haunted Black Forest cake. Whereas the moistness in a Black Forest cake comes from the cherries, here it comes from kalamata olives. Plus the briny, salty flavor of cured olives is not so far off from that of natural cocoa powder (both are slightly bitter and acidic but addictive). That flavor combines beautifully with the sweetness of vanilla and sugar. The effect is unique and deeply satisfying.

1. Preheat the oven to 350°F. Grease a 6-cup nonstick jumbo muffin tin with butter and dust lightly with flour.

2. Put the chocolate and butter in a heatproof bowl and set over a small pot of barely simmering water. Stir gently until melted and smooth. Remove from the heat, stir in the olives, and let stand until cool.

3. In the bowl of a standing mixer fitted with the whisk attachment, whisk the eggs and whites at medium speed until foamy. With the motor running, gradually add the sugar in a slow stream. Increase the speed to medium-high and whip until the eggs have tripled in volume, 4 to 5 minutes; the whipped eggs should hold the trail of the whisk.

4. Meanwhile, sift the flour and cocoa together into a large bowl. Add the chocolate and whisk until combined.

5. With a large rubber spatula, fold about one-third of the egg mixture into the chocolate mixture to lighten it, then fold in the remaining egg mixture until just combined. Divide the batter among the muffin cups. Bake until a toothpick inserted in the center of a cake comes out clean, 20 to 25 minutes. Let stand for 5 minutes.

6. Run a knife around the edges of the cakes. Place a large cutting board or platter over the pan and invert the pan and board; lift off the pan. Arrange the cakes on dessert plates, dust each one with cocoa powder, and put a dollop of crème fraîche and some chopped cherries on top. Serve warm.

1.5 BLACK COCOA

Part of what's special about this alternative is its deep, dark, intense color, which can usually only be achieved in a dessert with the use of black cocoa (available at KingArthurFlour.com). Black cocoa replacer, which is what gives Oreos their jet-black color, is a specialty whole-grain flour made of roasted barley. It's more economical and does the job just as well. You can mail-order it from the Wisconsin-based family-owned Briess Malt & Ingredients (Briess.com) or King Arthur Flour. Or you could certainly add a drop or two of black food coloring to mimic. To use black cocoa or black cocoa replacer in this recipe, simply substitute it for the natural cocoa.

8 tablespoons
(1 stick)
unsalted butter,
softened, plus
more for greasing
the pan

1¼ cups all-purpose
flour, plus more
for the pan

1 cup sugar

2 large eggs, at
room temperature

¼ cup natural
unsweetened cocoa
powder

½ teaspoon baking
soda

¼ teaspoon fine
salt

½ cup sour cream,
at room
temperature

¼ cup whole milk,
at room
temperature

3½ tablespoons
fresh beet juice
or red food
coloring

1 teaspoon vanilla
extract

Cream Cheese Ice
Cream (page 275)
for serving

1 teaspoon mint,
juliened
(optional)

SERVES 8 TO 10

RED VELVET TARTARE WITH CREAM CHEESE ICE CREAM

When I was running a restaurant in Atlanta called One Midtown Kitchen, one of my chefs made a red velvet wedding cake. There were crumbs on the cutting board, and from across the room, they looked like flecks of steak tartare. That observation made me realize that because I'm not a trained pastry chef, I am not encumbered by expectations that my cakes look textbook beautiful—and when you're making desserts at home, neither are you. This cake is all about having fun. Using fresh beet juice instead of food coloring will not give the cake the electric red color you might be used to, but it's a good natural substitute and does give it a deep maroon hue. I serve the cake crumbled on top of cream cheese ice cream, a gentle twist on the traditional icing accompaniment.

1. Preheat the oven to 375°F. Butter and flour a 9-by-13-inch glass baking dish.

2. In the bowl of a standing mixer fitted with the paddle attachment, cream the butter and sugar on medium speed until lightened, about 5 minutes. Add the eggs one at a time, beating well and scraping down the sides of the bowl with a rubber spatula after each addition.

3. Sift the flour, cocoa, baking soda, and salt together into a medium bowl. In a large liquid measuring cup or a small bowl, whisk the sour cream, milk, beet juice, and vanilla together until combined. With the mixer on low, add the flour mixture alternating with the milk mixture in 3 additions, beginning and ending with the dry ingredients and mixing until the batter is smooth. Stop the mixer and scrape down the sides of the bowl with a rubber spatula as necessary.

4. Pour the batter into the prepared pan and bake until a toothpick inserted in the center comes out clean, 20 to 25 minutes. Cool in the pan on a rack.

5. To serve, crumble the cake into very small pieces and scatter about 1 cup onto each dessert plate. Top with a scoop of ice cream and a few more cake crumbles. Garnish with mint, if using. Serve immediately.

| Unsalted butter for the paper cups | 3 large eggs
5 tablespoons sugar | ½ cup pastry flour | Sliced fresh berries, ice cream, or chocolate sauce for serving |

SERVES 8

E-Z BAKE INDIVIDUAL ANGEL FOOD CAKES

I grew up at the beginning of the dump-and-serve microwave revolution, and I both make fun of and embrace that fact. Microwaves were so exciting when they first became popular, with their promise of speed and efficiency; nowadays we use them mostly for microwave popcorn. But why not make use of something we all have sitting in our kitchens? This angel food cake is just as light and airy and tender as one baked in a regular oven. And a lot EZ-er.

1. Lightly butter the insides of eight paper coffee cups that are the Starbucks "tall" (12 ounces). With a sharp pointed knife, poke five or six slits evenly into the sides of each cup.

2. In the bowl of a standing mixer fitted with the whisk attachment, whip the eggs on medium speed until foamy. Increase the speed to medium-high and add the sugar in a slow, steady stream. Continue whipping until the eggs have tripled in volume, 6 to 8 minutes. Remove the bowl from the mixer stand and, using a fine-mesh strainer, sift the flour onto the top of the eggs. Using a large rubber spatula, gently fold in the flour until just incorporated.

3. Fill each cup two-thirds full of batter. Place in the microwave and cook on high for 30 seconds, or until the cakes are set. Cool the cakes in the cups for 5 minutes, then peel away the paper to release the cakes.

4. Serve the angel food cakes standing upright on dessert plates, with sliced berries, ice cream, or chocolate sauce on the side.

2.0 WHIPPED CAKE BATTER

Angel food cakes are prized for their light-as-air texture. I discovered that if you charge the cake batter in an iSi siphon, you can omit the laborious task of hand-whisking the egg whites and create a version that is just as ethereal.

Whisk together all the ingredients until smooth and transfer the batter to an iSi siphon (see page 14) and charge with 2 cartridges. Fill each cup two-thirds full of batter and proceed as directed.

FOR THE CHEESECAKE

1 cup heavy cream

A 3- to 4-inch piece Parmesan cheese rind

20 Biscoff cookies or ¾ cup graham cracker crumbs plus ¾ cup finely crushed gingersnaps

6 tablespoons (¾ stick) unsalted butter, melted

2 pounds cream cheese, at room temperature

½ cup finely grated Parmesan cheese, plus more for garnish

⅓ cup sugar

6 large egg yolks, at room temperature

2 teaspoons vanilla extract

FOR THE TOPPING

½ cup sour cream, at room temperature

2 tablespoons molasses

6 pitted Medjool dates, finely chopped

⅓ cup Marcona almonds or roasted whole almonds, chopped

SERVES 8 TO 10

PARMESAN CHEESECAKE WITH DATES + ALMONDS *(page 259)*

The inspiration for this dessert was to combine a cheese course and a dessert into one—like a cheese Danish. It was also born of the fact that I don't like to throw anything away, such as Parmesan cheese rinds, which can be so useful. When I go to the cheese counter at the supermarket, I often buy Parmesan rinds; there is a surprising amount of cheese left on them, and you can keep them in the freezer and then use them for flavoring everything from chicken stock to my Tomato Sauce (page 34) to the cream for this cheesecake.

1. Preheat the oven to 325°F. Position a rack in the lower third of the oven.

2. TO MAKE THE CHEESECAKE: Put the cream and Parmesan rind into a small saucepan and heat over medium-low heat until just beginning to simmer. Remove from the heat and let cool to room temperature, at least 15 minutes.

3. If using the cookies, put them in a food processor and process until finely ground. Transfer to a small bowl (or put the graham cracker and gingersnap crumbs in the bowl) and add the butter. Stir well until crumbs are evenly moistened. Press them into the bottom of a 9-inch springform pan.

4. Bake the crust until set and beginning to brown, 10 to 12 minutes. Remove from the oven and cool completely. (Leave the oven on.)

5. In the bowl of a standing mixer fitted with the paddle attachment, beat the cream cheese on medium-low speed until softened. Add the grated Parmesan and sugar, increase the speed to medium, and beat until the sugar dissolves and the mixture is fluffy, about 5 minutes. With the mixer on low, add the yolks one at a time, mixing well and scraping down the sides of the bowl with a rubber spatula after each addition. Remove the Parmesan rind from the cream and, with the mixer on low speed, add the cream to the cream cheese mixture, along with the vanilla, and mix until completely smooth, stopping to scrape down the bowl as necessary.

AERATED CHEESECAKE

There isn't a word more synonymous with molecular gastronomy than foam. Love the technique or not, this version is quite possibly the sweetest whipit imaginable. We take a cooked cheesecake and deconstruct it by pureeing it to a smooth paste, then loading it into an iSi syphon.

1 Preheat the oven to 300°F.

2 Follow steps 2 and 5 of the recipe, then pour the batter into an oven-safe bowl. Bake until the batter is set, approximately 1½ hours.

3 Put the batter in a blender or mixer and puree until smooth.

4 Pour approximately 2 cups of batter into an iSi siphon with a cream charge. Now you have an aerated cheesecake that you can use to top other desserts or ice cream, or just spray directly into your mouth. . . . I won't tell.

6. Pour the batter into the cooled crust and tap the sides of the pan several times to release any air bubbles. Bake for 1 hour and 20 minutes, or until the edges of the filling are set but the center is still slightly jiggly.

7. Meanwhile, in a small bowl, stir the sour cream and molasses together until combined. Mix the dates and almonds together in a small bowl. They will be very sticky and clump together.

8. Remove the baked cheesecake from the oven and, with your fingers, break apart the date-nut mixture and gently sprinkle it evenly over the surface of the cheesecake. Spoon the sour cream mixture evenly over the dates and nuts, leaving a ½-inch border around the edges. Return the pan to the oven and bake for 5 minutes. Turn off the oven, use a wooden spoon handle to prop the door open slightly, and leave the cheesecake in the oven to cool for 1 hour.

9. Remove the cheesecake from the oven and let cool to room temperature, then refrigerate for at least 4 hours, and up to 5 days.

10. When ready to serve, remove the cheesecake from the refrigerator and let stand at room temperature for 30 minutes. Remove the springform ring and, using a knife dipped in warm water and wiped dry before each cut, slice the cake. Serve with Parmesan sprinkled on top.

ICE CREAMS

Doing interesting things with ice cream—for example, adding unusual or even savory flavors or spices, or using dry ice to freeze it—is something I really enjoy doing, in part because there seems to be a collective cultural assumption of what "ice cream" is, and I want that notion to be more creative and fun. That can mean making ice cream a bit richer with cream cheese; taking the natural tartness of plain frozen yogurt and deepening it with buttermilk and ginger; or turning traditional Southern sweet iced tea into a creamy vanilla-spiked delight. I believe anything can work in ice cream form: All you have to do is believe. Here are a couple of flavor offerings, with a fun technique or two.

MAKES ABOUT 1 QUART

BUTTERMILK-GINGER FROZEN YOGURT

| A 4-inch piece fresh ginger, peeled and chopped | 2 cups low-fat buttermilk | 4 large egg yolks
¾ cup sugar | 1 cup whole milk |

1. In a large liquid measuring cup or a small bowl, combine the ginger and buttermilk. Refrigerate for at least 1 hour, and up to 3 hours.

2. Heat the milk in a medium saucepan over medium heat until hot but not boiling. Meanwhile, in a medium bowl, whisk the yolks and sugar together until combined. Whisking constantly, gradually add the hot milk to the egg yolks. Pour the mixture back into the saucepan, return it to medium-low heat, and stir constantly with a wooden spoon until it is thickened and coats the back of the spoon, 6 to 8 minutes. Remove from the heat.

3. Strain the buttermilk through a fine-mesh strainer into the milk mixture and whisk well to combine; discard the ginger. Strain the mixture into a medium bowl. Set the bowl in a slightly larger bowl filled with ice water and stir occasionally until the ice cream base is cold.

4. Freeze the ice cream in your ice cream maker following the manufacturer's instructions. Transfer to an airtight container and freeze for up to 1 month.

SWEET TEA ICE CREAM

2 cups sweetened
  iced tea,
  homemade or
  store-bought

2 cups whole milk
1 cup heavy cream

1 vanilla bean,
  split, seeds
  scraped out, seeds
  and pod reserved

4 large egg yolks
¾ cup sugar

1. Pour the tea into a small saucepan and bring to a simmer over medium heat. Cook until reduced by half. Remove from the heat and set aside.

2. In a medium saucepan, warm the milk, cream, and vanilla seeds and pod over medium-low heat until very hot but not boiling. Meanwhile, in a medium bowl, whisk the yolks and sugar together until combined. Whisking constantly, gradually pour the hot milk into the egg yolks. Pour the mixture back into the saucepan, return to medium-low heat, and stir constantly with a wooden spoon until it is thickened and coats the back of the spoon, 6 to 8 minutes. Remove from the heat.

3. Pour the reduced sweet tea into the milk mixture and stir well. Strain the mixture through a fine-mesh strainer into a medium bowl. Set the bowl in a slightly larger bowl filled with ice water and stir occasionally until the ice cream base is cold.

4. Freeze the ice cream in your ice cream maker following the manufacturer's instructions. Transfer to an airtight container and freeze for up to 1 month.

CREAM CHEESE ICE CREAM

2 cups 2% milk
3 tablespoons corn
  syrup

4 large egg yolks
½ cup sugar

6 ounces cream
  cheese, diced, at
  room temperature

½ teaspoon vanilla
  extract

1. Put the milk and corn syrup in a medium saucepan and heat over medium-low heat until hot but not boiling. Meanwhile, whisk the yolks and sugar together in a medium bowl. Whisking constantly, gradually pour the hot milk mixture into the eggs. Pour the egg mixture back into the saucepan, return it to medium-low heat, and stir constantly with a wooden spoon until it is thickened and coats the back of the spoon, 6 to 8 minutes. Remove from the heat, add the cream cheese, and whisk until completely melted and smooth. Whisk in the vanilla.

2. Strain the mixture through a fine-mesh strainer into a small bowl. Set the bowl in a slightly larger bowl filled with ice water and stir occasionally until the ice cream base is cool.

3. Freeze the ice cream in your ice cream maker following the manufacturer's instructions. Transfer to an airtight container and freeze for up to 1 month.

2.0 DRY ICE CREAM

Freezing ice cream with dry ice creates a unique effect: Dry ice is frozen compressed carbon dioxide, the same thing that carbonates your soda. (Dry ice is really cold; always wear gloves when you handle it, because frostbite can happen quickly—and don't try to eat it.) Because of its very low temperature, it's great for cooling stuff, and when it's exposed to room-temperature air, it immediately gives off vapors—that characteristic fog you see on music video sets. So, using it to freeze ice cream is not only supercool but also carbonates the ice cream. This is kind of trippy and works really well for some flavors (e.g., strawberry) and not so great for others (tomato). As the ice cream stands, like your can of soda, it will lose its carbonation (which is fine).

To freeze ice cream using dry ice, wearing protective gloves, add several large chunks of dry ice to a food processor and pulse until pulverized into a powder. Put the ice cream base into the bowl of a standing mixer fitted with the whisk attachment and turn it on to medium speed. Drop spoonfuls of the dry ice powder into the mixer until the ice cream is very thick and frozen like soft-serve ice cream. Use immediately, or transfer to an airtight container and freeze until ready to use.

DON'T
EAT THIS

As a chef, working with recipes is natural for me. We all use recipes, even for non-food items. Here are some *possibly* helpful recipes for things you shouldn't eat.

375

QUICK-FIRE HAIR GEL

¼ cup rendered
  duck fat, at room
  temperature

3 tablespoons
  liquid nitrogen
  in a metal spritz
  bottle

Rub the duck fat through your hair as desired. Moving quickly, apply the liquid nitrogen to your hair, adding more for additional crunchy texture.

PLEASE READ THIS

Touching liquid nitrogen with your hands for short periods of time won't hurt you, but prolonged contact will burn you just like hot oil would. So please use gloves.

COPPER POT CLEANER

½ cup white vinegar

½ cup all-purpose
  flour

½ cup kosher salt

In a small bowl, combine the vinegar, flour, and salt. Dip a coarse scrub brush or pad into the mixture and start your scrubbing.

MOUTHWASH

½ teaspoon baking
  soda

4 to 5 ounces water

1 or 2 drops mint
  extract

In a small bowl, mix the baking soda, water, and mint extract. Pour into a cup, take a swig, and gargle.

LIQUID HAND SOAP

1 bar unscented
  soap

1 gallon water

1 teaspoon extract
  of your choice,
  such as lemongrass
  (optional)

2 iSi NO2 charges
  (optional)

1. With a grater that you would use for Parmesan cheese, grate the soap bar into a large bowl.

2. In a large pot over high heat, bring the water to a boil. Add the grated soap and stir to dissolve, about 2 minutes. Remove the pot from the heat and let the mixture sit at room temperature to cool, stirring every once in a while.

3. Stir in your optional aroma extract. (Lemongrass and cilantro will make you smell like a market in Thailand.) Pour the liquid into a pump dispenser and wash your hands with it. If you want super foamy hand soap, add the liquid to an iSi and charge it 2 times.

ACKNOWLEDGMENTS

TO MY FAMILY: There isn't really a condensed way to thank you. My wife, Jazmin; my kids, Riley and Embry; you inspire me every single day, and the fun spirit of our lives documented in this book is all due to you.

TO THE BLAIS AND FLAMAND SIDES OF MY FAMILY: Thank you for being my biggest fans and supporters while also reminding me of where I came from.

TO ALL OF THE COOKS I WORKED SIDE-BY-SIDE WITH FOR SO MANY YEARS AT SO MANY PLACES: I remember, and I often channel those times when we were grinding it out seven days a week.

TO THOMAS KELLER + DANIEL BOULUD: I was a little chef for a little time for both of you, but your influence has been and continues to be, a driving force in my life. Thank you for the opportunities.

TO ALL THE COOKS WHO HAVE WORKED FOR ME: We all know who does all the work in a restaurant. Thanks for carrying me on your shoulders, hearts, and knives.

TO MY BUSINESS PARTNERS, RON STEWART, BARRY MILLS, BOB AMICK + TODD RUSHING: You all continue to impress me in so many ways. Thanks for being a part of all of it.

TO MY MANAGER, CAMERON LEVKOFF AT THE CEA + MY AGENT ADAM NETTLER AT CAA: I never thought I would ever type that. You make my life more exciting every day. Thanks for opening so many doors. And where are we with that last deal? ;)

TO WES MARTIN + KELLY ALEXANDER: I could not have put together this book without your help. Your experiences in food writing and recipe testing helped bridge my thoughts to paper, and some of my restaurant-kitchen recipes to your stovetops. Much thanks for the struggle; it certainly was worth it.

TO MY PR TEAM: Thanks for blowing up my e-mails with recipe requests and last-minute bookings. And, Pamela Spiegel, thanks for coming in from Brooklyn early . . . and on a Saturday.

TO MY EDITOR, EMILY TAKOUDES + THE TEAM AT CLARKSON POTTER: Thanks for putting up with me and giving me the opportunity to live out the dream of being an author. I'm looking forward to many more. I promise it will be easier next time!

TO MICHAEL PSALTIS AT THE CEA: It's amazing to think it only took a few years! Thanks for your patience, wisdom, and friendship.

TO THE TEAM THAT COOKED THIS BOOK, BRAD, JASON, MARK + SPENCER: Thanks, as always, for making it happen. You are some of my favorite people.

TO MEGAN + STACI: Thank you for making me pretty.

TO ANDREA + ELI: You both consistently remind me of why we do this. No one knows my food better, and both of you continue to push me and my food daily. Andrea, I look forward to writing *your* cookbook one day.

TO ALL OF THOSE I YELLED AT, FIRED ON THE SPOT, OR AT A MINIMUM STRESSED OUT BECAUSE I WAS GOING CRAZY ABOUT SOMETHING: Half of you deserved it. The other half, I'm sorry. It was a phase.

TO THE TEAMS AT FLIP BURGER BOUTIQUE: It truly is one of my biggest pleasures to see you grow. Thanks for every day.

TO THE TEAMS AT THE SPENCE: It's all about making people happy. Let's keep cooking one plate at a time and serving up "relentless hospitality."

TO ALL THE FINE FOLKS AT BRAVO + MAGICAL ELVES: Thanks for turning this rocky uphill climb into an escalator. I consider you all family.

AND LAST BUT NOT LEAST, TO MY FANS, ALL THE "BLAISIANS" OUT THERE: You have made me more responsible and your kindness and enthusiasm for my work is never forgotten.

INDEX

Note: Page references in *italics* indicate photographs.

THE END